LEARNING FROM
RUSSIA'S RECENT WARS

LEARNING FROM RUSSIA'S RECENT WARS

Why, Where, and When Russia Might Strike Next

Neal G. Jesse

Rapid Communications in Conflict and Security Series
General Editor: Geoffrey R.H. Burn

CAMBRIA PRESS

Amherst, New York

Requests for permission should be directed to
permissions@cambriapress.com, or mailed to:
Cambria Press
100 Corporate Parkway, Suite 128
Amherst, New York 14226, USA

Library of Congress Cataloging-in-Publication Data on file.

ISBN: 9781621965411

To Katie, Oliver, Miles, and all our cats

TABLE OF CONTENTS

LIST OF TABLES

ACKNOWLEDGMENTS

This book would not have been possible without the contribution of many, many people. The origins of this book lay in many areas of my academic life, all of which I need to acknowledge.

One source of this study lies in my previous published research on small-state foreign policy, and in particular my examination of the Russian threat to the Baltic nations. I am indebted to John Dreyer for his work on my most previous book and the insights that were produced from my discussions and collaboration with him. The comparative theory approach used in this book is derived from the excellent typology that John and I created for our book together. Likewise, my work on hegemonic powers and small state response to them has also contributed to this current work. I thank Steven Lobell and Kristen Williams for providing me with key understandings of the international system that are the backbone for my theoretical arguments.

Another source of this study lies in my lifelong interest in Russian (and Soviet) history and politics. I must thank my instructors at UCSB and UCLA for their excellence in preparing me for writing this manuscript. In particular, I commend the Russian language instructors and teaching assistants at both schools who managed to impart upon me my knowledge of the Russian language. It has proved invaluable in the preparation of this work.

I have to thank Bowling Green State University (BGSU) for providing me with a faculty improvement leave which allowed me to pursue this book project. I also would like to thank the German, Russian, and East Asian Language (GREAL) department for numerous discussions about Russia that have informed my research. Likewise, I acknowledge a grant from the University of Michigan many years ago that gave me access to documents and research on Russia that were unavailable to me at my host institution.

I need to thank and acknowledge those who attended my presentations at the 2019 and 2018 Annual Meetings of the Midwestern Political Science Association in Chicago and the 2017 Annual Meeting of the International Studies Association in Baltimore. I presented at these conventions earlier versions of material included in the final manuscript. I thank all the panel participants and audience guests who commented and thus improved my understanding of the material.

I also would like to thank two research assistants in the Masters of Public Administration (MPA) program in the BGSU Political Science Department. Both Nic Bush and Tyler Kepschull labored endlessly tracking down resources and reading over drafts, while also grading for my introductory course. Without their help, this book would never have been completed.

A debt is also owed to the anonymous reviewers who labored through the various manuscript drafts of this book. Their sharp critiques and keen eyes led to a substantial improvement in the finished product. The professional work of reviewing long manuscripts is tedious and not often recognized for its value. Thus, I thank the reviewers immensely for their service to my book and to the profession, for without them this book would be much poorer.

It would be very remiss of me if I neglected the encouragement and advice of Geoffrey Burn at Cambria Press. It was initial discussions with Geoffrey at the ISSS-ISAC 2016 meeting at Notre Dame University in South Bend, Indiana, that led to the germination of this project. At our subsequent meeting at the ISA In Baltimore, Geoffrey helped bend my ear toward focusing on Russian foreign policy and asymmetrical warfare as the main theme of the current manuscript. Geoffrey was also very understanding as I missed deadlines. For all of this, I thank him very much. I also thank everyone else at Cambria Press who has labored on behalf of publishing my work. Although I do not know all their names, I thank them for all that they have done.

Of course, even with all this assistance, errors and omissions most certainly have worked their way into the book. All such mistakes are my sole responsibility, and I take ownership of them.

Last, and most importantly, I thank my family for all the support and love that they have provided. My wife and children have put up with the disruption of our lives that writing a book tends to produce. The instances are too numerous to list here, but one example would be all the mornings when I got up at the crack of dawn to get writing done on the book and then forgot to make breakfast for the boys or get coffee ready for my wife, emerging from my basement only around noon to greet them. Their understanding allowed me to produce this work.

LEARNING FROM
RUSSIA'S RECENT WARS

CHAPTER 1

THEORIES OF RUSSIAN FOREIGN POLICY

RUSSIAN GOALS IN THE CONTEMPORARY WORLD

To Western observers, Russian foreign policy can often appear a bit opaque. This is due to many factors. Some scholars argue that there has been a striking inability of general international relations theories to explain historical Russian/Soviet foreign policy behavior.[1] Another argument is that due to the authoritarian or autocratic nature of Soviet and Russian governments, there exists a relative lack of information outside of the Soviet Union/Russia about how foreign policy is made by domestic actors.[2] There is also the seeming paradox of Russian actions that run counter to their own national interest, such as the Russian intervention in eastern Ukraine.[3] Do these missteps represent fundamental errors in Russian foreign policy, or are they signs that Western understanding of Russian foreign policy is not finely tuned?

There are also factors related more to domestic politics, social norms and identity. Andrei P. Tsygankov argues that Russian foreign policy cannot be disentangled from the search for a Russian national identity.[4] Thus, one can argue that Russian foreign policy originates more from an inherent national quest than realist structural considerations. On top of this, the changing strategies pursued by Russia, sometimes in only a matter of years or decades, also add to the overall complexity.[5] To this list we can add a pair of structural factors. The two dramatic regime changes in the twentieth century (i.e., from Russian Empire to Soviet Union and from Soviet Union to Russian Federation) present points of discontinuity.[6] On top of this, the change of the international system from bipolarity and Cold War, to eventual unipolarity post-1991, adds another interruption into the time series. Thus, any examination of Russian foreign policy must account for this inherent complexity.

The exploration of Russian foreign policy by scholars and military analysts creates, as one might assume given the factors enumerated earlier, a mountain of published work. With some degree of simplification, I see these works divided into five basic approaches to understanding Russian foreign policy. First, there are the theoretical works mostly written by academics that cover a range from the study of grand strategies and themes to ideas and identity.[7] Second, there are scholarly works that focus more on the historical trajectory of Russian foreign policy as a means to gauge the contemporary foreign policy.[8] Third, there are a series of reports and papers, mainly written at the war colleges, think tanks, and government agencies, that assess contemporary Russian events, documents, actions, and such related areas to look for clues as to the current strategic aims of Russian foreign policy.[9]

Fourth, there exists a wealth of work on individual parts of Russian foreign and/or defense policy by experts on those topics. The range and extent of such research is vast, but some examples include the role of Russian soft power and propaganda,[10] military reform,[11] the politics of energy,[12] civil-military relations,[13] the influence of the *Siloviki*,[14] domestic politics,[15] and Russia's hybrid warfare.[16] The fifth area of research contains works on specific geographical regions or countries. Some examples include Russian foreign policy toward the Arctic region,[17] Georgia,[18] Ukraine,[19] the Black Sea,[20] Crimea,[21] Eastern Europe,[22] Eurasia,[23] and the Caucasus.[24] Research that combines these approaches exist as well; for example, hybrid warfare in certain regions, such as in Romania[25] or Crimea.[26] It also is worth noting, that a good portion of this literature relies on primary sources for some of its information, including documents and speeches directly by Russian foreign policy makers and politicians and that these sources are a foundation across all the different types of research.[27]

Important in my examination of Russian foreign policy is trying not to descend into one of two intellectual pitfalls. The first is categorizing Russian foreign policy as so unique that no theoretical or comparative approach can explain it. This sort of exceptionalism argument might seem to make sense initially, but it is inherently not overly useful. For example, if we were to say that the unique combination of autocratic government, crony capitalism, post-communist experience, and great power aspirations make Russian foreign policy unique, we would not only fail to explain how Russian foreign policy has changed so often since 1991 but also create a non-parsimonious argument that surely falls under the weight of all its unspoken assumptions and Byzantine web of relationships.

The second pitfall is the slavish application of theory to Russian foreign policy. The researcher must always be aware that theories generated by Western international relations scholars may not directly apply to Russia. In particular, the application of theories generated during the Cold War period need critical examination before one forces the Russian experience into theoretical confines. Charting a path between these two pitfalls requires careful application and testing of theory, while also taking into account the complexity and peculiarity of Russian foreign policy, especially the unique cultural sources.

Broadly, there are three different schools of thought in comparative foreign policy: structural theories, domestic factor theories, and social constructivist/ideational theories. Quite often the implications and predictions of these different schools are not directly compared. One exception is Jesse and Dreyer's examination of small states in which they tease out how each school of theory predicts very different sources of foreign policy and foreign policy change.[28] If we are to explore Russian foreign policy, it is important to apply all three schools without bias or prejudice.

THREE SCHOOLS OF COMPARATIVE FOREIGN POLICY

Theorizing about foreign policy cannot be divorced from general theories of international relations. International relations theories focus on explaining and understanding the interaction of states in the international system. Over the course of the last century, three broad schools have emerged in the discussion of the fundamental sources of state behavior: realist, domestic factor, and social constructivist. Each of the three rely on very different assumptions about the primary source of state behavior and the resulting foreign policy choices of states. In brief, realism emphasizes the structure of the international system, and in particular the symmetry/asymmetry of power relationships between states; domestic factor theories focus on sources and interests internal to each state, including such sources as economic sectors, political institutions, political parties and actors, public opinion, regime type, and policy processes; and social constructivist theories point to identity, shared norms, understandings, common values, and the conceptualizations of identity as the drivers of state behavior. I shall take each of these three schools in turn, focusing on how each could be useful in understanding Russian foreign policy.

Realist Theories of Foreign Policy Behavior

Realist theories are fundamentally about structural factors and are state-centric in their determination of the locus of foreign policy development. Building on the work of Kenneth Waltz and the more foundational work of Thomas Hobbes, realism sees the international system as anarchical.[29] Realism thus emphasizes "the central role of the state, the primacy of state survival, and the self-help nature of the system."[30] Each state exists in this perpetual state of war, always striving to maintain its security in a hostile environment without any overarching governance or law.

Security is a prerequisite for state survival, and this need for security dominates foreign policy choice. Security is primarily based on a state's ability to generate power in all its different forms, both hard and soft, and is derived from natural resources, industrial capacity, population size, cultural agents, and a myriad of other factors.[31] Power is transformed into state capacity for coercion and/or persuasion in the international system. An important concept in realist thought is that a gain in power by any state leads to a decline in the relative power of other states. Yet, in this zero-sum conceptualization of the international system, as one state's security increases, other states must surely perceive a weakening in their security. Thus, the simultaneous pursuit of security by all states in the international system leads to an overall reduction in state security and the potential for conflict. Realist scholars refer to this phenomenon as the security dilemma.[32] In realist thought, there is no such concept as the "secure state" as all states are plagued by the perception of insecurity. Moreover, each state sees the potential for increasing its security by increasing its power, even if it already has a great degree of capability and power: each increase, no matter how marginal, produces more security.

Given the centrality of the state in realist thought, there are plenty of definitional issues surrounding the concept of the state. Power and capability can be not defined as solely material resources (e.g., population, military personnel, number of missiles) because power, in reality, also has intangible components. The entire concept of soft power relies on the realization that not all power can be quantified, and that power can take many forms, be they diplomatic, political, interpersonal, or transactional. Yet, despite the difficulties in defining power and capability, certain useful categorizations predominate in realist studies of international relations, chiefly the division of the world's states into great powers and minor powers.[33] Great powers fundamentally shape the nature of the international system through the application of their greater power.[34]

Middle powers and small powers must seek strategies to survive given their weaker position.[35]

Building upon the work of Robert L. Rothstein, who identifies that alliance formation by states did not follow from absolute measures of state power, Robert O. Keohane argues that the power of a state cannot be defined solely through absolute measures, but rather it can be better defined in comparison to the power of other states in the system.[36] He classifies states by the degree to which they can alter or define the international system: system-determining, system-influencing, system-affecting, and system-ineffectual.[37] Keohane states that his categorical names correspond to the more traditional terms of great, secondary, middle, and small.[38]

Still, problems remain in defining clear boundaries between the categories, and there most likely will never be "a precise definition that is beyond argumentative dispute, reasonable objection, or empirical confusion."[39] Studies that explore definitions of states do not agree on a single typology, with studies using different definitions and different terms to categorize the size of states.[40] For the purposes of this study, we will use the typology of Jesse and Dreyer that builds upon the comparative power approach:

- **Superpower:** state that is never weak interacting with any other state at the global, regional, or sub-regional level.
- **Great state:** state that is weaker than a superpower at the global level, but stronger than non-great states at global level, regional level, and sub-regional level.
- **Middle state:** state always weak at global level, weaker than great states at regional level but stronger than other states at regional and sub-regional level.
- **Small state:** state always weak at global and regional levels, but strong at sub-regional level.

- **Microstate:** state always weak at all levels, unless dealing with other micro states.[41]

In particular, Russian belief in their "natural" status as a great power means that Russia should be an equal with any great powers in their region. If Russia truly sees itself as a Eurasian power, it can only be a great power if it is on par with Germany, France, the United Kingdom, Japan, and China. One can reasonably argue that with the end of the Soviet Union, Russia fell from superpower status to middle-power status. The events of the 1990s illuminated the relative decline as while Russia thought it was cooperating with the West as an equal (i.e., a great power), it soon realized that the West was dictating to Russia—a clear sign of a power asymmetry.

Another issue in the realist literature is the concept of hegemony. A hegemon is "a state that simultaneously dominates several regions of the globe and that as a unit comprises its informal and/or formal empire."[42] While unipolarity defines the contemporary international system, again because of the American preponderance of power, the concept of hegemony defines the degree to which the sole superpower dominates, monitors and impacts the international system. Hegemony relies on three components: 1) a preponderance of power in a single state, 2) that state's awareness of its position and its willingness to use its power in the international environment, and 3) that state's shaping on the international system through international institutions and regimes.[43] Importantly, the presence of the hegemon, and its interests, might pervade the system but this does leave room for other powers, including great powers, to maneuver and/or resist the hegemonic power's interests.[44]

Realist literature has developed over a number of decades since Waltz's work, and variants of realism have been proposed. Without digressing into a theoretical discussion that is not directly relevant to this work, distinctions between offensive and defensive realism need a short elaboration. Classic defensive realism posits that the anarchical system promotes states to seek survival through self-help that is not, in and of itself, offensive in nature.[45] In other words, states will seek to maintain a balance in the international system. Typically, states would seek defensive alliances in order to maintain the status quo. Offensive realism, in contrast, asserts that the anarchical system promotes states to act aggressively and that such behavior leads to great power conflict.[46] What both versions of realism have in common is that the structure of the international system leads states to take foreign policy action.

In conclusion, realist theories point to the following predictions. First, a change in the structure of the international system should lead to a change in foreign policy by the affected states.[47] This change may be due to many factors, such as a declining hegemon, an increase in power by a great state, and a new alliance by a number of states. No matter the source, a change in a relative power relationship in the system should produce changes in foreign policy by states that now perceive that their security is weakened. Second, a lack of change (or one may say, a continuity) in the structure of the international system should lead to no change in a state's foreign policy.[48] When relative power relationships maintain a status quo, states should continue with previous foreign policies.

Domestic Factor Theories of Foreign Policy Behavior

Unlike Waltz's work in the realist school, there is not one canonical work that defines domestic factor theories of foreign policy. Rather, most domestic factor theories are by-products of scholarly work examining the nature of politics within the state, both comparative theories of domestic politics and empirical observations of individual states. Thus, domestic factor theories are more a set of different ideas that all rely on the same fundamental belief: foreign policy originates from forces within the state, not from outside.

Therefore, domestic factor theories fundamentally reject the "statist" approach of realist theories.[49] The basic realist conceptualization of the state as a self-help, security-seeking, autonomous actor is an oversimplification of the foreign policy making process within any individual state.[50] Rather, foreign policy is the product of powerful competing interests within the state. Each different societal actor possesses a different set of opinions, interests, and preferences over foreign policy. These interests are articulated to and channeled through the domestic set of political institutions.[51] The resulting foreign policy is the product of this domestic competition for control of state policy-making. Domestic interests and actors who successfully capture the main institutions of the state have a greater degree of control over the resulting foreign policy. Research identifies that well-organized groups with specific interests have a greater propensity for capturing the state policy-making apparatus than diffuse interests or less-well organized groups.[52] Thus, foreign policy is the result of the struggle of organized actors to capture the levers and institutions of state control, with the resulting foreign policy matching the interests of the successful actor(s).

The number of possible domestic actors that could potentially contribute to foreign policy formulation is quite large. In general, such a list would include political parties, interest groups, social movements, business organizations, trade unions, formal institutions (e.g., courts, parliament), and individual actors of all types.[53] Just a brief extension of this concept to Russian foreign policy would include such domestic actors as Vladimir Putin, Dmitri Medvedev, Foreign Minister Sergey Lavrov, the Security Council, the State Duma, the Ministry of Defense, Rosneft, the *Siloviki*, and the LDPR.

Consequentially, the predictions from domestic factor theories differ significantly from those of realist theories.[54] A change in the societal actors who control or capture the key domestic institutions may lead to a change in foreign policy, even if nothing changes in the international structure. Likewise, a change in the relationship between domestic institutions (e.g., a change in the constitutional organization and distribution of power between a presidency and a legislature, between the government and the courts) also could trigger a change in foreign policy. Similarly, a change in the interests of a ruling set of domestic actors also can lead to a change in foreign policy choice.

Thus, a change in the actors who dominate the apparatus of foreign policy making should lead to a change in foreign policy.[55] On the flip side, during periods of no or little change in the domestic actors who control the state, foreign policy should not fundamentally change.[56]

Social Constructivist Theories of Foreign Policy Behavior

The final school of thought, and by far the most contemporary, is the theory of social constructivism. Originating in the late 1990s from work of scholars of European politics, social constructivist theories place the development and practice of norms at the heart of politics.[57] Norms are defined as the beliefs, values, and acceptable behaviors associated with a nation's primary identity.[58] Identity and interest are separate from material power and any autonomous state's interest. Each state's identity and interest generate from long-term historical, domestic, and social processes that interact with the international system.[59] Moreover, international organizations and organizations can teach states what the norms of the international society are or should be. In short, each nation (and the state by which it is represented) develops a common and shared set of norms and behaviors, and these norms and behaviors distinguish one nation from another.

A nation can be defined as "a political/state community of common affinity, identity, and solidarity, the association of a people, usually defined by a certain culture and kin sentiments, with a particular state."[60] This definition suggests that as a nation adopts a set of norms and behaviors, it also establishes its own unique perspective through which it views the actions of other nations and states. It is the interaction of each state's "national" perspective that has consequences for the structure of the international system.[61] In essence, each nation views the international system through its own unique nationalist lens. Through this perspective, each nation views its own actions and the actions of other nations in a different light than how these same actions are viewed by other nations. A consequence of unique national perspectives is that nations will most likely not agree fundamentally on the nature of the international system, the intention of other nations, or even the fundamental values and beliefs of each nation.

Another distinguishing feature of social constructivism is how its proponents view one of the fundamental assumptions of realist thought: the anarchical state. Social constructivists reject the assumption that the anarchical state is natural or the permanent state of the international system. Rather, they see the anarchical system as the construct of the interaction of states whose beliefs and identities have intentionally or unintentionally created exactly such a system.[62] In other words, the anarchical state exists strictly because it benefits one or more powerful states, which promote the continuance of such a system.

While there has been some social constructivist work on large states such as Russia,[63] a good deal of social constructivist work on foreign policy has centered on smaller, neutral states.[64] This literature stresses that change in the international system does not automatically produce change in small-state foreign policy. If the structural change sets off a soul-searching look at national identity and norms, it may lead to a change in identity. It is argued that this is the case of continental European neutrals such as Sweden and Austria where gradual shifts have happened.[65] However, if the nation does not change its identity, values, or norms, there will not be a change in that state's foreign policy. A good example of this is the long-term continuation of unarmed neutrality by Ireland.[66]

In summary, social constructivism is a more complex and comprehensive theory than either realism or domestic factors theory, mainly because the latter two tend to emphasize either external power or internal power, respectively, as the sole driver of foreign policy. In a nutshell, in social constructivist theory, change in foreign policy occurs from any one or more of the following: 1) establishment of a new norm, 2) the ending of a

previously established norm, 3) the development of a new identity, and/
or 4) the changing of an established identity.[67] None of these four possible
changes would occur in a very short period of time. Norms and identity
are not so elastic as to bend with the wind every few years. Thus, change
in foreign policy is generally should be infrequent and usually associated
with the sort of long-term change in norms that occurs over decades
and generations. Alternately, a sudden, dramatic change in norms might
occur with the abrupt demise of one regime and the establishment of
a radically different regime, as was the case for the USSR in December
1991 when it was replaced with a new democratic and capitalist Russia.

COMPARING THEORIES OF FOREIGN POLICY BEHAVIOR

The three separate schools of thought lead to differing predictions of
what drives foreign policy behavior. Jesse and Dreyer summarize these
differences in regard to small-state foreign policy behavior.[68] Generalizing
from their summary, we apply their conclusions to all states:

Realist Theory:

- States should react to changes in the international structure.
- State behavior should be generalized by either bandwagoning with
  dominant/powerful states or balancing against them.
- Foreign policy is centrally determined by the position of the state
  in the international system.

Domestic Factors Theory:

- The interplay and competition between domestic actors determine
  foreign policy.
- The foreign policy of the state responds slowly to changes in the
  international structure due to domestic actors' reluctance and/or
  inability to change their interests or opinions.
- Changes in which domestic actors control the state will lead to
  changes in foreign policy.

Social Constructivist Theory:

- Foreign policy follows the contours of a nation's norms and identity.

- Changes in the international structure or domestic politics will not necessarily produce foreign policy change.

- Long-term and gradual change in norms and identity leads to foreign policy change.

Table 1 shows the predictions of the three theories. In the first column, realism predicts that Russian foreign policy should be different in a unipolar world than the Soviet foreign policy that existed in a bipolar world. In the second column, domestic politics predicts a number of policies. When Yeltsin assumes the Russian presidency, his foreign policy should be different from the policies followed by the CPSU. The rise of Vladimir Putin to the presidency in 2000 should also signal a new foreign policy. As I detail a bit later, the Beslan School Siege created a permissive atmosphere for Putin to reorganize Russian politics through a reshaping of domestic institutions. Thus, domestic politics would predict 2004 as a key moment for foreign policy change as well. After that, there is no substantial change to the arrangement of domestic politics in Russia until 2014–2016. Even the dual arrangement of Boris Yelstin and Dmitry Medvedev to switch positions from 2008–2012 does not truly constitute a change in the domestic actors who control the Russian state. However, the conflict in Ukraine and the 2016 Foreign Policy Concept suggest a changing Russian view of the international system, revealing that Russian interests may have changed.[69]

The third column displays the predictions of social constructivist theory. Change only happens with major societal upheavals or the establishment of a new regime. Certainly, the change from the socialist state of the USSR to a capitalist, liberal, and democratic constitution not only replaces the institutions of power but also signals the promotion of a new set of norms. Of course, not all Russian citizens or elite quickly adopted the new norms, nor have the norms been universally accepted inside Russia, even by 2020. Recent literature suggests that the slowly built autocratic kleptocracy under the guidance of President Putin has eroded the norms of liberalism and democracy and replaced them with oligarchy, nationalism, and corruption.[70]

Table 1. Predictions of Three Theories.

	Realism	Domestic Factors	Social Constructivism
1979-1991 Cold War	Bipolar world	CPSU Domination	Communism/ State Socialism
1991-2000	Unipolar world	Yeltsin's Presidency	Free market capitalism/ liberalism
2000-2004		Putin Pre-Beslan	
2004-2008		Putin Post-Beslan	
2008-2012		Medvedev Presidency	
2012-2014/2016		Putin's Second Presidency pre-Ukraine/ Foreign Policy Concept	Kleptocracy/ Autocracy
2014/2016+		Post-Ukraine/ Foreign Policy Concept	

In the remainder of the book, I examine the degree to which Russian foreign policy fits with any of these predictions. I argue that to the degree that any of the three theories can accurately predict Russian state behavior, Western policy-makers get a better understanding of the broad contours of Russian foreign policy. And of course, any greater understanding should help Western policy-makers shape more productive relations with Russia, be it through confrontation, cooperation, or any combination of the two. In particular, knowing what truly drives Russian foreign policy, be it the international structure, domestic forces, or identity politics, can help Western policy-makers determine when, where, and why Russian aggression might occur—with the goal of finding ways to resist such aggression.[71]

RUSSIAN FOREIGN POLICY AND DEFENSE GOALS

Applying the three comparative theories of foreign policy is not easy. Russian foreign policy can sometimes seem complex and inscrutable to the outside observer. As a starting point, the Russian Foreign Policy Concept of 2016 contains 108 separate points that can provide a great deal of guidance.[72] The document starts with an enumeration of the key national interests of Russia (Section I. General Provisions). Not surprisingly, this section outlines the importance of defense policy; that is, national security and the defense of Russian sovereignty and territory as a bedrock of foreign policy. At the same time, included in this section are a commitment to "strengthen the rule of law and democratic institutions," "create a favorable external environment," "strengthen Russia's position in global economic relations," "strengthen Russia's role in international culture," and a host of other objectives.

One of the most important parts of the Russian Foreign Policy Concept is the fourth article which outlines Russia's understanding that the international system is becoming more multipolar (Section II. Modern World and Foreign Policy of the Russian Federation). This statement fundamentally places Russia's understanding of the world at odds with

American leadership of a single, unified global order. Of equal importance is the phrase buried in Article 4 that sees power in the system shifting toward the Asia-Pacific region; a region over which Russia and China would have greater influence. In Section III of the Russian Foreign Policy Concept, Russia's priorities are listed (Section III. Priorities of the Russian Federation in Overcoming Global Challenges Shaping a Fair and Sustainable World Order). Highlights of this section are Russia's stated commitment to the rule of law (such as support for the United Nations Charter), as well as its commitment to strengthening international security (such as nuclear nonproliferation), supporting international cooperation on economics and the environment, pursuing international human rights, and delivering information support for Russian Federation activities.

While it is beyond the scope of this work to provide a detailed description of the many different actors involved in the making of Russian foreign policy, a brief sketch here will illustrate the complexity. Fundamentally, the President of the Russian Federation "sets the State's foreign policy guidelines, directs the country's foreign policy and, as the head of state, represents the Russian Federation in international relations."[73] The Security Council plays a coordinating role, by both preparing proposals for the President and also guiding policy implementation.[74] According to the Russian Foreign Policy Concept, the Foreign Ministry "develops the grand strategy" of foreign policy.[75] However, as Putin has consolidated most executive powers, including foreign policy, into the office of the president, the foreign ministry has been much more involved in policy implementation than formulation.[76] Others involved in foreign policy include the prime minister, both houses of parliament, the Ministry of Defense, the constituent entities of the Russian Federation, and many others. Thus, while there are a lot of actors involved in foreign policy, over time the presidency has become the key actor. Moreover, the personalistic nature of Russian domestic politics that makes personal relationships central to policy-making also impacts the policy-making process in foreign policy.

Andrew Monaghan makes it clear that from among this complexity it is unlikely that Russia, a substantial number of important political actors, or even President Putin, has a "grand strategy" in pursuing Russia's goals.[77] He also argues that while Western observers often over-prescribe strategic intent to Russia's actions, seeing a plan to either overthrow NATO or end American global hegemony, observers and analysts inside Russia see instead a lack of a clear strategy and reactive foreign policy decisions.[78] Yet, he argues that foreign policy actors in Russia do have a strategic agenda to try and achieve foreign policy objectives. Thus, given what may not be a coherent or grand strategy, there is still strategic planning and therefore Monaghan argues that Russia's broad foreign policy goals can be ascertained. From all this complexity, there are three general foreign policy and defense goals on which observers of Russia have some fair agreement.

Russia as a Great Power

The end of the Soviet Union was a particularly traumatic time for the Russian people. It signaled the end of the centuries-long project of empire building and expansion. Russia lost territory that it had held since the seventeenth century.[79] Its superpower status vanished, fourteen former Soviet Socialist Republics became independent, and its economy shrank precipitously. Political, societal, and economic turmoil wracked the Russian Federation, and politics became a chaotic free-for-all as old and new actors angled for a position of authority in the new Russian state. Even with this dramatic decline in Russia's power and global standing, Russian elite did not give up on the idea that Russia still had a destiny as a great power.[80] That Russia seeks great power status is a common conclusion among Western analysts of Russian foreign policy.[81] Alexander Sergunin calls Russia a "reformist state" that is "unsatisfied with the existing rules of the game."[82] Christian Thorun's look at the changing nature of Russian foreign policy relies on a long examination of the changing Russian definitions of its foundations for great power status.[83] Marcel H. Van Herpen painstakingly discusses the similarities between

Russia's historic quest for empire and Putin's new imperial designs.[84] Russia's quest for great power status is at the heart of Tsygankov's analysis Russian national identity and its changing foreign policy.[85] Others note that Russia's quest for great power status is fundamentally driven by insecurity as they potentially are underachieving as a great power.[86] Contemporary assessments of Russia's power also claim that great power status is the primary basis for Russia's security and foreign policies.[87] Lilia Shevtsova argues that "ambitions to be a great power" are a part of an enduring "Russian System" of governance.[88] Therefore, one overarching goal is Russia's attempt to regain great power status.

Friendly Relations with Its Neighbors

Samuel Charap and Timothy J. Colton argue that one of Russia's main foreign policy goals is the maintenance of friendly relations with its neighbors.[89] Following the color revolutions of 2003–2005, Russia identified that regime change was both first a product of western interference, with statements by Defense Minister Sergei Shoigu supporting this idea, and second antithetical to continued Russian influence in the region. While the idea that the color revolutions were Western plots is not representative of the overall truth behind the regime changes, the second idea certainly is correct from the Russian perspective. Importantly, the color revolutions sought to replace authoritarian regimes with more democratic governments. Charap and Colton reject the idea that Russian foreign policy thus became anti-democratic; instead they suggest that Russian policy became counter-revolutionary.[90] Russia associated regime change with countries becoming more pro-Western and thus any destabilization of the status quo would inherently lead to the new governments having less affinity with Russia. In their view, Russia is neither promoting authoritarian regimes nor opposing democratic governments, but rather seeking friendly neighbors of any stripe.

Rebuilding Defense Capabilities as a Tool for Foreign Policy
The 2004 Russian presidential election was a pivotal moment for Russian foreign and defense policy. The election returned Putin to power for a second four-year term with a mandate from the public. An important event early was the Beslan school siege of September 2004. In the wake of the siege, Putin instituted a number of domestic reforms that would have long-term consequences for Russian foreign and defense policy. Putin used the post-Beslan climate to push the Duma to pass greater anti-terrorism laws that helped the Russian government restrict independent media and non-governmental organizations. Putin also reformed the federal system by eliminating the direct election of the heads of Russian federal subjects and replaced it with a system whereby they would be appointed by the Russian President and approved by the local parliaments. Intelligence and law enforcement agencies also became more centralized under the Russian president's control. In short, the series of domestic reforms that Putin instigated post-Beslan led to the Russian president have a much greater freedom of action in all matters, including foreign policy.

For the next four years President Putin would begin reforming the Russian military and defense industries. Putin sought to convert a mostly conscripted armed forces into a contract (or volunteer) force. He also sought to trim the bloat in the officer ranks that made the armed forces too top-heavy. In 2007 he appointed Anatoly Serdyukov as Defense Minister and ordered him to engage in an anti-corruption effort. This led to the desired purging of the officer ranks. Putin also ordered the development of a re-armament plan to rebuild the Russian armed forces which had deteriorated slowly but surely since the fall of the Soviet Union. Importantly, this had to be combined with a revitalization of the Russian defense industry which had declined for close to two decades. The short-term goal of this rearmament was to revitalize the defense of Russia; the long-term goal was to establish a strong armed forces as a tool for foreign policy.

The 2008 Russia-Georgia War exposed that the armed forces were still in need of substantial reform. The overall assessment by the Russian military command was that the Russian armed forces performed poorly. In particular, the Army and Air Force were determined to not have been sufficiently combat ready. The problem in these commands was not limited to a single area but encompassed issues of lack of equipment, outdated vehicles, a failure of satellite GPS systems, failures of leadership, failures of troop training, an imbalance of headquarter staff to combat personnel, and an overall lack of command and control. From 2008 to roughly 2014, both Medvedev and then Putin would concentrate on building a strong defense force as a foundation for a successful foreign policy. In particular, a series of rearmament plans and changes in the Minister of Defense would address the need to rebuild the military while actions to improve economic performance would help with generating more funds for defense spending.[91] At the time of writing in early 2020, plans to rearm and rebuild the Russian armed forces continue.

The contribution of defense policy to foreign policy is most evident in the tasks of the Ministry of Defense (MoD). As of March 2019, the stated objectives of the MoD are:

- Deterring the military and political threats to the security or interests of the Russian Federation
- Supporting economic and political interests of the Russian Federation
- Mounting other-than-war enforcement operations
- Using military force.[92]

The first two stated objectives clearly support the basic foreign policy interests of the Russian state. In this way, defense is the foundation for foreign policy. The third objective corresponds with the development inside the armed forces of nonconventional forces, such as cyber warfare assets. While there is much debate about the influence of the writings of General Valery Gerasimov and the so-called "Gerasimov Doctrine," there is little debate that the Russian armed forces have expanded their nonconventional capabilities since 2013.[93] Overall, since 2008 the Russian state has pursued the revitalization of defense assets as an undergirding for a strong foreign policy.

The MoD tasks align with what Russia sees as threats to the Russian state. Broadly outlined, the contemporary threats are 1) the strength of opposing militaries, such as those of China and the United States, 2) instability in states on Russia's borders, both to the west and south, and 3) "the combination of failing states, sociopolitical conflicts, and international terrorism" that pose unknown risks to Russian interests.[94] The Russian view of its national security centers on a preoccupation with NATO actions in Europe that borders not just on suspicion but perhaps paranoia.[95] As such, defense policy (i.e., the use of the armed forces and other assets to defend the Russian state) is often a fundamental backbone of Russian foreign policy, with the latter trying to mitigate possible threats to the secure defense of Russia.

CONCLUSION

Overall Russian goals are fairly straightforward: rebuild defense capacity, create a ring of friendly relations with its neighbors, and increase Russian power and influence in the pursuit of great power status. Exactly how Russia seeks to achieve these goals is of course a complicated story. In the next chapter I apply the comparative foreign policy theories to a selection of Russia's post-Soviet wars and aggressions. The goal is to determine why, when, and where Russia's foreign policy intervened in its neighbors' affairs. The goal of the subsequent chapters will be to highlight how knowledge of the past aggressions can help us predict any future aggressions.

Notes

1. Christian Thorun, *Explaining Changes in Russian Foreign Policy: The Role of Ideas in Post-Soviet Russia's Conduct towards the West* (New York, Palgrave Macmillan, 2009) 4; Alexander Sergunin, *Explaining Russian Foreign Policy Behavior: Theory and Practice* (Stuttgart,Ibidem-Verlag, 2016), 27.

2. Daniel Treisman, ed., *The New Autocracy: Information Politics and Policy in Putin's Russia* (Washington, DC, Brookings Institute, 2017).

3. Samuel Charap and Timothy J. Colton, *Everyone Loses: The Ukraine Crisis and the Ruinous Contest for Post-Soviet Eurasia* (London, International Institute for Strategic Studies/Routledge, 2017); Sergunin, *Explaining Russian Foreign Policy Behavior*, 59.

4. Andrei P. Tsygankov, *Russia's Foreign Policy: Change and Continuity in National Identity* (Plymouth, UK, Rowman & Littlefield, 2013).

5. Thorun, *Explaining Changes in Russian Foreign Policy*, 46.

6. Olga Oliker, Christopher S. Chivvis, Keith Crane, Olesya Tkacheva, and Scott Boston, *Russian Foreign Policy in Historical and Current Context: A Reassessment* (Santa Monica, RAND Corporation, 2015), 2–4.

7. Sergunin, *Explaining Russian Foreign Policy Behavior*; Thorun, *Explaining Changes in Russian Foreign Policy*; Andrew Radin and Clint Reach, *Russian Views of the International Order* (Santa Monica, RAND Corporation, 2017); Marcel H. Van Herpen, *Putin's Wars: The Rise of Russia's New Imperialism*, 2nd Edition (New York, Rowman & Littlefield, 2015); Andrew Monaghan, "Putin's Russia: Shaping a Grand Strategy?" *International Affairs* 89, no. 5 (2013): 1221–1236; Jeffrey Mankoff, *Russian Foreign Policy: The Return of Great Power Politics*, 2nd Edition (New York, Rowman & Littlefield, 2012); Nikolas Gvosdev and Christopher Marsh, *Russian Foreign Policy: Interests, Vectors, and Sectors* (Los Angeles, Congressional Quarterly Press, 2014); Maria Raquel Freire and Lucinda Simao, "The Modernisation Agenda in Russian Foreign Policy," *European Politics and Society* 16, no. 1 (2015): 126–141.

8. Oliker, et al., *Russian Foreign Policy in Historical and Current Context*; Charles K. Bartles, "Getting Gerasimov Right," *Military Review* 96, no. 1 (2016): 30–38; David E. McNabb, *Vladimir Putin and Russia's Imperial Revival* (New York: CRC Press, 2016); Igor Sutyagin, "Driving Forces in Russia's Strategic Thinking" in *Ukraine and Beyond: Russia's Strate-*

gic Challenge to Europe edited by Janne Matlary and Tormod Heier (New York, Palgrave, 2016), 85–100; Tsygankov, *Russia's Foreign Policy*; Christoph Zürcher, *The Post-Soviet Wars: Rebellion, Ethnic Conflict, and Nationhood in the Caucasus* (New York, New York University Press, 2007).

9. Samuel Charap, Alyssa Demus, and Jeremy Sharpino, *Getting Out from "In-Between": Perspectives on the Regional Order in Post-Soviet Europe and Eurasia* (Santa Monica, RAND Corporation, 2018); Defense Intelligence Agency (DIA), *Russian Military Power: Building a Military to Support Great Power Aspirations* (Washington, DC, DIA, 2017); Keir Giles, *The Turning Point for Russian Foreign Policy* (Carlisle, Strategic Studies Institute and U.S. Army War College, 2017); Matthew R. Slater, Michael Purcell, and Andrew M. Del Gaudio, editors, *Considering Russsia: Emergence of a Near Peer Competitor* (Quantico, Marine Corps University Press, 2017).

10. Marcel H. Van Herpen, *Putin's Propaganda Machine: Soft Power and Russian Foreign Policy* (New York, Rowman & Littlefield, 2016).

11. Roger N. McDermott, *The Reform of Russia's Conventional Armed Forces: Problems, Challenges, and Policy Implications* (Washington DC, Jamestown Foundation, 2011).

12. Agnia Grigas, *The Politics of Energy and Memory between the Baltic States and Russia* (Burlington, Ashgate, 2013).

13. Thomas Gomart, *Russian Civil-Military Relations: Putin's Legacy* (Washington, DC, Carnegie Endowment for International Peace, 2008).

14. Andrei Soldatov and Michael Rochlitz, "The Siloviki in Russian Politics," In *The New Autocracy: Information Politics and Policy in Putin's Russia* edited by Daniel Treisman (Washington, DC, Brookings Institute, 2017), 83–108.

15. Treisman, *The New Autocracy.*

16. Andrew Monaghan, "Putin's Way of War: The 'War' in Russia's 'Hybrid Warfare,'" *Parameters* 45, no. 4 (2016): 65–74; Alexander Lanoszka, 'Russian Hybrid Warfare and Extended Deterrence in Eastern Europe." *International Affairs* 92, no. 1 (2016): 175–195 (2016).

17. Elana Wilson Rowe. Editor. *Russia and the North* (Ottawa, University of Ottawa Press, 2009).

18. Carolina Vendil Pallin and Fredrik Westerlund, "Russia's War in Georgia: Lessons and Consequences," *Small Wars & Insurgencies* 20, no. 2 (2009): 400–424; Güner Özkan, "Spoils of a War: Impact of Georgia-Russia War on Russian Foreign and Security Policies in the 'Near Abroad.'"

Akademic Bakis 6, no. 11 (2012): 35–64; Julie A. George, *The Politics of Ethnic Separatism in Russia and Georgia* (New York, Palgrave Macmillan, 2009).

19. Lawrence Freedman, "Ukraine and the Art of Limited War," *Survival* 56, no. 6 (2014): 7–38; Roy Allison, "Russian 'Deniable' Intervention in Ukraine: How and Why Russia Broke the Rules," *International Affairs* 90, no. 6 (2014): 1255–1297.

20. Daniel Hamilton and Gerhard Mangott, editors, *The Wider Black Sea Region in the 21st Century: Strategic, Economic and Energy Perspectives* (Washington, DC, Center for Transatlantic Business Relations, 2008); Fiona Houston, W. Duncan Wood, and Derek M. Robinson, editors. *Black Sea Security: International Cooperation and Counter-Trafficking in the Black Sea Region* (Washington, DC, IOS Press, 2006).

21. Constantine Pleshakov, *The Crimean Nexus: Putin's War and the Clash of Civilizations* (New Haven, Yale University Press, 2017).

22. Douglas Mastriano, *A U.S. Army War College Assessment on Russian Strategy in Eastern Europe and Recommendations on how to Leverage Landpower to Maintain the Peace.* (Carlisle, Pa, Strategic Studies Institute and U.S. Army War College Press, 2017).

23. Mikhail A. Molchanov, *Eurasian Regionalisms and Russian Foreign Policy* (Burlington, Ashgate, 2015).

24. Robert W. Schaefer, *The Insurgency in Chechnya and the North Caucasus: From Gazavat to Jihad* (Santa Barbara, Praeger, 2011); Stephen F. Jones, editor, *War and Revolution in the Caucasus: Georgia Ablaze* (New York, Routledge, 2010); Fariz Ismailzade and Glen E. Howard, editors, *The South Caucasus 2021: Oil, Democracy and Geopolitics* (Washington, DC, The Jamestown Foundation, 2012).

25. Daniel-Cornel Stefanescu, "Particularities of Preparing Romania's Territory in Case of the Country's Implication in a Hybrid War," *Scientific Research and Education in the Air Force-AFASES* (2016): 657–662.

26. Mehmet Seyfettin Erol and Safak Oguz, "Hybrid Warfare Studies and Russia's Example in Crimea," *Akedemik Bakis* 9, no. 17 (2015): 261–277.

27. For example, *Doctrine of Information Security of the Russian Federation.* Ministry of Foreign Affairs, December 5, 2016; *Foreign Policy Concept of the Russian Federation,* November 30, 2016, Ministry of Foreign Affairs of the Russian Federation; Valery Gerasimov, "The Value of Science is in the Foresight: New Challenges Demanding Rethinking the Forms and Methods of Carrying out Combat Operations," *Voyenno-Promyshlennyy Kurier (Military Industrial Courier).* (2013); *Russian National Security*

Strategy, Text of 31 December Russian Federation Presidential Edit 683 approving appended text of "The Russian Federation's National Security Strategy. December 2015.

28. Neal G. Jesse and John R. Dreyer, *Small States in the International System: At Peace and At War* (Lanham, Lexington Books, 2016).

29. Kenneth Waltz, *Theory of International Politics* (New York, McGraw Hill, 1979); Thomas Hobbes, *Leviathan: With Selected Variants from the Latin Edition of 1668*, Ed. Edwin Curley. (Indianapolis, Hackett, 1994).

30. Neal G. Jesse, "Choosing to Go It Alone: Irish Neutrality in Theoretical and Comparative Perspective," *International Political Science Review* 27, no. 1 (2006) 7–28, p.13.

31. Joseph S. Nye Jr., *Soft Power: The Means to Success in World Politics* (New York, Public Affairs, 2004).

32. Waltz, *Theory of International Politics*

33. John J. Mearsheimer, *The Tragedy of Great Power Politics* (New York, W.W. Norton, 2001).

34. Paul Kennedy, *The Rise and Fall of the Great Powers: Economic Change and Military Conflict from 1500 to 2000* (New York, Vintage Books, 1987).

35. Mearsheimer, *The Tragedy of Great Power Politics*; Annette Baker Fox, *The Power of Small States: Diplomacy in World War II* (Chicago, University of Chicago Press, 1959); Robert L. Rothstein, *Alliances and Small Powers* (New York, Columbia University Press, 1968).

36. Robert O. Keohane, "Lilliputians' Dilemmas: Small States in International Politics," *International Organization* 23, no. 2 (1969): 291–310.

37. Keohane, "Lilliputians' Dilemmas," 295–296.

38. Ibid., 296.

39. Jesse and Dreyer, *Small States in the International System*, 5.

40. Jesse and Dreyer, *Small States in the International System*; Keohane, "Lilliputians' Dilemmas"; David R. Mares, "Middle Powers under Regional Hegemony: To Challenge or Acquiesce in Hegemonic Enforcement," *International Studies Quarterly* (1988): 453–471; Trygve Mathisen, *The Functions of Small States in the Strategies of the Great Powers* (Oslo, Scandinavian University Books, Universitetsforlaget Oslo-Bergen-Tromsö, 1971); K. P. Mueller, *Strategy, Asymmetric Deterrence, and Accommodation: Middle Powers and Security in Modern Europe* (Princeton, Ph.D. Dissertation, 1991), Anders Wivel and Kajsa Ji Noe Oest, "Security, Profit, or Shadow of the Past? Explaining the Security Strategies of Microstates" *Cambridge Review of International Affairs* 23, no. 3 (2010): 429–453.

41. Jesse and Dreyer, *Small States in the International System*, 10–13.

42. Steven E. Lobell, *The Challenge of Hegemony: Grand Strategy, Trade, and Domestic Politics* (Ann Arbor, University of Michigan Press, 2003), 8.

43. Kristen P. Williams, Steven E. Lobell, and Neal G. Jesse, editors, *Beyond Great Powers and Hegemons: Why Secondary States Support, Follow, or Challenge* (Stanford, Stanford University Press, 2012), 7.

44. Neal G. Jesse, Steven E. Lobell, Galia Press-Barnathan, and Kristen P. Williams. "The Leader can't Lead when the Followers won't Follow." In Williams et. al. *Beyond Great Powers and Hegemons: Why Secondary States Support, Follow, or Challenge* (Stanford, Stanford University Press, 2012), 1–30, pp. 11–17.

45. See, for example, Waltz, *Theory of International Politics*.

46. Mearsheimer, *The Tragedy of Great Power Politics*.

47. Jesse and Dreyer, *Small States in the International System*, 34.

48. Ibid., 34.

49. Ibid., 40.

50. Miriam Fendius Elman, "The Foreign Policies of Small States: Challenging Neorealism in Its Own Backyard," *British Journal of Political Science* 25, no. 2 (1995): 171–217.

51. James G. March and Johan P. Olsen, "The New Institutionalism: Organizational Factors in Political Life," *American Political Science Review* 78, no. 3 (1984): 734–749; James G. March and Johan P. Olsen, *Rediscovering Institutions: The Organizational Basis of Politics* (New York, The Free Press, 1989); Kathleen Thelen and Sven Steinmo, "Historical Institutionalism in Comparative Politics" in *Historical Institutionalism in Comparative Politics* edited by Sven Steinmo, Kathleen Helen, and Frank Longstretch (New York, Cambridge University Press, 1992), 1–32.

52. Mancur Olson, *The Logic of Collective Action: Public Goods and the Theory of Groups* (Cambridge, Harvard University Press, 1971).

53. Jesse and Dreyer, *Small States in the International System*, 41.

54. Ibid., 48–53.

55. There is of course the possibility that in any change in dominant actors that the interests of those coming into power match exactly the interests of those being removed. In such a case one would not expect any difference in foreign policy. Such an alignment of common interests should be rare. However, in the next section social constructivist theories provide one possible argument as to how this might occur.

56. There is the possibility that a stable dominant actor might have a significant change in its interests during the period in which it is in power, which would then precipitate a change in foreign policy. Proving such

an incidence would require a robust analysis of exactly how and why such interests changed in a very short period of time.

57. Alexander Wendt, *Social Theory of International Politics* (Cambridge, Cambridge University Press, 1999).

58. Martha Finnemore and Kathryn Sikkink, "International Norm Dynamics and Political Change," *International Organization* 52, no. 4 (1998): 887–917.

59. Emanuel Adler, "Seizing the Middle Ground: Constructivism in World Politics," *European Journal of International Relations* 3, no. 3 (1997): 319–359; John Gerard Ruggie, "What Makes the World Hang Together?: Neo-Utilitarianism and the Social Constructivist Challenge," *International Organization* 52, no. 4 (1998): 855–885.

60. Azur Gat, *Nations: The Long History and Deep Roots of Political Ethnicity and Nationalism* (New York, Cambridge University Press, 2013), 26.

61. Ted Kopf, "The Promise of Constructivism in International Relations Theory," *International Security* 23, no. 1 (1998): 171–200.

62. Ruggie, "What Makes the World Hang Together?"

63. Anne L. Culnan, *The Social Construction of Russian Resurgence: Aspirations, Identity, and Security Interests* (Baltimore, Johns Hopkins University Press, 2009).

64. Christine Agius, *The Social Construction of Swedish Neutrality: Challenges to Swedish Identity and Sovereignty* (Manchester, Manchester University Press, 2006); Christine Agius and Karen Devine, "Neutrality: A Really Dead Concept? A Reprise," *Cooperation and Conflict* 46, no. 3 (2011): 265–284; Annike Björkdahl, *From Idea to Norm-Promoting Conflict Prevention* (Lund, Sweden, Lund University, 2002); Annika Björkdahl, "Norm Advocacy: A Small State Strategy to Influence the EU," *Journal of European Public Policy*, 15, no. 1 (2008): 135–154; Karen Devine, "Stretching the IR Theoretical Spectrum on Irish Neutrality: A Critical Social Constructivist Framework," *International Political Science Review* 29, no. 4 (2008): 461–488; Jessica L. Beyer and Stephanie C. Hofmann, "Varieties of Neutrality Norm Revision and Decline," *Cooperation and Conflict* 46, no. 3 (2011): 285–311; Laurent Goetschel, "Neutrals as Brokers of Peacekeeping Ideas?" *Cooperation and Conflict* 46, no. 3 (2011): 312–333; Jesse, "Choosing to Go It Alone," Hans Löden, "Reaching a Vanishing Point? Reflections on the Future of Neutrality Norms in Sweden and Finland," *Cooperation and Conflict* 47, no. 2 (2012): 271–284; Christine Ingebritsen, "Norm Entrepreneurs: Scandinavia's Role in World Politics," *Cooperation and Conflict* 37, no. 1 (2002): 11–23.

65. Agius, *The Social Construction of Swedish Identity*; Ulrika Möller and Ulf Bjereld, "From Nordic Neutrals to Post-Neutral Europeans: Differences in Finnish and Swedish Policy Transformation," *Cooperation and Conflict* 49, no. 1 (2010): 363–386.
66. Jesse, "Choosing to Go It Alone,"; Neal G. Jesse, "Contemporary Irish Neutrality: Still a Singular Stance," *New Hibernia Review* 11, no. 1 (2007): 74–95.
67. Jesse and Dreyer, *Small States in the International System*.
68. Ibid.
69. The argument is that Russian aggression in Crimea and actions in Eastern Ukraine signal a new willingness by the Russian state to act unilaterally in Eastern Europe. This unilateral action displays a calculated disregard for the American-led hegemony. The 2016 Foreign Policy Concept crystalizes this idea with its deliberate and unequivocal declaration of a multipolar international system. In short, Russia is announcing its desire, even if it has not yet been realized, for a multipolar system to replace the current unipolar system. The exact time of the change in domestic interests cannot be precisely timed, so I have chosen to represent the period from 2014–2016 as the time of change.
70. As Treisman argues in *The New Autocracy*, the Russian autocracy is not a typical repressive regime state but an "informational autocracy," in which control over media and information is the greatest asset of Putin and his supporters.
71. The concluding chapter of this book contains recommendations for Western policy-makers based on the evidence and arguments from the first seven chapters.
72. Foreign Policy Concept of the Russian Federation.
73. Ibid.
74. Mankoff, *Russian Foreign Policy*, 55–56.
75. Foreign Policy Concept of the Russian Federation.
76. Mankoff, *Russian Foreign Policy*, 54.
77. Andrew Monaghan, *Power in Modern Russia* (Manchester, Manchester University Press, 2017), 1–15.
78. Ibid., 3–4.
79. Mankoff, *Russian Foreign Policy*, 3.
80. Ibid., 3.
81. Jakob Hedenskog, Vilhelm Konnander, Bertil Nygren, Ingmar Oldberg, and Christer Pursiainen, editors, *Russia as a Great Power: Dimensions of Security under Putin* (Abingdon, Routledge, 2005).

82. Sergunin, *Explaining Russian Foreign Policy Behavior*, 25.

83. Thorun, *Explaining Changes in Russian Foreign Policy*, 28–50.

84. Van Herpen, *Putin's Wars*, 9–87.

85. Tsygankov, *Russia's Foreign Policy*, xxv–xxviii.

86. Hanna Smith, "Russia as a Great Power: Status Inconsistency and the Two Chechen Wars," *Communist and Post-Communist Studies*, 47, no. 3 (2014): 355–363.

87. Slater, et al., *Considering Russia.*

88. Lilia Shevtsova, *Putin's Russia* (Washington, DC, Carnegie Endowment for International Peace, 2003), 16.

89. Charap and Colton, *Everyone Loses.*

90. Ibid., 77–78.

91. This material is covered in much more depth in Chapter 3.

92. Ministry of Defense, *Tasks*, 2019, http://eng.mil.ru/en/mission/tasks.htm, accessed March 12, 2019.

93. I cover the development of Russian non-conventional assets in Chapter Four and the increased use of cyber warfare in Chapter Five.

94. Daniel Goure, "Moscow's Visions of Future War: So Many Conflict Scenarios so Little Time, Money and Forces," *Journal of Slavic Military Studies* 1, no. 27 (2014): 63–100, p. 69.

95. Goure, "Moscow's Visions of Future War," 69.

CHAPTER 2

RUSSIA'S POST-SOVIET WARS, AGGRESSIONS, AND INTERVENTIONS

WHY, WHEN, AND WHERE

Conflict in the former Soviet Socialist Republics that ring Russia, in what is typically termed the "near abroad," demonstrates the role that a post-Soviet Russia expects to play in the Eurasia region. According to Boris Yeltsin in 1993, while Russia was not intending to reconstruct its former empire or even to put back together the territory that encompassed the Soviet Union, Russia sought to obtain "special powers as guarantor of peace and stability" in the region around Russia's new borders.[1] Roger E. Kanet summarizes the three objectives of Russian involvement in the many post-Soviet Wars as follows: First, Russia intended to maintain its regional dominance. Second, the Russian military leadership used the wars as a way to impose unity on the both the declining armed forces and the former states of the Soviet Union. Third, the Russian involvement in these conflicts was justified as a means to protect Russian minorities in the newly independent states.[2]

The interpretation of Russian military engagement in the post-Soviet world mirrors the three theoretical approaches in chapter 1. From the realist perspective, Russia seeks to achieve a greater regional hegemony both to dominate weaker neighbors but also as a means toward establishing itself as a great power. From the domestic perspective, Russian aggression was driven by a need for internal organization after the collapse of the Soviet Union. Last, from the social constructivist perspective, Russian aggression sought to unite a transnational Russian community that had been scattered by the breakup of the USSR and was engaged in a mass nationalist mobilization.[3] This chapter explores Russian aggressions in the "near abroad," and in particular, in the "in-between" states,[4] with aim of elucidating the underlying reasons for each action and contributing to our understanding of Russian foreign policy through the three theoretical perspectives.

BORIS YELTSIN'S WARS: THE EARLY CONFLICTS

Just before Yeltsin had time to settle in as President of Russia, his military was involved in a number of conflicts on Russia's borders, including the Nagorno-Karabakh dispute in which an Armenian-majority region of Azerbaijan sought independence began in 1988 while the USSR was still intact. When the USSR collapsed and both Armenia and Azerbaijan declared their independence, the unsettled issue of Nagorno-Karabakh escalated into full-scale conflict. The Nagorno-Karabakh Armenians were heavily armed, supported by both the Armenian government and mercenary forces. As Yeltsin took power, the Russian government began to provide covert aid to the Nagorno-Karabakh Armenians mainly to protect a sizable ethnically Russian minority in the territory. The conflict went on for a couple of years with the better-armed Armenian forces securing Nagorno-Karabakh. Azerbaijan was forced to recognize the de facto independence of Nagorno-Karabakh but did not concede the territory to Armenia.[5] At the time of writing this book, there was an ongoing brokerage of negotiations between the independent republic,

Armenia and Azerbaijan by the Minsk Group (comprised of Russia, the United States and France). As of January 2020, the situation remains unresolved.

Important to the conflict was the presence of an ethnic Russian minority. Ted Hopf argues that the presence of more than 25 million Russians living in the fourteen former Soviet Socialist Republics would surely influence Russian foreign policy.[6] Russia would be able to use the presence of a Russian population as both a reason for Russian involvement in the conflict and a source of leverage over the direction of the conflict. A recurring pattern in the post-Soviet conflicts is that the leaders of the other states with a Russian-minority population or a Russian military contingent must always weigh the possibility of Russian intervention. And importantly, the leaders of the smaller states must certainly recognize that any Russian involvement has the potential to become grossly asymmetrical compared to the capabilities of the smaller state, should Russia desire it to be so.

Russian involvement in the civil war of Tajikistan demonstrates this principle. After the declaration of Tajik independence from the USSR, a power struggle emerged between the former communists, now organized as reformers and in control of the government after the 1991 presidential election, and separatist groups mainly comprised of both liberal reformers and Islamic elements. The presence of an old Soviet military unit in Tajikistan at the time of independence played a large role in the ensuring conflict. Originally comprising Tajik conscripts and a core of Russian officers, the unit disintegrated during the Tajjik independence. In 1992 Yeltsin sent Russian forces to bolster the unit and renamed it the Russian 201st Motorized Rifle Division. At an estimated fighting strength of between 7,000 and 10,000, the division could plausibly determine the course of the conflict between the government and the rebels, and this is exactly what it did.

Yeltsin ordered the 201st to act as peacekeepers and to secure the Tajik-Afghanistan border.[7] Russia and the Tajik government, feared that Islamic veterans (mujahideen) of the Russia-Afghanistan war would flow across the border to help the rebels. Despite the neutral-sounding objective of the 201st's deployment, in reality they supported the government as the unit found itself fighting against Islamic elements which were always on the side of the resistance. The fighting intensified in 1992 and 1993, leading to tens of thousands of casualties and over a million displaced people. The conflict ended with the government victorious, but the country was left in ruins and devoid of any central authority. Chaos and sporadic fighting continued up to 1997 when a comprehensive peace agreement was signed under the auspices of an observer mission led by the United Nations (UN). The 201st Motorized Rifle Division established a base in Tajikistan in 2004, and the Russian government has an agreement to maintain the base until the year 2042.[8]

Another conflict in which Russia interjected itself was in Moldova. The roots of the conflict began in 1989 when the Supreme Soviet of the Moldavian Soviet Socialist Republic declared Moldovan the official language. Ethnic Slavs worried that this was the first in a possible series of steps that would see the Russian language marginalized, Slavic culture removed, and Moldova eventually unify with Romania. The far eastern territory of Transnistria, landlocked and bordered by Ukraine, was primarily a slavic region with less than 40 percent of the population ethnically Moldovan. Tension escalated rapidly in 1990 as a Moldovan nationalist group won parliamentary elections and separatists in Transnistria declared a separate Pridnestrovian (as the territory is known in Russian) Soviet Socialist Republic. Soviet President Mikhail Gorbachev refused to recognize the new Pridnestrovian SSR but also cited the Moldovan lack of respect for ethnic minorities as the cause of the secession movement. Thus, Soviet foreign policy presaged Russian foreign policy: defense of Russian minorities would lead to Russian interference in a former Soviet Republic.

In November 1990, fighting broke out between volunteer forces of the Moldovan government and the Transnistria separatists. The struggle intensified in 1992 as both government and separatist forces attempted to gain control of the ex-Soviet weaponry stationed in Moldova. Under an agreement of the former fifteen Soviet Socialist Republics, negotiated in late 1991 and early 1992, Moldova was to create a new defense ministry and assume control of most of the equipment of the Soviet 14th Army in Moldova, which had two of its four bases in Moldova, with some equipment slated to be transported to Ukraine.[9] While technically the Russian forces were neutral, and as part of a series of cease-fires they would be a peacekeeping force, in practice the 14th Army was sympathetic to the separatists. The on-the-ground reality seemed linked to the respective commander of the 14th Army, as initially the 14th Army did little to stop separatists from raiding its weapons caches. Later with a new commander and the support of President Yeltsin, the 14th Army transferred its weapons (per the agreement mentioned earlier) to the Moldovan defense ministry in spring 1992. Given the Russian and Ukrainian minorities in Transnistria, volunteers from both countries entered Moldova and fought alongside the separatists.[10]

The events of the early summer of 1992 determined the final course of the conflict. With newly acquired equipment, the Moldovan forces began to retake territory from the separatists. However, fighting in the city of Bendery threatened the transfer of 14th Army equipment moving from Moldova to Ukraine. The new commander, General Major Alexander Lebed, was under orders to protect the transfer by all means necessary. He ordered the 14th Army to defend its position. Its subsequent artillery strike destroyed the attacking Moldovan army forces. This show of overwhelming force ended any thought of further action by the Moldovan government in Transnistria, effectively ending the conflict.

To this day Transnistria remains one of the "frozen" post-Soviet conflicts. The international community does not recognize it as an independent nation. Yet, the Moldovan government does not have the ability to retake the territory because of the implicit support of Russia. The situation is similar to that of Nagorno-Karabakh, now known as Artsakh by the inhabitants of the region, in which a kind of halfway status quo prevails since the cessation of armed conflict. The separatist regions act as if they were independent, but they have no international status as such. Moreover, neither region would be able to stay independent without the backing of Russia. Thus, the Russian foreign policy to protect a vulnerable Russian minority has created a position by which Russia must support the governments of the separatist regions, however ineffective the leaders of those governments might be. This predicament displays the inherent costs of Russian foreign policy to intervene on behalf of Russian minorities in former Soviet republics: Russia gets locked into a long-term commitment to the populations of these regions without any effective and clear means to resolve or better the situation. Such a result appears to foreshadow Russian intervention in Ukraine in 2014.

This exact situation would play out in another of Yeltsin's early wars: the separatist movements in Georgia from 1991 to 1993. In April 1991, Georgia declared its independence from the Soviet Union. The fledgling Georgian government declared that it would assume sovereignty over the two autonomous oblasts of Abkhazia and South Ossetia. Tensions between Georgians and Ossetians had been simmering for a few years as Ossetian separatists had been trying to gain more autonomy under the Georgian SSR. The annulment of their autonomous oblast set the stage for direct conflict. In December 1990 the Georgian government declared a state of emergency and moved troops into South Ossetia. Fighting between some newly formed Georgian units and the mainly volunteer separatist militias raged from 1991 to 1992 without any clear winner. During this stage of the conflict, human rights abuses were common as both ethnic groups, and the armed combatants representing them, targeted vulnerable villages and towns mainly as a means of revenge.[11]

Russian involvement in the conflict is a matter of contention. While President Yeltsin maintained that Russian involvement was mainly as peacekeepers "to keep the warring sides apart" the Russian involvement also furthered their foreign policy goal of tying former Soviet Republics to Russia.[12] As in the Transnistria conflict, volunteers from Russia participated on the side of the separatists. There is also some evidence that Russian equipment made its way to the separatist militias.[13] As in the previously mentioned conflicts, the separatist resistance was able to hold most of its ground mainly through the tacit support of Russia. A brokered cease-fire led to Georgia acquiescing to a divided South Ossetia in which the separatists controlled the majority of the territory in a *de facto* independence.

This pattern played out in Abkhazia in a similar fashion, though on a larger scale. As in South Ossetia, Abkhaz separatists agitated for independence from Georgia in the late 1980s, in which a series of minor scuffles required a deployment of mainly national guard troops to quell. It is important to note that one-third of the population at the time in the Abkhazia oblast were Russian, making it one of the largest ethnically Russian regions of Georgia. Abkhaz separatists attacked in June 1992 and declared independence from Georgia in July of that year. A swift attack by Georgia quickly routed the separatists. The now-more-desperate separatist movement declared what amounts to a guerrilla and terrorist war against the Georgian government, to which the Georgian military commander Giorgi Karkarashvili responded by announcing that Georgia would pursue a policy of genocide against the Abkhaz people if resistance continued. The resulting ethnic conflict was brutal and led to thousands of Abkhaz and tens of thousands of ethnic Georgian civilians killed by the warring parties. Internal displacement of civilians numbered in the hundreds of thousands. Georgia occupied most of the breakaway territory but had no desire to remain there indefinitely.

Russia, technically neutral in the conflict, negotiated a cease-fire in September 1992. As Georgian forces retreated as part of the cease-fire, the Abkhaz separatists attacked. The Abkhaz forces were supplied by Russia, as they now possessed tanks and other heavy equipment, and made great progress. Further, the Russian navy blockaded the Georgian seaport near Gagra where most of the fighting was taking place. Russian involvement escalated with Russian airstrikes on Georgian positions, Russian artillery bombardments of Georgian-held towns, and the introduction of Russian airborne troops. In early 1993 it was clear that Russian intervention was having the desired effect as Abkhaz separatists were back in control of most of their territory. The Georgian parliament appealed to the United Nations and European Union, declaring that Russia had launched an undeclared war on Georgia.

The end result was similar to the other conflicts: Abkhazia became a *de facto* independent region without international recognition, yet it was recognized as independent by Russia. So once again, Russia committed itself to defending a Russia minority and an ethnic separatist movement in a former Soviet republic. Taken together the four independent regions in these conflicts (Artsakh, Transnistria, South Ossetia, and Abkhazia) would in 2001 start discussions to form a commonwealth between them. This would eventually be formalized in 2007 as the Community for Democracy and Rights of Nations (also known as the Commonwealth of Unrecognized States).

As a form of foreign policy, the Russian aggression under Yeltsin's first administration appears on its face to have been counterproductive as it created a hostile relationship with neighboring countries and committed Russia to supporting weak, separatist governments for an indeterminate amount of time into the future. Yet, there was one major gain for Russia in these actions: Russian support of separatists allowed Russia to exert pressure on the governments of the former Soviet republics of Moldova and Georgia. Thus, Russian involvement might come at a continued cost but establishes Russian influence over its former satellites. The proactive Russian policies also allowed Yeltsin to appease nationalist elements in the Russian Duma while simultaneously garnering support among the Russian population, who generally supported the protection of Russian minorities in the former Soviet Republics.

Yeltsin's Nightmare: War in Chechnya

But everything did not go well for Yeltsin's foreign policy, particularly in the region of Chechnya where domestic and foreign policy collided. The area of the North Caucasus has historically been a source of much instability, including during the expansion of the Russian Empire, in the aftermath of the Russian Revolution and Civil War, and during World War II when the native populations were moved as part of a forced relocation.[14] Inherent in this instability is the realization that the centuries-long expansion of Russian interests into the North Caucasus inevitability created a multiethnic Russian Empire/Soviet state. The people of the North Caucasus have more in common with their neighbors in the South Caucasus (e.g., Georgians), the Middle East and Afghanistan than with the Russian community. In addition, the inhabitants of the North Caucasus region (e.g., the Chechens, Circassians, Ingush, and Dagestanis) possess deep grudges against the Russians that date back centuries.[15] This region had historically been part of the Muslim world, something alien to both the Eastern Orthodox Russian Empire and the atheist Soviet Union.

It is with the demise of the Soviet Union that the alienness of Chechnya (and other North Caucasus nations) came to the fore. The loosening of the Soviet reins under Gorbachev led to a renewed sense of Islamic nationalism tied with a renewal of cultural and national identity.[16] Importantly, the leaders in Chechnya had been raised or born in Kazakhstan during the time of the Stalin imposed exile.[17] When the Soviet Union fell and the socialist republics of the South Caucasus became independent states, the Autonomous Soviet Socialist Republics of the North Caucasus were quietly integrated into the new Russian Federation. Russia's desire to retain its territorial integrity after the loss of the other fourteen former Soviet republics meant that Yeltsin had no interest in having territory inside the Russian federation lead to a further fragmentation and diminution of Russian territorial sovereignty.

The tension between the more independence-minded Chechens and the state-preservation goals of Yeltsin came to head with the election of Dzhokhar Dudayev as President of Chechnya in October 1991. Dudayev declared Chechnya independent of Russia, to which Yeltsin declared a state of emergency in Chechnya in November. Initially, both sides decided that negotiation was the preferred path to resolving the conflict. From 1992 to 1993, the sides met several times to try and arrive at a solution. Whether either or both were willing to comprise is still a matter of debate, but recent scholarship argues that unlike the other regions of the North Caucasus that formalized agreements with Yeltsin's Russia, the military leaders of Chechnya seemed less or not at all interested in doing so.[18] During this time there was an exodus out of Chechnya of non-Chechen citizens, primarily the Russians who asserted that they were being discriminated against by the new Chechen authorities.

With this debate aside, a domestic factor inside Russia eventually led to conflict: Yelstin's weakening grasp on the Russian Duma. Duma elections in December 1993 did not lead to a majority for the pro-government parties. As 1994 dragged on, Yeltsin found it harder and harder to impose his will on a Duma in which the parties that supported him were faltering. At the same time, the legislature could not provide support or guidance for Yeltsin, his political advisors were pressing for direct and perhaps belligerent action toward Chechnya. Yeltsin needed a policy success in order to regroup his legislative allies and to garner public support. Yeltsin's Defense Minister Pavel Grachev assured him that a Russian military victory over the Chechens would be easily achieved, perhaps in as short a time as two hours. This culminated in the Russian-aided coup attempt by a warring Chechen faction against Dudayev in November 1994 that ultimately failed.[19] The failed coup was embarrassing to the Russian president. The capture of Russian soldiers by Chechen units only made the matter worse for Yeltsin who now faced public ridicule for the disastrous action.

In the face of this defeat, Yeltsin decided to double down. In the name of restoring constitutional order, he authorized a full-scale Russian invasion of Chechnya which began in December 1994. Massive aerial bombardment of Chechen cities resembled the strategic bombings of World War II. Some cities were leveled so flat that they resembled parking lots for automobiles. Days after the air campaign, Russian units crossed into Chechnya and vastly outnumbered the anticipated opposing Chechen units. Despite many setbacks due to poor organization, the use of conscripted soldiers, a lack of training in modern urban warfare, and equipment problems, the overwhelming asymmetry in troops led to an unstoppable Russian advance. Chechen resistance to the initial Russian invasion lasted for about two months, but the overwhelming superiority of the Russian units could not be matched with ferocity by the Chechen resistance for very long.

Chechen forces retreated to the capital of Grozny which suffered through a months-long siege by Russian forces. The destruction of the city was vast, both from fighting on the ground and Russian aerial bombardment, with the Russians seizing control in March 1995. As the Chechen resistance scattered, this led to an expansion of the war in many ways, including the following four: First, it led to a moving of the main battlefields in the war to the lowland areas and the mountains, which proved a difficult battleground for the Russian units. Second, the war entered into the public discourse in Russia, particularly as heavy Russian casualties were beginning to arrive back home in coffins. Not surprisingly, the unpopularity of the war surged among the Russian populace. This led to a dramatic decline in Yeltsin's support in the December 1995 Duma election. Viktor Chernomyrdin was retained as Prime Minister but could no longer count on any long-term support in the legislature. The unpopularity of the war also was a factor in the lead up to the 1996 Russian Presidential election. The Communist Party Leader Gennady Zyuganov held the largest share of seats in the Duma and would be a serious challenge to replace Yeltsin.

The third way which added to the expansion of the war was the Chechen rebels turning to terrorism as a new tactic. On June 14, 1995, a group of around 150 Chechen rebels assaulted and captured a police station and city hall in Budyonnovsk. Eventually, most of the terrorists fled the government buildings and captured the local hospital where they took more than 2,000 hostages. The leader of the rebels, Shamil Basayev, demanded that Yeltsin end the Russian war in Chechnya. Yeltsin responded with intransigence, signaling that he would do everything possible to end the siege. After multiple attacks by Russian special forces failed to dislodge the terrorists, Russian Prime Minister Viktor Chernoymyrdin negotiated directly with Basayev over the phone.[20] The negotiated agreement between the two allowed the Chechen rebels safe passage to Dagestan and secured the release of the hostages. The resulting political reaction in Russia was a disaster for Yeltsin and his government. The Duma passed a (non-binding) vote of no confidence while the Security Minister Sergei Stepashin and Interior Minister Viktor Yerin both lost their positions. And as might be expected, the Russian population turned even further against the war and the government that appeared ineffective in either protecting civilians or bringing the war to a decisive end. Further terrorist attacks by Chechen (and other) rebel groups in the Caucasus would further undermine support for Yeltsin among both the Duma and the Russian population.

The fourth way the war expanded was how it exploded into the international consciousness both in the region and all around the world. In the Caucasus the Chechen fight against the occupying Russian forces galvanized sympathy from other minority groups. Resistance to Russian demands increased in both Dagestan and Ingushetia. Volunteers from Georgia and elsewhere contributed to the fighting strength of the Chechen rebels. The Chechen separatists were also helped by their connections to the wider Muslim community, and, in particular, the more extreme Islamist groups such as Al-Qaeda.[21] In Western Europe and North America, Western nations were criticizing Russian involvement in Chechnya. Criticism typically centered around two linked aspects of the conflict: the indiscriminate Russian bombing of civilians and the humanitarian crisis. For example, while Yeltsin was trying to court Western aid at the G-7 meeting in Canada, he had to deflect discussions of the Russian campaign in Chechnya.

Meanwhile on the ground in Chechnya, the Russian forces were preforming poorly. An over-reliance on air power led to reducing Chechnya to rubble. The resulting urban warfare in a demolished land-scape was hellish for the ill-trained, poorly equipped, and demoralized Russian soldiers. Chechen rebels employing guerrilla tactics would hit swiftly and then vanish into the hills and mountains. Russian units took Grozny on a number of occasions, only to have the Chechens take it back at a later date. This similar situation played out all over Chechnya: Russian units could not systematically eliminate the Chechen resistance. With a presidential election looming, Yeltsin sought a way to end the conflict. Negotiations between the Russian government and the Chechen rebels culminated in the Khasav-Yurt Accord of August 31, 1996, effec-tively ending the First Chechen War. Chechnya remained in Russia, but it was more akin to an autonomous republic than an integrated region.

The effects of the war on Russia were profound. The poor performance of the Russian military would lead to recriminations all around, with the military leadership blaming the government for its poor decisions, while the Yeltsin government blamed the military for its lack of preparedness and poor tactics. The Russian populace was stunned at the failure of both the military and the government. Russians expected their military to be on par with that of a great power; defeat by a local band of Islamic separatists was a shock. In this chaotic environment in which factions inside Russia pointed fingers at each other, reform could not, and certainly would not, be accomplished. The Russian military performance seemed to have learned little from its defeat in Afghanistan and appeared to replicate that performance in Chechnya.[22]

The First Chechen War undid almost all of the political gains that Yeltsin had made through more successful foreign policy in the South

Caucasus. Yet, despite both the political and military bungling of the war, the overall thrust of foreign policy was both consistent with other Russian actions and largely successful: Russia would fight to both preserve the unity of the Russian state and intimidate minorities on the periphery of the Russian state. Using the publicly spoken rationale of protecting Russian-minority populations, Russian foreign policy combined realist objectives with social constructivist motivations: it projected power against its neighbors to force them into a more pro-Russian set of policies under the guise of protecting minority Russian communities. This point needs some emphasis here. It can be argued that the 2008 Russian-Georgian War was some sort of turning point where Russian foreign policy became more assertive and aggressive. As has been made clear in this chapter, Yeltsin's foreign policy was inherently assertive and aggressive against its neighbors even during the 1990s. The real difference in 2008 will be the underlying challenge by Putin to the international order and American hegemony, not the overall level of Russian aggressiveness in defending its interests.

THE SECOND CHECHEN WAR: FROM YELTIN'S WAR TO PUTIN'S WAR

Yetsin's nightmare in Chechnya was far from over. After a lull from 1996 to 1999, fighting would eventually resume. During the interwar period, Chechnya's economy disintegrated, and the Chechen government could barely impose sovereignty and authority over Grozny let along the countryside, while terrorist attacks on Russian military, police, and civilians slowly intensified. The Chechen resistance also became more radicalized as the situation within Chechnya worsened. On August 1999, an attack on Dagestan by Chechen separatists provided the impetus for a resumption of direct, armed conflict and the start of the Second Chechen War.

The Russian government, still in Yeltsin's hands but with an increased awareness that Yeltsin was preparing a successor ahead of the 2000 presidential elections, moved rapidly to subdue Chechnya. From August to September, Russia unleashed another massive aerial bombing campaign, reducing Chechnya to more rubble. The Russian military prepared for an invasion, but Yeltsin was hesitant to resume a land war that had cost him so dearly once before. In October the new Prime Minister, Vladimir Putin, moved decisively. He nullified the legitimacy of the local authorities in Chechnya and ordered the invasion. On October 12, Russian forces started the invasion, supported by missile strikes against key Chechen positions. The assault moved rapidly, sweeping Chechen resistance aside. Russian units reached Grozny in December, and by February 2000 they had taken the Chechen capital. Putin established his direct rule over Chechnya a few months later, and major military operations would cease soon thereafter. By 2003, rule of Chechnya would transfer to a local government that while technically autonomous would in fact be subject to Russian dominance. Guerrilla and terrorist resistance would continue until 2009 when Chechen separatists ended their campaign against Russian occupation.

Yeltsin's war in Chechnya became Putin's war in Chechnya, but with vastly different results both militarily and politically. Understanding the inherent unpopularity of Russian action in Chechnya, Putin brought the Second Chechen War to an end as quickly as possible. Yet, he had one weapon in his arsenal that Yeltsin did not—his decision to rule over Chechnya directly from Moscow. Putin's centralization of political control over the troubled and rebellious republic foreshadowed his centralization of political authority in Russia more broadly. To the people of Russia, Putin's campaign in Chechnya was a success, as it limited the long-term exposure of Russian troops. Chechen terrorism would continue to be a thorn in Putin's side, but one that he could potentially turn to political advantage.

Putin's Peace: 2000-2008
The end of the Second Chechen War ushered in a period of relative calm between Russia and its neighbors. Putin's focus was mainly on

consolidating his power, both through forming the United Russia party to institutionalize his control of the Duma and by dominating domestic politics in various ways. Putin also needed to find a way to rebuild the Russian economy while simultaneously weakening the power of the oligarchs. Initially, Putin sought cooperation with the West to reduce international criticism of Russia that had built over its actions in Chechnya and to secure much-needed funding. The September 11, 2001, Al-Qaeda terrorist attack in the United States allowed Russia to play the role as another major state committed to fighting international terrorism. This renewed Russian cooperation, combined with the view of Western nations who saw Putin's election as a welcome change from Boris Yeltsin's chaotic administration, led to some optimism about the future of Western-Russian relations. Yet, Europe was still wary about a new Russian ruler who seemed more intent on a vertical, statist model of rebuilding Russia rather than a democratic, European model.[23]

If there was any sense that Russia was at war during the period 2000–20008, it would be as part of the American-led international war on terrorism. This is not to say that Russia was a key participant in the American campaign, but rather that Putin found Russia engaged in its own struggle against international terrorism much like the United States. However, in Russia's case, it was a terrorism that originated in the Russian wars of the 1990s. A number of apartment bombings across Russia took place in the 1990s, but while Chechens or Dagestanis were suspected of the acts, no conclusive proof has yet been provided. In the 2000s, the conflicts that had mostly been contained within the Caucasus now spilled over into Russia. Coinciding with the ending of the Second Chechen War in 2000, Basayev and other Chechen separatists, often in conjunction with international Islamic elements, began a campaign of terror against the Russian population. The 2002 Dubrovka Theater siege in Moscow being the first large-scale act by Chechen-affiliated terrorists. The pumping of a fentanyl-derived toxic agent into the theater by Russian security services, resulting in the estimated deaths of 200 hostages and injuries to roughly 700 more, stunned the Russian population. Paradoxically, it did not lead to a criticism of the Putin government, but rather a rallying around the president and an increase in his support among the public.

The 2004 Beslan School Hostage Crisis is a pivotal event. The aftermath of this siege saw Putin tighten his control on Russian politics and society, greatly paving the way for the autocratic government that currently exists in Russia. On September 1, 2004, a cadre of terrorists seized an elementary school in the town of Beslan in North Ossetia, taking more than 1,100 hostages, mainly children. The terrorist cadre had been sent by Shamil Basayev with demands that Russian occupying forces withdraw from Chechnya and that Chechen independence be recognized by the Russian government. On the third day of the siege, a number of explosions (with the exact nature and cause of the explosions still a subject of much dispute) inside the school started a series of events leading to a full-scale assault by Russian forces, led by the Federal Security Service (FSB), on the hostage takers. The attack was poorly coordinated and included the use of heavy rocket fire and T-72 main battle tanks. In the chaos, more than 300 hostages were killed and more than 700 injured.

Nationalists and others in the Duma criticized Putin for the loss of lives in the counterterrorism efforts. They pointed out that a key base of his 2000 presidential election platform was effective counterterrorism policies.[24] In response to the criticism, Putin took advantage of the Beslan siege to start a series of changes in Russian politics that would centralize power in the presidency. To make these changes, he needed a base of support, and he found it in the Russian population. In the aftermath of the Beslan School Siege, the Russian populace made a predictable call for stronger counterterrorism measures and a restriction on the movement of Chechens into Russia. In response, Putin eliminated direct election of the local governors of federal subjects, instead creating a system of presidential nomination and local legislative confirmation. This would allow the Russian president to create a series of governors who would follow the president's decisions and not be an independent source of decision-making. Putin passed a law eliminating the single-member districts in elections to the Duma, thus consolidating the control of parties over individual Duma members. This reform also had the effect of reducing the number of independent candidates. In addition, a number of anti-terrorism measures were passed through the Duma, giving greater authority to the government to restrict coverage of events by the media and to regulate foreign-funded non-governmental organizations (NGOs).

These immediate reforms were followed by legislation in 2006 and 2007 to assign the lead role in counterterrorism to the FSB. Among the changes were an increased legal use of wiretapping, FSB control over the military in counterterrorism operations, the authority to shoot down passenger planes, the outlawing of propaganda or messaging that supports or justifies terrorism, and the punishment of political or ideological vandalism with incarceration. A law allowing the Russian president to use all measures of force outside the Russian borders against terrorism was also passed; this law effectively allows the Russian president to order the assassination of any opponent in any country.[25]

This period also saw the consolidation of support for Putin and his prime minister Dmitry Medvedev into the single United Russia party. This move created majority support for the pair who now ruled in a "tandemocracy." As Putin's second four-year term was running out in 2007, he designated Medvedev as the heir apparent to the presidency. The March 2008 election saw Medvedev elected president. He quickly appointed Putin as his prime minister. Exactly which man was the more powerful from the period of 2008 to 2012 is a matter of speculation and not the concern of this book. The key takeaway is that the two were in agreement on most issues of foreign policy. Later in the book, I discuss Medvedev's efforts during his term as president to reform the Russian military. The reader can safely assume that Putin was in concordance with all the efforts that Medvedev made, and perhaps it can be inferred that Putin was a key proponent of the Medvedev actions. In either case, the year 2008 would prove to be not only the source of change in the Russian president but also of great importance to Russian foreign policy.

2008 WAR REEMERGES IN THE CAUCASUS, AND RUSSIAN AGGRESSION RETURNS TOO

The first true European war of the twenty-first century began in August 2008 between Russia and Georgia. Yet, the groundwork for the war started as early as 2004 when Mikheil Saakashvili was elected President of Georgia. One of his top priorities was to restore Georgian control to South Ossetia and Abkhazia. Under the guise of police operations, such as anti-drug smuggling, Georgian security forces began incursions primarily into South Ossetia. In 2007 Saakashvili arranged a pro-Georgian administration to be installed in South Ossetia. Russia promptly refused to recognize this new government.[26]

At this point, Georgian and Russian domestic politics combined with international relations to create a volatile situation. In March 2008, South Ossetia and Abkhazia petitioned Russia to recognize their independent status from Georgia. The Russian Duma passed a resolution asking President Medvedev to do exactly that. At a NATO summit in Bucharest in April 2008, the American President George W. Bush gave his support to the wishes of Georgia and Ukraine to start a membership plan to join NATO. President Putin (who was still president until Medvedev assumed the role in May) was at the Bucharest summit and made it explicitly clear that he considered such a move by either or both nations to be a direct security threat to Russia.

Returning to Russia, President Putin issued a decree establishing ties between Russia and the two separatist Georgian republics. By late April, both Russia and Georgia were mobilizing troops and moving them to the border between the two countries. Since 2003, Georgia had been reforming its military, mainly because it was weaker than the ragtag units of the separatists.[27] The reform efforts went forward with the assumption that a likely, eventual adversary would be Russia.[28] One consequence of this reform was that by 2008, the Georgian armed forces were superior to the armed militias of the separatists, perhaps spurring Georgian aggression.[29] From April to July, the situation slowly deteriorated. Russia increased the number of its peacekeepers in both South Ossetia and Abkhazia, separatist militias attacked pro-Georgian politicians and political institutions, Georgian police stepped up their involvement in both regions, and separatist leaders were victims of both successful and unsuccessful assassination attempts. In July, Russian aircraft flew over South Ossetia, in apparent violation of Georgia's territorial sovereignty. To add an international dimension, both the United States and Russia started military exercises in the Caucasus on exactly the same day—July 15. Of note is that at the conclusion of the Russian exercises on August 2, the Russian troops did not leave the area.[30]

Events inside South Ossetia in the first week of August began to move rapidly and produced a spiral of conflict. Clashes between Ossetian separatists and Georgian peacekeepers, mortar exchanges initiated by both sides, bombings, Georgian sniper attacks, and other actions intensified the already-volatile situation. Georgian forces launched an offensive on August 7 and moved into South Ossetian territory. The overall goal of the Georgian attack was to quickly overrun the south Ossetian capital of Tskhinvali and close off the Trans-Caucacus Motorway via which Russian troops would arrive.[31] An emergency meeting of the Russian Security Council, chaired by the now-President Medvedev, asserted that Russia was ready to protect both its peacekeepers and the Russian citizens in South Ossetia.[32] Again, Russia would couch its interventionism into a neighboring country as defense of Russian citizens and maintaining peace.

Russian units counterattacked on the night of August 8 and began to push the Georgian troops back almost immediately. Russia launched aerial bombardments of both Georgian units and Georgian cities, including the Georgian capital of Tbilisi. Simultaneously the Russian Black Sea fleet began to blockade the Georgian coast and occupied the crucial port of Poti. The Russian offensive from Abkhazia quickly overran Georgian resistance and moved south into Georgian territory. At the same time, the Russian offensive in South Ossetia pushed Georgian units out of the territory and Russian units continued south into Georgian territory.

Coinciding with the Russian military offensive was an undeclared cyberwar by Russia against Georgia.[33] On August 7, Russia launched a series of denial of service (DoS) attacks against Georgian government websites.[34] Further DoS attacks occurred against Georgian media while government websites were defaced. The attacks effectively shut down sites belonging to the Georgian Ministry of Defense, Supreme Court, and other governmental bodies. In the next few days, attacks crippled the largest Georgian bank, the Georgian parliament, media organizations, and many other Georgian businesses. David Hollis argues that the cyberattacks were coordinated with the air, land, and sea attacks, amounting to a coordination of war into the fourth dimension of the Internet that had not previously been done.[35] Cyberattacks continued until late August when Georgian cybersecurity efforts blocked all further (alleged) Russian attacks.

The warring parties agreed to a cease-fire negotiated by the French President Nicolas Sarkozy (who represented the entire European Union in the negotiations) on August 12. Russian troops occupied both Abkhazia and South Ossetia while withdrawing from other areas of Georgia. Russia also recognized the independence of the two separatist republics. The war was costly to Georgia, with more than 2,000 personnel injured or killed, and hundreds of armor, artillery, and other heavy armaments destroyed or lost.[36] Russian losses were more limited with an official tally of 67 killed, of which 48 were from hostile fire and the remainder mainly from accidents.[37] Russia lost six aircraft, but half of the planes were either directly or most likely downed by friendly fire.[38]

Following the Russian withdrawal, Georgia ended its diplomatic contacts with Russia and accused it of launching an aggressive war in order to seize Georgian territory. To this day, Russian troops still occupy the two territories in violation of the cease-fire agreement and Russia still considers the two territories to be independent of Georgia. Moreover, later agreements conceded to Russia the right to occupy military bases in both regions.[39]

Taken in a larger context, Russian foreign policy in the Russian-Georgian War reflects the fundamental and underlying realist aspects of Russian security concerns.[40] The Caucasus are a vital geostrategic region for Russia. Georgian overtures to NATO were bound to provoke a Russian response, as a primary goal of Putin by the late 2000s was to prevent any further encroachment of NATO toward Russian borders. Still, there were domestic and ideational factors that helped push Russia toward action. The presence of Russian citizens galvanized domestic support both among the public and in the Duma. The actions of President Saakashvili and the Georgian offensive provided all the cover that Putin needed to claim that the Russian actions were in self-defense and to protect the independent people in Abkhazia and South Ossetia.

The larger goal of preventing any further former Soviet Republics from flirting with NATO membership was also strengthened. It did not escape Russia's notice that none of the Western powers came to Georgia's aid in meaningful way. The message was clear: Russia could assert its foreign policy dominance over its "near abroad" and the West either would not or could not challenge it. This message was resoundingly clear in other states such as Ukraine, which saw an immediate growth in pro-Russian political agitation.[41] Thus, the Russian-Georgian War of August 2008 led to many political gains that the Kremlin believed validated its actions.

Yet, the war also revealed many shortcomings of the Russian military.[42] Within months of ending the war, the Russian military would start its largest restructuring and reorganization in decades.[43] Why was such an overhaul needed when Russian forces seemed to achieve all of their military objectives during the short war? The underlying truth is that the Russian military underperformed in many ways. First, there was a breakdown in coordinated command and control. In particular, the use of incompatible communications equipment between the air and ground forces reduced coordination of strikes.[44] Both failures in intelligence operations and tactical formation compounded the command and control problems. The Russian units were successful against their Georgian opponents despite these issues because of the overwhelming differences in numbers. According to one estimate, the Russian military budget is thirty times that of the Georgian military and the total Russian force projection is forty times greater.[45]

Second, the superior Russian numbers hid "three major deficiencies related to Russian military personnel: a shortage of well-trained troops, the nonexistence of sufficient first-line units, and deficiencies within the leadership structure."[46] At least 30 percent of the Russian soldiers were conscripts with little training. Chief of the General Staff Nikolay Makarov estimated that less than 20 percent of Russian units were battle ready, with too many units full of officers and bereft of enlisted personnel.[47] Third, Russian equipment was generally outdated, leaving Russian troops ill-equipped to fight effectively.[48] Therefore overall, the military suffered from employing Soviet-era tactics with Soviet-era technology with ill-trained and ill-equipped personnel who lacked morale. The reform of the Russian military is the subject of the next chapter, but at this point the reader should note the disjunction between the military and political success of the Russian campaign in Georgia and the glaring deficiencies that were exposed in the Russian armed forces. Foreign policy had been successful, but the underlying weakness in the defense forces has been exposed.

2014 RUSSIAN INTERVENTION IN UKRAINE

The Russian invasion of Georgia was overt, with Russian military units directly engaging with Georgian forces and invading Georgian territory. The Russian intervention in Ukraine in 2014 following the collapse of Viktor Yanukovich's presidency and the Euromaiden protests would be a covert operation in which Russia would try to conceal its involvement. Over the course of a few months, Russia would seize the valuable territory of Crimea and support the Donbass rebellion in Eastern Ukraine in the Luhansk and Donetsk Oblasts. While the international reaction to the Russian war in Georgia was muted, the reaction from the West in regard to Russian actions in Ukraine was swift and severe. Russia has paid a great price for its intervention in Ukraine; examining why it did so helps illuminate key points about Russia's foreign policy.

The Russian Empire conquered Crimea in 1783, overrunning the Tartars and taking the territory away from the Ottoman Empire. During the nineteenth century, Ukraine was divided between the Austria-Hungarian Empire and the Russian Empire at the Dnieper river. Following the Russian Revolution and subsequent Civil War, Ukraine and Crimea were annexed into the nascent Soviet Union in 1921 and 1922, respectively. During World War II, Crimea was the site of the mass deportation of Crimean Tartars and other minorities from Crimea to Central Asia by Stalin for what he perceived as their pro-Nazi sympathies. The Tartars would subsequently return to Crimea in 1991.[49] Russians have traditionally viewed Ukraine as an important heartland of the Russian Empire, with Crimea having a special place because of its incorporation into the empire by Catherine the Great. The presence of the Russian Black Sea Fleet home at Sevastopol provides a key defense component as it allows Russia access to the Mediterranean.

Relations between Ukraine and Russia remained close after the fall of the Soviet Union. Ukraine eventually gave up its possession of Soviet nuclear forces in return for Russian assurances of the sovereignty and inviolability of Ukrainian territory. Ukraine allowed Russia to lease the base at Sevastopol so that its fleet could remain in the Black Sea. Ukraine and Russia negotiated a series of agreements over energy transport, primarily natural gas, from Russia through Ukraine to the rest of Europe. Still, disputes between Ukrainian and Russian businesses over both the price of the gas and the cost of its transport grew in stature to become full-blown international disputes during the 1990s and early 2000s. In 1998 Gazprom, the Russian natural gas exporter, and Naftogaz, the national natural gas and oil company of Ukraine, signed a contract managing the transport of natural gas from Russia through Ukraine. That same year, Gazprom accused Naftogaz of diverting gas transits and responded by suspending energy transfers to Ukraine. Negotiations between the two corporations in 2006 became acrimonious when agreement could not be reached on gas price increases, transit fees, and methods of payment.[50] One source of the dispute between Russia and Ukraine was Turkmenistan, which began to raise prices in 2004.[51] Again, Gazprom shut off supplies and caused a European crisis as the reduction also led to shortages in other European countries. In 2009 a dispute erupted over gas prices and Ukrainian debt payments to Gazprom. In a recurring pattern, gas shipments to and through Ukraine were reduced severely, setting off a Europe-wide crisis. International lenders agreed to loan money to Ukraine so that it could maintain a reliable payment schedule to Russia. While the Gazprom shutoff forced Ukraine to make good on its debts, an unintended consequence was the growing distrust of European countries regarding the reliability of energy supplies from Russia, particularly those moving through Ukraine. Under Vladimir Putin's leadership, Russia has effectively further weaponized energy as a source of foreign policy leverage and Ukraine still transports about three-fourths of Russian natural gas exports to Europe, maintaining Ukraine as a continued target of Russian energy foreign policy.[52]

Therefore, the Kremlin has a large incentive to influence or force Ukraine into the Russian orbit of satellite states. Ukraine is both a buffer against Western influence and a transit for Russian influence to flow into the West. Importantly, the eastern half of Ukraine has a large Russian minority. Since independence, Ukraine has been torn between a Ukrainian population that tends to look to Europe and a Russian population that focuses east toward Moscow. The 2004–2005 Orange Revolution in Ukraine displayed the ethnic tension and division within that country. A disputed election and subsequent protest led to the defeat of the Kremlin-backed candidate Viktor Yanukovich and the ascension of ethnic Ukrainian candidate Viktor Yuschenko to the presidency. After the subsequent and tumultuous half decade of politics in Ukraine led by Yuschenko, Yanukovich ran for and won the 2010 presidential election. This set the stage for the events that would define contemporary Ukraine.

Putin quickly urged Yanukovich to join the Russian-led Customs Union (with Russia, Kazakhstan, and Belarus).[53] The passing by the Ukrainian legislature of a Russian language law in 2012, which permitted Russian to be the official language in certain eastern portions of Ukraine, led to protests, particularly in the Western half of Ukraine. The protests grew as the Yanukovich-directed legislature began to end discussions between the European Union (EU) and Ukraine over a trade-association status for the latter. Russia imposed a series of economic sanctions against Ukraine over the protests, which were growing into mass demonstrations by early 2013. Events moved quickly in November 2013 after Yanukovich canceled negotiations with the EU and instead agreed to a large loan-and-trade agreement with Russia. Hundreds of thousands of demonstrators gathered in the Maiden square (leading to the protests being named the Euromaiden protests) to protest Yanukovich's government. The president's signing of repressive laws in January 2014 led to bloody confrontations between security forces and protestors. In February, the protests spread to many cities in western Ukraine. European Union mediation led to an interim government being formed and charges being brought against Yanukovich for the murder of protesters. He fled the country and turned up days later in Russia.

In late February 2014, Russia responded. Following the establishment of the interim government, pro-Russian protests against it broke out in Crimea on February 23 and continued for days. On February 27 and within days of Yanukovich fleeing Kiev, masked and armed men in green uniforms without any identifying patches or insignia (and thus called the "little green men" by locals and the media) began seizing government offices, military bases, and road checkpoints in Crimea. These men disarmed Ukrainian units and quickly cut off Crimea from the rest of Ukraine. There can be little doubt that the majority (if not all) of these "little green men" were indeed Russian soldiers and most likely special operations forces.[54] At the time Putin denied that the soldiers were Russian, instead insisting that they were part of local militias.[55] It is important to note that the intrusion of the soldiers coincided with the appearance of a letter on March 1 from Yanukovich asking Russia to intervene in Ukraine. That same day both houses of the Russian legislature authorized Putin to use force to occupy Crimea and protect the Russian population there, as roughly 60 percent of the population in Crimea was ethnically Russian.[56]

A new, autonomous Crimean parliament authorized a referendum to establish the future of Crimea via the following questions: did the citizens of Crimea wish to secede from Ukraine and become a part of the Russian Federation or did the citizens of Crimea wish to be an autonomous community within Ukraine? Before the referendum was to be held, Russian troops swarmed out of the base at Sevastopol as permitted by the Russian parliamentary act. There is also credible evidence that other Russian units entered Crimea (or were already present) and helped in subduing all resistance. By March 2, Crimea was effectively under Russian control. It is in this atmosphere that the subsequent referendum took place on March 16. The Ukrainian government declared the referendum unconstitutional, but they had little actual control over events in Crimea. The official report from the Crimean parliament was that 95 percent of voters approved union with Russia; however this number is certainly inflated. The next day the Crimean government announced it was an independent republic, began to nationalize private property in Crimea, and requested that Russia admit the new republic into its federation. That same day Putin recognized the breakaway republic of Crimea and authorized the inclusion of Crimea and Sevastopol as federal subjects in the Russian Federation. Crimea was now a Russian possession.

The actions of the Russian units display a level of planning similar to the invasion of Georgia. There can be no doubt that Russian forces were prepared to take the Crimean peninsula and a plan was clearly in place. Exactly when the planning began is not clear, but Bartles and McDermott believe that "Russia probably had some form of contingency planing for a Crimean annexation...most likely, preparations for the campaign began days or weeks before Yanukovych's escape."[57] This should come as no surprise given that 1) the instability inside Ukraine for over a decade and 2) the strategic importance of Sevastopol to Russian projection of power into the Black Sea and further. Having only a single naval port on the Black Sea is more a strategic weakness than a strength. Russia was never going to gamble with the possibility of that port falling into Ukrainian hands, especially any pro-Western Ukrainian government. In a speech on March 18, Putin also gave a separate realist rationale for Russian action: the inappropriate eastward expansion of NATO into a nation with a sizeable Russian population.[58]

There are, however, differences between the Russian intervention in Georgia in 2008 and its actions to seize Crimea in 2014. Bartles and McDermott point out that in the latter, the Russian "force mix and application of strategy represents something new and experimental in Russian military power."[59] While the reasons for the Russian action were similar in both cases (the protection of ethnic Russians against hostile local forces; the need to prevent the breakdown of order in a territory on the Russian border), "from a tactical/operational perspective these were very different situations, and in several senses the campaigns were conducted in much different fashions."[60] The war with Georgia was a large-scale conventional conflict in which a large number of elements of the Russian armed forces were thrown into the conflict against an opponent with some credibility to resist. The operation in Crimean campaign was accomplished mainly through highly specialized units with a commitment to not engage in a direct, shooting confrontation.[61] Moreover, Russian military planners had every reason to believe that the Ukrainian units possessed "low military capabilities and low levels of combat readiness" and thus were not likely to provide any meaningful resistance.[62]

Yet, the seizure of Crimea came at a great cost. The European Union reached out to the new Ukrainian government and within a year signed a trade agreement with them. This was exactly the opposite of what Russia wanted. The G-7 kicked Russia out of the G-8 and canceled its meeting in Sochi, Russia. The United States and the European Union placed a series of sanctions on Russian citizens and companies associated with Putin and/or the invasion of Crimea. Canada, Switzerland, and Australia also independently established similar sanctions. Generally, the sanctions have three effects: restricting access of targeted persons and companies from Western capital and financial markets, embargoing exports to Russia of high-technology energy equipment, and embargoing exports to Russia of dual-use or military equipment. The intent of the sanctions is to hit Russia where it would hurt the most—the energy sector and access to the vast supply of Western capital. There is evidence that the sanctions have hurt the Russian economy and have reduced overall Russian economic growth.

But Russian intervention in Ukraine also included its support for the Donbass Rebellion. In March 2014, while events were moving quickly in Crimea, pro-Russian protests against the interim Ukrainian government also took place in the eastern Donetsk and Luhansk Oblasts. The pattern of events was quite similar to Crimea: rebels seized government buildings, "little green men" appeared to help with seizing important sites and bases, the rebels declared their independence from Ukraine, the rebels declared new independent Republics, the new governments sought help from Russia to secure this new independence, and quite quickly actual Russian military units entered the region.

The pretext for Russian intervention was the same as for Crimea: to protect a Russian-minority population from the despotic rule of an illegitimate Ukrainian government. The Donbass region was conquered by the Russian Empire in the late eighteenth century, and the more urban and industrial areas quickly became inhabited by Russian speakers, with the Ukrainian population mainly living and working in the countryside. By 2014, roughly 40 percent of the population in the Donbass region was ethnically Russian.

But the Donbass region differed from Crimea in three very important ways. First, it did not have any important Russian base akin to the one in

Sevastopol. In short, Russian troops in the Donbass were not protecting any important geostrategic military asset. From a pure realist perspective, the Russian intrusion into the Donbass could only be seen by foreign observers as a land grab. Second, while the overwhelming majority of the population in Crimea was Russian, the majority in the Donbass was Ukrainian. This meant that popular support for the rebellion was unlikely to be from them. Third, and of great importance to how the conflict would subsequently unfold, the Donbass could not be geographically isolated from Ukraine by cutting off a small isthmus, as had been done by Russian forces in Crimea. This allows Ukrainian police units, security units, and military units to move against the Donbass rebellion without having to dislodge a Russian presence directly.

The Donbass rebellions have bogged down into a long, slow war between the Ukrainian government versus the Russian-supported rebels. Russian intervention to help the rebels includes efforts such as providing funding and equipment; advising and training rebel units; encouraging Russian private citizens to fight for the rebels; and directing Russian military participation such as cross-border shelling, the use of Russian drones, the presence of Russian special operations forces, Russian armored units and equipment operating on Ukrainian territory, and Russian-directed cyber warfare attacks against Ukraine, among other actions.

The question that one must ask at this point is why Russian participation has not become more overt. Scholars tend to point to the implication that a declared war by Russia against Ukraine, or at least the clear use of Russian military units to support the Donbass rebellions, would most likely lead to an even stronger Western reaction. What Russia probably fears is that in that instance NATO would have a clear rationale for putting its presence into Ukraine, which is, of course, the exact opposite of what Putin wants. In addition, the use of covert forces allows Putin to maintain a plausible deniability of Russian action, even with the obvious nature of Russian involvement. There are also the practical lessons that the Russians have learned from their intervention in the Donbass region.

Roger N. McDermott argues that assessments of the Russian performance identifies many key areas in which the Russian military can improve, including better control of proxy forces, better articulation of objectives, increased use of modern weapon and hardware systems, better use of electronic weapons, better integration of agencies, and other issues.[63]

Interestingly, Russian action in the Donbass rebellion appears to have produced little gain for Russia and come at a cost. The Donbass region has slowly sunk into economic decline, the rebels appear no close to seceding from Ukraine, and increased lawlessness has made the region (unlike the fairly stable and prosperous Crimea) an unappealing addition to the Russian Federation. At the same time, the Ukrainian government has signed a trade agreement with the EU and moved closer to the West. The only positive result for Russia is that Russia has prevented Ukraine from moving closer to NATO.

Russian action in Ukraine has hurt Russia both domestically and on the international stage. The negative impact of sanctions on the Russian economy are most likely secondary to the general weakness and lack of global competitiveness in the Russian economy and the downturn of oil prices in 2014–2015.[64] Russia's relations with Europe have deteriorated, with nations (such as Germany) that previously were less confrontational with Russia moving further toward confrontational relations more associated with the United Kingdom or United States.[65] Further, Russian aggression has served to heighten the security needs of smaller East European countries (such as the Baltic nations) who now seek even greater reassurances from NATO about their commitments. On the balance sheet, the seizure of Crimea can be labelled a Russian foreign policy success, but Russian intervention in the Donbass rebellions is at best a stalemate and at worst a costly mistake in which neither the West, Ukraine, nor Russia can be considered a winner.[66]

CONCLUSION: THE WHY, WHEN, AND WHERE OF RUSSIAN AGGRESSION TOWARD ITS NEIGHBORS

The question of why Russia intervened in the preceding conflicts is complicated; it cannot explained by a single theory, but rather a combination of theories. The common link to all of the wars was the realist desire of Russian foreign policy to control the buffer zone around Russia's borders and extend Russian influence. When the pretext of protecting a Russian minority exists (as it did in Georgia and Ukraine), Russia asserted this rationale to bolster its claim for action. In this manner, a long-term objective to regain great power status and to dominate the Eurasian region combined with domestic and/or social constructivist factors to push Russia toward action.

Further, Russian actions are more aggressive and assertive to the degree that Russia believes that Western reaction will be limited. This explains why Russian action in Chechnya was the most direct and brutal for it was a "domestic" issue inside the Russian Federation. Direct war against Georgia also fit the pattern as Russia estimated that the West would not directly intervene ... and Russia was correct. Where the West has some interest, such as Ukraine, Russia has acted in a covert way, trying to maintain plausible deniability while still pursuing its foreign policy goals.

Importantly, Russian intervention, particularly following the 2008 Georgian War, displays a few clear patterns. Samuel Charap argues that the Russian use of force comes "after other non-kinetic means have been tried and are seen to have failed."[67] Moreover, the use of force has been limited to "just enough force to get the policy job done, but not more."[68] Russian intervention thus seeks to secure a high-value political objective using only the most necessary means without undue escalation of force. Russia also portrays "the use of force in all these cases as consistent with international law."[69] Russia thus creates a façade of legitimacy while also paying lip service to the basic principles of international standards. This couching of armed intervention in such terms can buy the time and space necessary for the Russian intervention to succeed before Western powers can effectively check Russian actions.

The answer to "when" Russia decided to intervene shows the influence of domestic factors to determine the specific timing of Russian action. Russian decisiveness in the Second Chechen War was partially a product of the change in presidents from Boris Yeltsin to Vladimir Putin. The timing of Russian operations in the 2008 Russia-Georgia War had a great deal to do with Russian reaction to aggressive actions from the Georgian government forces. Likewise, as events in Ukraine spiraled out of control under Ukrainian President Viktor Yanukovich, Russia's hand was forced to either intervene or capitulate to the pro-democracy and pro-Western developments inside Ukraine.[70]

The answer to "where" in these instances tends to have one or both of the following criteria: a territory on the border or periphery of Russia and/or the presence of a Russian-minority population. The first factor points to the realist nature of Russian intervention, in other words, to maintain influence and control over countries on Russia's border. The latter factor points to the affinity between the ethnic Russians who live in the Russian Federation and those ethnic Russians who now live in other countries due to the fall of the Soviet Union. This affinity not only provides an ideational rationale for Russian action but is also a strong argument by domestic actors as to why Russian intervention is necessary. We will return to these general observations later in the book.

NOTES

1. Boris Yeltsin. "Speech of Boris Yeltsin to Members of the Civic Union," ITAR-TASS, March 1, 1993.
2. Roger E. Kanet, "The Return of Imperial Russia," In *Conflict in the Former USSR* edited by Matthew Sussex (Cambridge, Cambridge University Press, 2012), 15–34.
3. Quite importantly, Gorenburg argues that a mass nationalist mobilization can occur independent from domestic theories, such as elite struggles for control of the Russian state.
4. Near Abroad is a general term for the nations that lie on Russia's borders both to the east and the south, and typically refers to those that were former members of the USSR. The term "In-Between" refers specifically to those nations that lie between Russia and Eastern Europe and those that lie between Russia and Turkey. The latter list comprises Belarus, Ukraine, Moldova, Georgia, Armenia and Azerbaijan. Chalyi argues that Armenia and Belarus should not not be this group as both are members of the Eurasian Economic Union (EAEU) and Collective Security Treaty Organization (CTSO). While Chalyi's argument has some merit, I do not seek to resolve this dispute here. Thus, in this book I accept the placing of the two countries into the In-Between group. Charap et. al., *Getting Out from In-Between*; Oleksandr Chalyi, "Approaches to Resolving the Conflict over the States In-Between," In Charap, Samuel, et al. *Getting Out from "In-Between": Perspectives on the Regional Order in Post-Soviet Europe and Eurasia* (Santa Monica, RAND Corporation, 2018). 33–40.
5. Gvosdev and Marsh, *Russian Foreign Policy,* 173.
6. Ted Hopf, "Russian Identity and Foreign Policy in Estonia and Uzbekistan," In *The Sources of Russian Foreign Policy after the Cold War* edited by Celeste A. Wallander (Boulder, Westview Press, 1996), 147–171`.
7. Gvosdev and Marsh, *Russian Foreign Policy,* 173.
8. TASS (Russian News Agency), "Russian Military Conduct Antiterrorist Drills in Tajikistan," February 29, 2016, https://tass.com/defense/859627 , AU: Please provide URL], accessed June 5, 2018.
9. In 1989 the Soviet 14th Guards Army comprised four divisions, of which the 28th Guards Motor Rifle Division was in Chernomorskoe, Ukraine, and the 180th Motor Rifle Division was in Belgorod-Dnestrovsky, Ukraine. The 86th Guards Motor Rifle Division was in Balti,

Moldova. Importantly, the 59th Guards Motor Rifle Division was located in Tiraspol, Moldova—which was the unofficial capital of the Pridnestrovian SSR. Vladimir I. Feskov, Vladimir I. Golikov, K. A. Kalsihnikov, and Sergei A. Slugin *The Soviet Army in the Period of the Cold War* (Tomsk, Finland, Tomsk University Press, 2013). 104–105.

10. Alexi Arbatov, "Military Reform: From Crisis to Stagnation," In *The Russian Military* edited by Stephen E. Miller and Dmitri Trenin (Cambridge, MIT Press, 2004), 95–120.

11. Tracey German, "Abkhazia and South Ossetia: Collisions of Georgian and Russian Interests," *Russie Nei Visions*, no. 11 (Paris, Institut Français des Relations Internationales, 2006), 6–8.

12. See, for, example, Mankoff, *Russian Foreign Policy*, 238.

13. Evidence of direct Russian action is difficult to chronicle. However, there are accusations that materials were passed to separatists. See, for example, Nikola Cvetkovski, *The Georgian-South Ossetian Conflict*, Danish Association for Research on the Caucasus, https://www.caucasus.dk/chapter4.htm, Accessed January 2, 2020.

14. Ariel Cohen, *Russia's Counterinsurgency in North Caucasus: Performance and Consequences—The Strategic Threat of Religious Extremism and Moscow's Response* (Carlisle, Strategic Studies institute and U.S. Army War College Press, 2014), v, 3–5.

15. Cohen, *Russia's Counterinsurgency in North Caucasus*, 1–3.

16. Vakhit Akaev, "The History and Specifics of the Islamic Renaissance Today in the Chechen Republic," *Central Asia and the Caucasus* 12, no. 3 (2011): 97–102.

17. Svante E. Cornell, *The "Afghanistization" of the North Caucasus: Causes and Implications of a Changing Conflict—Russian Homegrown Insurgency: Jihad in the North Caucasus* (Carlisle, Strategic Studies Institute and U.S. Army War College Press, 2014), 121.

18. Ibid., 128–129.

19. Ilyas Akhmadov and Miriam Lanskoy, *The Chechen Struggle: Independence Won and Lost* (New York, Palgrave MacMillan, 2010), 12–13.

20. Cohen, *Russia's Counterinsurgency in North Caucasus*, 24.

21. Ibid., 27.

22. Ibid., 30–33.

23. Angela Stent, "Putin's Power Play in Syria: How to Respond to Russia's Intervention," *Foreign Affairs* 95, no. 1 (2016): 106–113.

24. Tsygankov, *Russia's Foreign Policy*, 161.

25. Thomas F. Remington, *Politics in Russia,* 7th edition (New York, Rout-ledge, 2012), 71.
26. In this section, I briefly sketch the history of the Five-Day War. For a more detailed and comprehensive account of events, please see Anton Lavrov, "Timeline of Russian-Georgian Hostilities in August 2008," in *Tanks of August,* edited by Ruslan Pukhov (Moscow, Centre for Analysis of Strategies and Technologies, 2010), 37–76.
27. Lavrov, "Timeline of Russian-Georgian Hostilities in August 2008," 37–38.
28. Vyacheslav Tseluiko, "Georgian Army Reform under Saakashvili Prior to the 2008 Five Day War," In *Tanks of August,* edited by Ruslan Pukhov (Moscow, Centre for Analysis of Strategies and Technologies, 2010), 9–36, p. 15.
29. Anton Lavrov, "Russian Air Losses in the Five Day War against Georgia," In *Tanks of August* edited by Ruslan Pukhov (Moscow, Centre for Analysis of Strategies and Technologies, 2010), 99–106; Tseluiko, "Georgian Army Reform under Saakashvili Prior to the 2008 Five Day War," 32–33.
30. Lavrov, "Timeline of Russian-Georgian Hostilities in August 2008," 43.
31. Ibid., 42.
32. Roy Allison, "Russia Resurgent? Moscow's Campaign to 'coerce Georgia to Peace', *International Affairs* 84, no. 6 (2008): 1145–1171, p. 1158.
33. I detail the Russian efforts in chapters 4 and 5.
34. McNabb, *Vladimir Putin and Russia's Imperial Revival,* 118–119.
35. Davis Hollis, *Cyberwar Case Study: Georgia 2008* (Small Wars Foundation, 2011), http://smallwarsjournal.com/blog/journal/docs-temp/639-hollis.pdf, accessed June 13, 2018, p. 8.
36. Lavrov, "Timeline of Russian-Georgian Hostilities in August 2008," 75.
37. Anton Lavrov, "Russian and Allied Losses," In *Tanks of August* edited by Ruslan Pukhov (Moscow, Centre for Analysis of Strategies and Technologies, 2010), 129–138, pp. 131–135.
38. Interestingly, by the end of the fighting, the Georgian armed forces were still numerically an equal to the opposing Russian units. Of course, the total Russian domination of the air negated this seeming equality. Lavrov, "Russian Air Losses in the Five Day War against Georgia," 104–105; Anton Lavrov, "State of the Georgian Army by the End of Hostilities," In *Tanks of August* edited by Ruslan Pukhov (Moscow, Centre for Analysis of Strategies and Technologies, 2010), 107–114.
39. Gvosdev and Marsh, *Russian Foreign Policy,* 178.

40. Beat Kernen, and Matthew Sussex, "The Russo-Georgian War: Identity, Intervention, and Norm Adaptation," In *Conflict in the Former USSR* edited by Matthew Sussex (Cambridge, Cambridge University Press, 2012), 91–117, pp. 92–96.
41. Gvosdev and Marsh, *Russian Foreign Policy*, 178.
42. Roger N. McDermott, "Russia's Conventional Armed Forces and the Georgian War," *Parameters* 39, no. 1, 2009: 65–80, p. 67; Athena Bryce-Rogers, "Russian Military Reform in the Aftermath of the 2008 Russia-Georgia War," *Demokratizatsiya* 21, no. 3 (2013): 339–368, p. 347.
43. Gregory P. Lannon, "Russia's New Look: Army Reforms and Russian Foreign Policy," *Journal of Slavic Military Studies* 24, no. 1 (2011): 26–54, p. 27.
44. Bryce-Rogers, "Russian Military Reform in the Aftermath of the 2008 Russia–Georgia War," 351.
45. Margarete Klein, "Military implications of Georgia war: Russian Armed Forces in need ofreform," In *The Caucasus Crisis: International Perceptions and Policy Implications for Germany and Europe* edited by Hans-Henning Schroeder (Berlin, SWP Research Paper, RP 9, 2008), 12–18, p. 14.
46. Bryce–Rogers, "Russian Military Reform in the Aftermath of the 2008 Russia–Georgia War," 352.
47. Ariel Cohen and Robert E. Hamilton, *The Russian Military and the Georgian War: Lessons and Implications* (Carlisle, Strategic Studies Institute and U.S. Army War College Press, 2011), 31–32.
48. Keir Giles, "Russian Operations in Georgia: Lessons Identified versus Lessons Learned," In *The Russian Armed Forces in Transition: Economic, Geopolitical and Institutional Uncertainties* edited by Roger N. McDermott, Bertil Nygren and Carolina Vendil Pallin (New York, Routledge, 2012), 1–20, p. 12.
49. McNabb, *Vladimir Putin and Russia's Imperial Revival*, 145–147.
50. Jonathan Stern, *The Russian-Ukrainian Gas Crisis of January 2006* (Oxford Institute for Energy Studies 2006), https://www.oxfordenergy.org/wpcms/wp-content/uploads/2011/01/Jan2006-RussiaUkraineGasCrisis-JonathanStern.pdf, accessed June 1, 2019.
51. Michael Fredholm, *Natural-Gas Trade Between Russia, Turkmenistan, and Ukraine: Agreements and Disputes. Asian Cultures and Modernity*, Research Report 15, 2008, http://gpf-europe.com/upload/iblock/2fa/fredholm.ukraine.russia.gas.rr15.pdf, accessed June 1, 2019.
52. McNabb, *Vladimir Putin and Russia's Imperial Revival*, 123–141.

53. Charap and Colton, *Everyone Loses,* 115.
54. In 2015 Putin declared February 27th "National Special Operations Forces' Day." The coincidence is not accidental (Radio Free Europe, "Putin Creates Special Operations Forces' Day."
55. McNabb, *Vladimir Putin and Russia's Imperial Revival,* 150.
56. Ibid., 150.
57. Charles K. Bartles and Roger N. McDermott, "Russia's Military Operation in Crimea: Road-Testing Rapid Reaction Capabilities," *Problems of Post-Communism* 61, no. 6 (2014): 46–63, p. 54.
58. As paraphrased in Charap and Colton, *Everyone Loses,* 129–130.
59. Bartles and McDermott, "Russia's Military Operation in Crimea," 46.
60. Ibid., 47.
61. Ibid., 55–59.
62. Ibid., 57.
63. Roger N. McDermott, "Does Russia Have a Gerasimov Doctrine?" *Parameters* 46, no. 1 (2016): 97–103, p. 102.
64. Charap and Colton, *Everyone Loses,* 158–159.
65. Ibid., 161.
66. Charap and Colton, *Everyone Loses.*
67. Samuel Charap, "Russia's Use of Force as a Foreign Policy Tool: Is There a Logic?" *PONARS Eurasia Policy Memo,* No. 443 (2016), http://www.ponarseurasia.org/sites/default/files/policy-memos-pdf/Pepm443_Charap_Oct2016_4.pdf, accessed 29 April 2019, p. 3.
68. Charap, "Russia's Use of Force as a Foreign Policy Tool: Is There a Logic?" 3.
69. Ibid., 4.
70. Charap and Colton, *Everyone Loses,* 127–131.

CHAPTER 3

RUSSIA'S EFFORTS TO REBUILD ITS ARMED FORCES FOR THE FUTURE

A capable Russian armed forces is the foundation for a strong defense policy; it is also a tool for the projection of power in Russian foreign policy. The current rebuilding of the Russian military can be viewed from two very divergent starting points: the Soviet military of the 1980s and the Russian military of the middle 1990s. The former was a formidable strategic and conventional force worthy of supporting the policy goals of a superpower. It had a global reach and capability second only that of the rival superpower, the United States. The latter was a mere fragment of the former. By the mid-1990s, the Russian military had degraded into a pale shadow of its Soviet predecessor. Understanding both the decline and rebuilding of the Russian armed forces helps us estimate its role in contemporary Russian foreign policy.

THE END OF THE SOVIET UNION AND THE
DRAMATIC SHRINKING OF THE RUSSIAN MILITARY

The Soviet Armed Forces typically numbered in the range from 3 to 4 million personnel and were deployed across the Republics of the Soviet Union and nations of the Warsaw Pact allies. With the collapse of the Soviet Union in 1991, the newly formed Russian Ministry of Defense assumed command of the pieces that would were not lost to the newly independent nations. Its first pressing problem was to relocate Russian military units and equipment from both Eastern Europe and former Soviet Republics onto Russian territory. Without an immediate strategic threat from NATO, the greater bulk of the Russian forces were maldeployed and needed to be moved.[1] In the process, most units transferred into the Russian Federation while others were either disbanded or formed the nucleus for the national armies of the former Soviet republics.[2]

Relocated units had to be stationed at existing Russian bases that had not previously housed frontline units. A reorganization of the overall command structure would also have to accommodate both the reduction in the number of units as well as the new integration of many units.[3] This movement inevitably led to a sharp decline in the overall size of the Russian military. A trickier issue pertained to units that were of great strategic importance to the Russian state and for which relocation would either be impossible or would sacrifice their strategic worth. The most important of such units was the Soviet/Russian Black Sea Fleet based at Sevastopol in Crimea. The naval base provides the only Russian access to the Black Sea and direct access to the Mediterranean. Russia was neither going to abandon this base nor turn it over to Ukraine. As a solution, the two countries eventually negotiated a lease agreement allowing Russia to maintain the base.

Moving Russian troops and equipment from host countries back onto Russian territory was the easiest part; dealing with the nuclear arsenal dispersed across Ukraine, Belarus, and Kazakhstan was not as simple. Both Russia and the international community feared that if the weapons remained in the host countries, they could potentially fall into the hands of rogue governments or terrorists. Another legitimate concern was that without a well-structured program of oversight, the nuclear weapons would eventually deteriorate into a state of disrepair that would increase the likelihood of a nuclear accident or contamination incident. After a period of negotiation, all the involved countries agreed to transport a number of the weapons to Russia while dismantling or destroying any remaining weapons. This coincided with a series of nuclear arms reduction treaties signed by the United States and Russia to limit the size of their nuclear arsenals (and of course, to reduce the cost to both nations of deploying and maintaining these arsenals).

Intentional downsizing of the military also played a part in the overall change. In order to decrease expenditures in the Soviet budget, Gorbachev initiated a round of downsizing in the 1980s that reduced overall military personnel from 5 million to 4 million.[4] Boris Yeltsin realized in the mid-1990s that reform was needed to professionalize the military. His attempts to end conscription, reduce the number of reserves, pare back the officer corps, and trim the military budget were largely unsuccessful. Indecisive supporters of Yeltsin, opposition parties in the Duma, and strong opposition from senior leaders in the armed forces prevented most of Yelstin's reforms from occurring. The result of Yeltsin's failed reforms led to the unintentional downsizing of the military from 4 million to 1.4 million personnel by 2000. This occurred mainly as a result of a reduced pool of possible conscripts, increased deferments, and retirement of active personnel.[5] When Putin succeeded Yeltsin as president, he assessed that the culmination of these trends in the 1990s left the military unready for combat.[6]

Overall, both the conventional and strategic assets of the Russian military were much weaker in the year 2000 than in 1991.[7] Funding for the Ministry of Defense also dropped a great deal, leaving most units undersupplied and troops underpaid. Morale within the armed forces was quite low, having not yet recovered from the failed campaign in

Afghanistan in the 1980s. On top of that, the quick deterioration of the armed forces in the 1990s left most units understaffed and without any clear goals or motivation. In such an environment, readiness of the mostly conscripted non-commissioned men declined greatly.

Similarly, the strategic missile force dropped precipitously from close to 40,000 warheads to roughly 15,000 by the middle of the 1990s (with further decline in the years after that).[8] However, unlike the conventional forces, the drop in the size of the Russian strategic force did not in any way reduce its overall capability, as the Russian strategic force was still roughly half of all warheads deployed around the globe. Its deterrent and/or strike capability was still assured. Noteworthy, too, is that the defense industry that once had a virtual monopoly on production and procurement within the Soviet Union, now found itself having to compete for arms sales against industries in the West, China, and elsewhere. In such an environment, the Russian defense industry, which had been the backbone of the Soviet military and was now the main source of procurement for the Russian military, also contracted.

The decline in the capabilities of the Russian armed forces did not go unnoticed. The need for reform, reorganization, and rebuilding was obvious. Both Defense Minister Pavel Grachev[9] and his successor Igor Sergeyev[10] sought to change the clunky old Soviet military organization that emphasized large-scale conventional units into a modern light and mobile organization.[11] In the late Soviet period, what was termed the Revolution in Military Affairs (RMA) had made its way into Russian strategic thinking, so the Ministry of Defense was not unfamiliar with its concepts and the need for reform that it championed. Yet, in the 1990s there was neither political support in the government nor Duma for reform of the military. In addition, there seemed to be no inclination to spend the funds necessary to reform the military.[12] Another component of the decline was the fracturing of the force agencies into from ten to sixteen distinct institutions, including the Ministry of Defense, Ministry of Interior, Federal Security Service, Federal Intelligence Service, and other institutions.[13] The *siloviki* (as the force agencies are called) are defined by their "uniformed personnel and/or command of their own militarized or armed formations."[14] Among all this reorganization and deterioration of the armed forces, Russia had more pressing matters: chiefly restarting its economy and organizing the Russian state.

The poor performance of the Russian armed forces in the First and Second Chechen Wars is a clear symptom of the poor state of the Russian military in the 1990s. Despite a need for reform, the Russian military failed to do so for all of the reasons detailed earlier. By one assessment, the Russian military "entered the first decade of the twenty-first century with a Soviet-era mobilization force structure almost completely equipped with out of date Soviet-era equipment (and) shortfalls in modern command, control, communications, computers, and intelligence, surveillance, and reconnaissance equipment and capabilities."[15]

PRE-GEORGIAN WAR REFORMS, 2000-2008

Reform of the Russians military in the first eight years of the twenty-first century was hampered by many factors. An initial obstacle was a reluctance to change the overall goal of the military that persisted since Soviet times: to fight a conventional war against NATO.[16] The eastward expansion of NATO in the 1990s, coupled with NATO's active campaign against Serbia in 1999, convinced many in Russian policy-making circles and the General Staff that Western aggression was a continuing threat.[17] Another factor was the continued inability of the Duma to address military reform in any systematic manner.[18]

The two wars in Chechnya planted seeds in the thinking among the politicians that reform of the military was a necessary. Putin, and the elite in the Russian government in general, criticized the readiness of the armed forces to fight insurgencies and regional wars. They lamented the poor morale and performance of a conscript army. In 2003 Putin attempted to convert the military to a professional, contract force of volunteers. His plan was to increase the annual number of volunteers from roughly 22,000 to 148,000 by 2008.[19] Putin also lowered the length of conscription from two years to a low of 12 months by 2007.[20]

In 2009 Putin announced the reforms as successful, but in 2010 the General Staff contradicted this assessment, calling the reforms a failure. The military had never bought into the reforms and had implemented them slowly and haltingly. The General Staff cut the estimate of the volunteer force down from Putin's 148,000 to 125,000. Yet even given that target, by 2010 the number of volunteers was only 100,000 annually.[21] In a pattern reminiscent of the Soviet era, and still a problem in Russia today, funds intended to create reform were instead diverted by politicians, administrators, and the military to procure weapons, raise salaries, or were lost to graft and corruption.

In February 2007 Putin appointed Anatoliy Serdyukov as Defense Minister. Serdyukov had been a furniture businessman in St. Petersburg in the 1990s and a familiar figure to Putin. After obtaining a law degree, he worked in the local tax ministry before being appointed by Putin in 2004 to run the Federal Tax Ministry of Russia; as such, Serdyukov was the first truly civilian Defense Minister.[22] Putin brought Serdyukov into the Defense Ministry with the charge of reducing the budget, cleaning up the corruption, and bringing the General Staff to heel. Serdyukov was also tasked with reducing the top-heavy nature of the military by trimming the officer ranks by more than half. His task was made easier by the post-Beslan School Siege reforms by which Putin centralized and consolidated political power into the Russian presidency.

However, there was still opposition to Serdyukov's reforms. The Chief of the General Staff, General Yuriy Baluyevsky, opposed and resisted Serdyukov. As a sign of the new political support Serdyukov had from Putin, Serdyukov was able to get Baluyevsky removed and replaced by the Putin-appointed General Nikolai Makarov. The direct appointment power of Putin now made Makarov more compellable and compliant with Serdyukov's demands. The Defense Minister would then set about purging the top generals, with all but three of the top 34 posts in the military changing hands under Serdyukov.[23] Serdyukov also tried to reduce corruption by bringing in his own outside inspectors to audit the defense budget.

POST-2008 GEORGIAN WAR REFORMS

By the start of the 2008 Russian-Georgian War, the reforms had just got underway and were not having a significant impact yet. As detailed in chapter 2, the overall readiness and performance of the Russian armed forces in the Georgian War was quite poor, despite the overall Russian strategic and political success in the war. Moreover, Russia began to realize that the Georgian War had been "fought exclusively with dated tactics, equipment, weapons and structures more suited to waging large scale conventional warfare."[24] Given this assessment and almost assuredly having the complete support of Putin and Medvedev[25], Serdyukov announced in October 2008 the most radical reforms of the Russian military to date. Athena Bryce-Rogers and others outline the main components of the intended reforms:

- Continue to shrink the overall size of the armed forces, with a target of one million by 2012
- Enforce the planned cuts of officers, with a goal of eliminating approximately 200,000 officers
- Change the structure of the armed forces from an egg-shape to a pyramid shape by reducing headquarter staff and increasing enlisted personnel
- Eliminate under-strength units and consolidate personnel into other units to bring them up to battle readiness
- Change the overall command structure from a regimental/division structure to a more flexible brigade system (along the lines of what NATO countries had already been doing)
- Improve the military educational system, and

- Modernize weapons systems and start a new weapons procurement program.[26]

These "new look" reforms were drastically needed to prepare the Russian armed forces to fight regional conflicts and local wars. Of note is the change from a regimental structure to a brigade system of organization. The former is highly centralized with all equipment being possessed by the division and only assigned to subordinate units as needed. It is a slow, cumbersome organization that has advantages when fighting large conventional war with divisions as the main tactical units. The brigade system allows for smaller units (e.g., brigades contain roughly 40 percent of the personnel compared to a division) to control their own equipment, to act with greater independence and flexibility, and to mobilize quickly. Overall, the brigade system should be better suited to address the emerging asymmetrical conflicts that are prevalent in the world today.[27]

The change to the brigade system also entailed Russia abandoning its centuries-old commitment to the mass mobilization principle.[28] In other words, the Russian military traditionally relied on a heavy conscript army in which a high percentage of eligible men would serve. This then creates a large reserve of previously enlisted men who can be mobilized quickly into divisions. Such a concept supports the idea that large-scale conventional war is likely and that quantity of manpower might be more useful than the quality of the manpower.

One assessment in 2009 found that the Russian command structure reform was quite successful with all brigades in "permanent readiness," although the precise definition of this readiness is not agreed upon.[29] However, there are others who doubt this level of success. Renz and Thorton argue that due to the "rushed, haphazard fashion" of the military reforms, overall success may prove difficult to achieve.[30] They point to the lack of modernization in the Russian defense industry, and in particular, its inability to develop new, sophisticated weapons. McDermott points out that "a weak planning capacity and inefficient support structures, as well as the limits of a beleaguered defense industry" will hold back the overall success of the reforms.[31] In a different tact, Renz argues that some of the underlying assumptions about the "flaws" in the Russian military might be exaggerated and/or misplaced.[32] She argues that the results of the Russian military reform are certainly "far from stellar," but that the Russian military is nevertheless still quite capable.[33]

Table 2. Russian Defense Spending.

Year	GDP (R bn)	Change real GDP as %	Def. Exp. (R bn)	Change real exp. as %	Defense exp. as % GDP
2016	86869	3.3	3377	5.4	3.89
2015	79725	3.1	3027	15.7	3.80
2014	73354	3.0	2489	12.4	3.39
2013	66515	2.4	2098	11.5	3.15
2012	62599	3.4	1812	10.2	2.90
2011	55800	4.3	1516	2.8	2.72
2010	46309	4.5	1277	-5.9	2.76

Source: The Military Balance, 2014: 164, Table 4.[34]

Coinciding with Serdyukov's efforts to reform the military was the beginning of the first concentrated attempt to rearm Russia in the post-Soviet period. President Putin announced in 2006 his desire to take increased revenues from the sale of energy and plough them into a plan of rearmament. The overall proposal became known as the State Armament

Plan 2015 (or SAP 2015). Putin intended to spend $189 billion to rearm the armed forces, with roughly 45 percent of the spending to modernize or replace equipment, most of which were still of Soviet-era origin.[35] If implemented successfully, SAP 2015 would increase defense budgets by a power of ten over the spending in 2000. In 2008, President Medvedev made a goal of SAP 2015 to rearm the military at a rate between 9 and 11 percent per year with a target of 70 percent modernization by 2020. When combined with the post-Georgian War reform efforts of Serdyukov, SAP 2015 signaled a major change in Russian policy. Russia would now reverse its decade-long declining defense spending and modernize its military.

But not everything went as expected. Any plan to rearm the military necessarily relies on the ability of the defense industry to produce the necessary equipment. The Russian defense industry had been in decline for the entirety of the 1990s, and it entered the 2000s in no better shape. By 2007 the defense industry was still using outdated Soviet designs for most of its models and had neither the expertise nor structure to produce the type of modern equipment that was needed.[36] For example, from 2008 to 2010 the defense industry was only able to support about a 2 percent increased rate of equipment replacement in the armed forces, far short of Medvedev's goal.[37] The global recession of 2008 also contributed to the decline in the Russian defense industry as the overall Russian economy declined from 2008 to 2010. The defense industry also suffered from the continued shortfall in research and development, which had historically been heavily financed by state spending, not the private sector.[38]

Unhappy with the pace of reforms, President Medvedev revised the State Armament Plan in May, 2009.[39] The new target date would be 2020 (and the new plan would be thus named SAP 2020) and would call for the eventual expenditure of 19.5 trillion rubles (or roughly US$616 billion). Roughly 70 percent of the spending supports new weapons and equipment with the rest almost evenly divided between repair/upgrades and research/development.[40] SAP 2020 is also quite forward looking, with 50 percent of spending going to the air force and aerospace defense, including procuring roughly 100 more spacecraft.[41] The plan calls for only around 30 percent of spending to occur within the first 5 years, with the remaining 70 percent to be spent from 2016 to 2020.[42]

The initiation of SAP 2020 in 2011 was quickly followed by a change in the Ministry of Defense. Serdyukov was sacked in 2012 and replaced with Sergei Shoigu. Shoigu was a civil engineer in the Soviet Union who during the Yeltsin administration became the Minister of Emergency Situations, a position in which he performed quite well. He continued in this post from 1991 to 2012, when in May of that year he was selected by the regional parliament as Governor of Moscow Oblast. In December 2012 after a power struggle between *siloviki* in the Putin administration and Serdukov, Putin appointed Shoigu as a neutral administrator of the Defense Ministry.

Shoigu quickly set about reforming the military along the lines promised by earlier reforms and Medvedev's SAP 2020. David E. McNabb summarizes the objectives of Shoigu's reforms:

- Increase combat readiness and capabilities
- Continue reducing personnel numbers
- Reorganize the overall structure of the armed forces and limit the number of officers
- Build a professional noncommissioned officer (NCO) system
- Reorganize and centralize military education
- Reorganize the military district system
- Transform land forces from a division system to a brigade system
- Reduce the number of units and bases
- Begin outsourcing logistic support
- Improve military housing and social services.[43]

Clearly the Shoigu reforms were an extension of all the previous attempts at military reform. If Russian rearming were to become an actuality and not just a desired goal, Shoigu would have to contend with the same difficulties that Serdukov faced. By one estimate in 2011, at least one-fifth of the Ministry of Defense budget was lost to corruption and theft.[44] However, by 2013 the Russian defense industry was making gains. By one estimate, the share of total global arms sales by the top six Russian defense companies rose by 28 percent and up to 5 percent of the total global sales.[45] In short, the Russian defense industry was bolstered by both SAP 2020, which was a renewed source of domestic purchasing, and the increased exporting of arms. At the same time the Russian government could now rely on the revived defense industry to help meet the demands of SAP 2020.

But the picture is not quite as rosy as it might seem. Although 2013 Russia's expenditure on defense and military expenditure was the third highest worldwide, it was not reaping proportionate returns.[46] Shoigu not only had to contend with the persistent corruption in the Russian defense industry as well as the inefficiency and cronyism inherent in the arms procurement process, but he also had to deal with two new problems in 2014. The first was the decline in the price of oil, and thus Russian energy sale revenues. The second was Western sanctions in the wake of the Russian seizure of Crimea and the conflict in Eastern Ukraine. The Western sanctions limited the transfer of weapons and weapon technology to Russia. Further, a "depressed global economy...declining prices for oil and gas, a depreciating currency, inflation, high interest rates, a declining rate of investment and underlying structural problems" all plagued the Russian economy after from 2014 and 2015.[47] This led to a decline in overall spending on national defense from 4.3% of the GDP to 4.0% in 2016.[48] We shall return to this topic a bit later in this chapter, for in the year 2013 and before the crisis in Ukraine, a new idea would be interjected into Russian military thinking.

THE GERASIMOV DOCTRINE AS A STARTING POINT AND NOT A COMPLETE DOCTRINE

Along with the attempt to reorganize, rebuild, and rearm the Russian military, a new way of thinking was introduced in 2013. A 2013 article by The Chief of the General Staff, General Valery Gerasimov, titled, "The Value of Science is in the Foresight: New Challenges Demand Rethinking the Forms and Methods of Carrying out Combat Operations" posited a potential new model for Russian application of force in future conflicts. The difficulties of the Chechen Wars of the 1990s and the Russian-Georgia War of 2008, when combined with the events of the 2011 Arab Spring uprisings, led Russian generals to thinking about how war had evolved in the past few decades. Importantly, Gerasimov argues that the Arab Spring was just as much a contemporary "war" as the more traditional wars in Chechnya and Georgia. He continues that the sort of regime change and regime destabilization that occurred, particularly in North Africa, was on the level of casualties, destruction, and consequences more similar to a conventional war. In short, Gerasimov proposed that nonmilitary means of achieving strategic goals had increased and that in some instances could exceed that of conventional military means of achieving the same goals.[49]

In his dissection of the Gerasimov Doctrine (as it is called in the West), Bartles suggests that Gerasimov frames his new thinking about warfare into the context of American actions post-1991. Gerasimov specifically outlined how the American-led actions in Iraq, Yugoslavia, Haiti, and Afghanistan from 1991 to 2004 were not just the "traditional" approach: select a target, search for a pretext for a military operation (e.g., WMDs, prevent genocide), then launch a military operation (e.g., invasion, bombing, etc.). Rather, Gerasimov argues that the United States and its allies used propaganda campaigns, NGOs, funding for pro-democracy groups, international organizations, and other covert actions prior to military intervention. In short, the West is already at war with the target country, but only in a clandestine fashion and one intended to produce agitation and civil unrest. The goal of such action is to lure the target government into repressive actions that then justify US-led reactions (e.g., sanctions, no-fly zones). Eventually either Western-directed peacekeepers or a Western-led military action completes the job.[50] McDermott agrees with Bartle's interpretation, that Gerasimov is not so much arguing that Russia pursue a hybrid strategy of warfare, but rather that the West is using such a tool for regime change.[51] Conclusively, Michael Kofman makes it clear that Gerasimov's writings were more a wake-up call within Russia for change than a forceful, document that had doctrinal impact and significance.[52]

Thus, a good way to read Gerasimov's writing is as a call for "Russian military scientists to advance fresh ideas" to counter Western use of hybrid warfare.[53] One implication is that Russia would have to develop hybrid resources of its own. If warfare was now to be conducted through both military and nonmilitary measures, Russia would not only have to rebuild and rearm its military, it would also have to build and arm its nonmilitary capabilities. Gerasimov estimated that the ratio of nonmilitary measures to military measures was on the order of 4 to 1. While this ratio is certainly just an estimate—Gerasimov quite rightly asserted that every war is unique, requiring a unique strategy and assets to be utilized in pursuit of policy goals—it is indicative of where foreign policy efforts, and thus governmental spending, should be placed. In chapters 4 and 5, I outline the continuation of this thought regarding the need for nonmilitary assets and how Russia has deployed them.

UKRAINE AND POST-UKRAINE DEVELOPMENTS ON THE RUSSIAN ECONOMY

The Russian participation in the Donbass region in the Ukrainian conflict since 2014, along with the Russian seizure of Crimea, changed the international environment in which Russian foreign policy operates. The Western sanctions aim to punish Russia for its actions in Ukraine and have had an impact. While the exact effect of the sanctions on Russian economic activity cannot be precisely determined, analysts believe that they have contributed to the overall decline, even if only a modest 0.5 percent of GDP.[54] After an initial recovery from the 2008 global recession, Russian economic growth faltered in 2013.[55] The fall continued for a number of years, as the overall strength of the Russian economy fell both in 2015 and 2016 by roughly around 2 percent of GDP.

However, it can be argued that the decline in oil prices contributed greatly to this decline, and certainly much more so than the sanctions. Russia is a net exporter of oil and natural gas, with these two sectors comprising roughly 60 percent of all Russian exports Moreover, these same products account for around 30 percent of Russian GDP. The price of oil on the international markets plays a major role in the Russian economy in many ways. The first is that when oil prices decline, as they did in the second half of 2014, the value of the Russian ruble falls with them. As the price of oil dipped to historic lows, by the end of 2014 the Russian ruble lost 59 percent of its value versus the American dollar.[56] Second, as revenues from export taxes on oil decline and the economy slid into recession, as the Russian economy did in 2015–2016, total government revenues decline. Russian government attempts to diversify the economy in the 2010s failed; over the decade, the "share of hydrocarbons in the country's exports has in fact steadily grown."[57]

Given its vulnerability to the global price of oil, Russia responded to the drop in the price by seeking deals with OPEC members to reduce supply. In December 2016, Russia reached an agreement with OPEC to reduce production starting in 2017. This has had some effect, despite some cheating on the agreement by some OPEC members, and has moved the price of oil up from its low of $25 a barrel to roughly $70 a barrel at the start of 2018. However, the price of oil will probably not stay at this level as production in the United States should continue to increase. The U.S. Energy Information Administration predicts the price of oil to fall to roughly $60 a barrel by the end of 2018 at to stay near that level throughout 2019.[58] This is not good news for Russia. During the recession of 2015–2016, Russia depleted its Reserve Fund (which at one point in the mid-2000s had more than $130 billion), and its Wealth Fund has sunk from a high of roughly $90 billion to just over $60 billion.[59] While Russia retains about a half-trillion dollars of foreign currencies in reserve, it cannot use those reserves to balance government budgets without eroding the strength of the ruble.

Thus, the effect of the Western sanctions against Russia for its intervention into Ukraine cannot be disentangled or independently accessed from the drop in oil prices that occurred at roughly the same time. The net effect of both these events was the Russian recession of 2015–2016 and the depletion of a significant amount of Russian reserve funds. This in turn has impacted Russian governmental budgets. The Russian government needs to avoid running large deficits for two reasons, both related to sanctions and the oil price drop. First, because of the sanctions, Russia finds it harder and more expensive to borrow money on the international markets. Second, the reduced reserves force Russia to either borrow the money at a high cost or to dip into its currency reserves (as stated earlier). Despite this clear incentive to balance the budget, deficits are still the norm. Russia has run a budget deficit every year from 20112 through 2017. Increases in the price of oil led to a modest surplus in 2018, but tentative forecasts for 2019 predict a return to a budget deficit near 3.0 to 3.5 percent of GDP. Overall government spending has also been declining in real terms (because of the falling value of the ruble), from a high in 2013 of around $425 billion to a low of roughly $230 billion in 2017, with a slight tick upward in 2018 to around $280 billion (figures for 2019 are not complete, but should be near those of 2018). While Russian government expenditures in rubles has held steady for a number of years, the value of that spending has dropped by almost half. This fall is only tempered by the fact that government spending on defense is almost entirely domestic, and thus most of that spending is not impacted by the decline in the purchasing power parity of the ruble. It is in this context that the Russian state must carry through with its rearmament plans.

SAP 2018–2027: THE GERASIMOV DOCTRINE, CONVENTIONAL WARFARE, OR BOTH?

So if the Russian military needs to be rebuilt and rearmed to fight a future conflicts, Russian rearmament plans would need to dovetail with Gerasimov's suggestions of increasing the nonconventional assets and simultaneously rebuilding the conventional armed forces while also not straining the fragile Russian governmental budget. Is this what we see? In February 2018, President Putin signed into effect the new ten-year State Rearmament Plan (known as SAP 2018–2027 or SAP 2027). The impetus for this new plan was that SAP 2020 was seen as having mixed results. The greatest success of SAP 2020 was in the modernization of the Russian Air Force. The defense industry was able to produce more fighter jets and other aircraft and deliver them relatively on time. The other branches of the Russian military did not perform as well. The Russian defense industry was not capable of producing the surface ships that the Navy demanded. The ground forces did not receive much funding in SAP 2020 (as the lion's share went to the Navy) and as such there was not much further upgrade post-2012. Overall, the results were uneven and highlighted both the corruption and deficiencies in the Russian defense industry.[60]

The need for SAP 2027 also arose from the inability of Russia to meet its SAP 2020 goals given the downturn in the Russian economy. The new plan calls for continued increases in defense spending, but all is not as it seems. As Julian Cooper points out, despite increases in absolute spending as measured in rubles, spending as a share of GDP declined in 2017 to 3.8% and military spending in real terms looks to have "declined in 2018 by more than five percent."[61] Cooper argues that this contraction "underlines the extend to which the years 2012 to 2015 were exceptional."[62] Thus, SAP 2027 forces Russian to determine as to which elements in SAP 2020 will be prioritized and which will see decreases in funding. At the time of writing in the Spring 2019, current analysis suggest that Russia is prioritizing "strategic nuclear forces [and] air defence systems" while reducing spending on fixed wing aircraft, helicopters, and naval ships.[63]

Even given these limitations, SAP 2027 is an ambitious project that allocates 20 trillion rubles (approximately US$357 billion) over the next ten years. Ninety-five percent of the funds are for military equipment procurement, repair, development, and acquisition while the remaining 5 percent is for construction of supporting infrastructure. It should be noted that the figure of 20 billion rubles is less than the 30–55 trillion that the Ministry of Defense sought from the budget.[64]

What exactly is in SAP 2027, and does it reflect any overall change in Russian strategic and military thinking along the lines of Gerasimov's thinking? First, SAP 2027 mostly postpones a number of large-scale, expensive projects, which were failures under SAP 2020. Two problems that emerged in SAP 2020 with large-scale projects (such as new aircraft carrier designs and strategic bombers) were first, the disjuncture between the strategic needs of the Russian military and the proposed use of these projects, and second, the inability of the Russian defense industry to develop and produce the intended weapons. Thus, SAP 2027 concentrates spending on weapons systems that are within reach of the Russian defense industry. Here again, we should note how the Western sanctions are impacting Russian defense procurement. Russia cannot go on Western international markets to purchase weapons or weapons components, thus forcing the Russian government to rely on a notoriously corrupt and inefficient domestic defense industry.

Summarizing current assessments of SAP 2027, targets of spending fall into the following key areas. First, the greatest share of spending is intended to equip and modernize the ground forces to better fight local and regional wars. Russian intervention in Ukraine has pointed to the continued need for conventional military units and equipment. In this light, SAP 2027 seeks to procure and deploy new tanks, new artillery, new ground-based missiles, a new short-range air-defense system, and self-propelled guns.[65] Second, SAP 2027 modernizes and upgrades the strategic nuclear force. It does so by deploying more strategic missiles aboard its submarine fleet. The strategic nuclear force will also be upgraded through development of land-based ICBMs, both silo and rail-based. In addition, more TU-60 strategic bombers are expected to resume production after 2021, with plans for a new design of strategic bomber being scrapped.[66]

Third, one of the biggest changes from SAP 2020 is the dramatic reduction in funding for the naval forces and the radical change in direction of the funding that remains. The naval forces enjoyed a great deal of funding from SAP 2020 but due to problems in procurement, development, and delivery of new ships, very little came from this spending. SAP 2027 cuts spending for the naval forces by almost 50 percent. Moreover, the reduced funding effectively stops development and deployment of new, large surface ships. This is a major change of direction. In 2008 then President Medvedev stated that the future of the Russian Navy was in large, aircraft carriers. This was in line with the Russian Admirals who wanted to build the world's second-largest aircraft carrier fleet. Complicating the matter was that Russia did not have a single defense company capable of building an aircraft carrier—the older Soviet aircraft carriers were built at a yard in Ukraine (including the single Russian aircraft carrier that remains in the fleet, the *Admiral Kuznetsov*, that launched in 1990). In fact, it is not clear that at the time of this writing that any Russian corporation currently has the capability to build any new aircraft carriers. This inability of the defense industry to deliver underscores both the inefficiency of the Russian defense industry as well as how sanctions are making this task even harder.[67]

Instead, SAP 2027 focuses on smaller ships, increasing the submarine fleet, and deploying more missiles systems. As Gorenburg notes, the move away from larger ships, such as the 14,000 ton *Lider*-class destroyers, to smaller ships, such as the 8,000-ton *Super Gorshkov*-class frigate, solves two problems. First, it creates smaller ships that can serve more roles, such as providing littoral combat support, while also increasing the armaments on the ships. Second, it is less costly to procure, purchase, and deploy the smaller ships. In this way the government is trying to get more ships for fewer rubles. It is important to note at this point that the Russian Navy's own doctrinal documents are at odds with this change. The navy still seeks to obtain more destroyers and aircraft carriers. This is despite the obvious reality that the Russian defense industry has a very limited ability to produce such ships and that the government its reluctant to fund these projects.[68]

A large part of the budget for the Russian Navy in SAP 2027 is allocated to a significant upgrade of the submarine fleet. In particular, the rearmament plan calls for deploying six more *Yasen-M* nuclear attack submarines. It also plans for the upgrading of a half-dozen older submarines and their redeployment. The SAP 2027 goal is to deploy a new submarine roughly every year. It is important to realize that this also was the goal of SAP 2020, although that goal was never achieved. SAP 2020 planned to produce 24 submarines (and 54 surface ships) from 2011 to 2024. The actual results were much less than that. Another ambitious goal of SAP 2027 is for the development and construction of a fifth-generation submarine by the mid-2020s. Russia will almost certainly miss this goal. The plan asks for the deployment of diesel-powered submarines of a number of classes over the next ten years, which is a more obtainable goal than the others.

The third, and perhaps most important part of the Naval budget, is spending on weapons systems. The 3M-54 *Kalibr* cruise missile has gained a reputation as a respectable multipurpose weapon. The *Kalibr* can be deployed on ships of any size, including the smaller frigates and corvettes, and packs a significant punch. It can be used both in an anti-ship role and also as a land-attack missile. The *Kalibr* is essentially a long-range cruise missile similar to that of the widely deployed American Tomahawk cruise missile. Russia has used the *Kalibr* missile extensively in Syria. With a range of roughly 1,000 miles, Russian ships of the Caspian Flotilla are able to hit targets in Syria with the *Kalibr*. The diesel-powered submarines in the Russian Navy are also able to deploy the weapon, although a version of the *Kalibr* with a more limited range of roughly half that of the surface fleet. SAP 2027 calls for deploying the *Kalibr* to pretty much every ship on which it can be fitted. This is a budget-friendly upgrade to the firepower of the Russian Navy that simultaneously increases the number of roles that the Navy can perform.

The final component of SAP 2027 is continued upgrading of the Russian Air Force. One of the few success stories of SAP 2020 was the deployment of modern aircraft, many fighter jets of many classes. SAP 2027 concentrates on increasing the number of support aircraft, including transport planes. Funding for unmanned aerial vehicles (UAVs) continues and builds upon the successful deployment of these weapons in SAP 2020. Funding also continues for the respectable S-400 surface-to-air missile defense system, first deployed in 2007. Russia has placed this system in Syria, has agreed to sell four of them to Turkey, and in negotiating with India about deployment of the system into that country.

CONCLUSION

SAP 2027 is the current incarnation of a long line of needed reforms of the Russian military. It builds upon the pressing need for reform post-2008 and the limited successes of SAP 2020. SAP 2027 on its face illustrates a change in the Russian strategic thinking about the use of its military while also trying to manage the federal budget. With the shift toward a lighter, more flexible and capable naval force, Russia seeks to give its forces greater firepower for fewer rubles. The continued streamlining and rearming of the ground forces shows both a consideration of conventional warfare but also the need for lighter, more mobile special operations units.

Of course, SAP 2027, much like SAP 2020, will only be successful if corruption and inefficiency in the military procurement process is reduced significantly. This is a big "if" because of the crony capitalism (or kleptocracy if you prefer) currency practiced in Russia.[69] With Putin's re-election in 2018, he is slated to be president until 2024. Therefore, Putin's system of government and dominance of the Russian economy through placement of *siloviki* into the state-owned enterprises (SEOs) most likely will continue unabated. The cost of this continued political and economic corruption on the rearming and rebuilding of the Russian military cannot be directly measured, but a good assumption is that it hampers its success. It is also important to note that SAP 2027 does not demonstrate a supposed shift away from a traditional military to a hybrid warfare model (à la the Western readings of Gerasimov). Rather, it illustrates the movement to a lighter, more flexible military that could contribute in a wider array of potential conflicts, including hybrid warfare.

Of clear importance to the success or failure of SAP 2027 is the simple realization that Russia must have an economy that rivals that of its opponents if it wants to spend like them. The Russian economy currently lags behind that of the United States, major European powers, Japan, and China in both productivity and size. Yet, Russia has immense energy and material resources that can provide a lifeline and backbone to the Russian economy. However, this is a double-edged sword—the over-reliance on natural gas and oil exports leaves Russia susceptible to Western sanctions and the global markets. Moreover, Russian economic competitiveness declined in the early 2000s, spurring the need for "quite substantial state investment...poured into lagging 'priority' sectors."[70] Chris Miller states that "since the beginning of the Putin era, Russia's leaders have had the following goals, in order of priority: maintaining power, expanding Russian influence abroad, and developing Russia's economy at home."[71] He goes on to say that as the Kremlin has strengthened central authority and sought to prevent popular dissent, it has allowed private business to engage in profitable enterprises only as long as it "does not contradict the previous two strategies." Consequentially, this system of "Putinomics [is] more conducive to political control but not to economic growth."[72] Thus, the state rearmament plans that I detailed in the previous chapter are unlikely to come to fruition as they rely on a healthy economy to provide the finances for government spending.

From this chapter, a couple of conclusions can be drawn. First, Russian efforts to modernize its armed forces have yet to be completed and are still a long way from their goal. Second, it appears that Gerasimov's ideas have had an impact, but they fall short of anything that we would want to term a "doctrine." Yet, his writings do indeed point to new ways that Russian foreign policy could seek to achieve its goals short of conventional warfare. The next two chapters investigate the degree to which Russia has sought to make up for shortcomings in its conventional forces through engagement in propaganda and information warfare, and the degree to which a hybrid model exists.

NOTES

1. Steven E. Miller, "Moscow's Military Power: Russia's Search for Security in an Age of Transition," In *The Russian Military: Power and Policy* edited by Steven E. Miller and Dmitri V. Trenin (Cambridge, MIT Press, 2004), 1–41, pp. 9–10.
2. Charles J. Dick, "A Bear Without Claws: The Russian Army in the 1990s," *Journal of Slavic Military Studies* 10, no. 1 (1997): 1–10.
3. Miller, "Moscow's Military Power."
4. McNabb, *Vladimir Putin and Russia's Imperial Revival*, 97.
5. Ibid., 98.
6. Rod Thornton, *Military Modernization and the Russian Ground Forces* (Carlisle, Strategic Studies Institute and U.S. Army War College Press, 2011).
7. Pavel K. Baev, *Russian Energy Policy and Military Power: Putin's Quest for Greatness* (New York, Routledge, 2008), 43–72.
8. Stockpiles of nuclear weapons and warheads are chronicled annually by the Federation of American Scientists. They have created Nuclear Notebooks since 1987, have estimated stockpiles back to 1945, and have provided (and continue to provide) their data to the Stockholm International Peace Research Institute (SIPRI) annual compiling of international statistics. A summary is available at https://fas.org/issues/nuclear-weapons/status-world-nuclear-forces/ with additional links on that page to the annual notebooks.
9. Minister of Defense 1992–1996.
10. Minister of Defense 1997–2001
11. Defense Intelligence Agency, *Russian Military Power.*
12. Carolina Vendil Pallin, *Russian Military Reform: A Failed Exercise in Defense Decision Making* (New York, Routledge, 2009), 6–14.
13. The difference between Renz's listing of ten agencies and Cooper's listing of sixteen relies on Cooper's more general interpretation of force in which the service typically has non-militarized personnel. Bettina Renz, "Russia's 'Force Structures' and the Study of Civil-Military Relations," *Journal of Slavic Military Studies* 18, no. 4 (2005): 559–585; Julian Cooper, "The Funding of Power Agencies of the Russian State," *The Journal of Power Institutions in Post-Soviet Societies*, 6/7 (2007), www.pipss.org.

14. Renz, "Russia's 'Force Structures' and the Study of Civil-Military Relations," 561.
15. Defense Intelligence Agency, *Russian Military Power*, 12.
16. Pallin, *Russian Military Reform*, 9–11.
17. William D. Jackson, "Encircled Again: Russia's Military Assessed Threats in a Post-Soviet World," *Political Science Quarterly* 117, no. 3 (2002): 373–400.
18. Pallin, *Russian Military Reform*, 12–14.
19. Arbatov, "Military Reform."
20. McNabb, *Vladimir Putin and Russia's Imperial Revival*, 98.
21. Ibid.
22. Bryce-Rogers, "Russian Military Reform in the Aftermath of the 2008 Russia-Georgia War," 346.
23. Ibid.; McDermott, *The Reform of Russia's Conventional Armed Forces*, 142–143.
24. Darl R. Herspring and Roger N. McDermott, "Serdyukov Promotes Systemic Russian Military Reform," *Orbis* 54, no. 2 (2010): 284–301, p. 295–296.
25. President Medvedev gave a speech in September 2008 where he emphasized the need to modernize the Russian armed forces (McDermott, 2009b: 68).
26. Bryce-Rogers, "Russian Military Reform in the Aftermath of the 2008 Russia-Georgia War"; McNabb, *Vladimir Putin and Russia's Imperial Revival*; Major Kasparas Mazitans, "Russian Armed Forces Military Reforms and Capability Development (2008–2012)," *Baltic Security and Defence Review* 16, no. 1 (20124): 5–45.
27. Lannon, "Russia's New Look," 39–40.
28. Roger N. McDermott, "The Restructuring of the Modern Russian Army," *Journal of Slavic Military Studies*, 22:4 (2009): 485–501; Bettina Renz and Rod Thorton, "Russian Military Modernization: Cause, Course, Consequences," *Problems of Post-Communism* 59, no. 1 (2012): 44–54.
29. Thornton, *Military Modernization and the Russian Ground Forces*, 23–24.
30. Renz and Thornton, "Russian Military Modernization," 52.
31. Roger N. McDermott, "Russia's Armed Forces and Future Warfare: The Brain of the Russian Army--Futuristic Visions Tethered by the Past," *Journal of Slavic Military Studies* 27, no. 4 (2014): 4–35, p. 33.
32. Bettina Renz, "Russian Military Capabilities after 20 Years of Reform," *Survival* 56, no. 3 (2014): 61–84, p. 62.
33. Renz, "Russian Military Capabilities after 20 Years of Reform," 78–79.

34. One important caveat is that defense expenditure in Russia is notoriously difficult to quantify precisely. Soft budget constraints allow the Ministry of Defense, among other force agencies, to move money into their budget with little transparency. Thus, the number listed are of course estimates. Julian Cooper, "The Russian Economy Twenty Years after the End of the Socialist Economic System," *Journal of Eurasian Studies* 4, no. 1 (2013): 55–64.

35. Bryce-Rogers, "Russian Military Reform in the Aftermath of the 2008 Russia-Georgia War," 361; Klein, "Military Implications of Georgia War," 13–15.

36. Cohen and Hamilton, *The Russian Military and the Georgian War*, 60–62.

37. Dmitry Gorenburg, *Russia's State Armaments Program 2020: Is the Third Time a Charm for Military Modernization* (PONARS Eurasia Policy Memo 125, 2010), http://www.ponarseurasia.org/sites/default/files/policy-memos-pdf/pepm_125.pdf, accessed June 21, 2018

38. Julian Cooper, "The Innovative Potential of the Russian Economy," *Russian Analytical Digest* 88, no. 1 (2010): 8–12, p. 9.

39. Herspring and McDermott, "Serdyukov Promotes Systemic Russian Military Reform," 292.

40. McNabb, *Vladimir Putin and Russia's Military Revival*, 106.

41. Ibid., 106.

42. Defense Intelligence Agency, *Russia's Military Power*, 20.

43. McNabb, *Vladimir Putin and Russia's Military Revival*, 100.

44. Bryce-Rogers, "Russian Military Reform in the Aftermath of the 2008 Russia-Georgia War," 367.

45. SIPRI (Stockholm International Peace Research Institute), *Yearbook* (Oxford, Oxford University Press, 2014), 206–207.

46. SIPRI, *Yearbook*, 183.

47. Julian Cooper, "The Military Dimension of a More Militant Russia," *Russian Journal of Economics*, no. 2 (2016): 129–145, p. 136.

48. Ibid., 136.

49. Gerasimov, "The Value of Science is in the Foresight."

50. Charles K. Bartles, "Getting Gerasimov Right," *Military Review* 96, no. 1 (January/February 2016): 30–38.

51. Roger N. McDermott, "Does Russia Have a Gerasimov Doctrine?" *Parameters* 46, no. 1 (Spring 2016): 97–105.

52. Michael Kofman, "Raiding and International Brigandry: Russia's Strategy for Great Power Competition," *War on the Rocks*, June 14, 2018, https://warontherocks.com/2018/06/raiding-and-international-

brigandry-russias-strategy-for-great-power-competition/, accessed September 2, 2019.

53. McDermott, "Does Russia Have a Gerasimov Doctrine?" 101.
54. Edward Hunter Christie, "Sanctions after Crimea: Have they Worked?" *NATO Review Magazine* (2016), https://www.nato.int/docu/review/2015/ russia/sanctions-after-crimea-have-they-worked/EN/index.htm, accessed June 25, 2018; Darko Janjevic, "Western Sanctions on Russia: Lots of Noise and Little Impact," *Deutsche Well* (2018), http://www.dw.com/en/ western-sanctions-on-russia-lots-of-noise-and-little-impact/a-43271200 , accessed June 25, 2018.
55. Julian Cooper, "The Russian Economy: The Impact of Sanctions and Falling Oil Prices, and the Prospects for Future Growth," *Russian Analytical Digest* 160 (2014): 2–4, p. 2.
56. Greg DePersio, "How does the Price of Oil Affect Russia's Economy?" *Investopedia,* April 30, 2018, https://www.investopedia.com/ask/answers/ 030315/how-does-price-oil-affect-russias-economy.asp, accessed June 26, 2018.
57. Cooper, "The Russian Economy," 3.
58. Jacob L. Shapiro, "An Oil Price Increase is Not Enough for Russia," *Geopolitical Futures,* January 17, 2018, https://geopoliticalfutures.com/oil-price-increase-not-enough-russia/, accessed June 26, 2018. The price of oil at the time of writing (December 24, 2019) is $66.72 for Brent Crude.
59. Shapiro, "An Oil Price Increase is Not Enough for Russia."
60. Pallin, *Russian Military Reform.*
61. Julian Cooper, *Russian Military Expenditure in 2017 and 2018, Arms Procurement and Prospects for 2019 and Beyond* (2019), https://static1. squarespace.com/static/55faab67e4b0914105347194/t/5c615f9fee6eb02f5 351f2f3/1549885344986/Russian+military+expenditure+in+2017+and+2 018+by+Cooper.pdf, accessed May 1, 2019.
62. Cooper, *Russian Military Expenditure in 2017 and 2018, Arms Procurement and Prospects for 2019 and Beyond.*
63. Ibid.
64. Dmitry Gorenburg, *Russia's Military Modernization Plans: 2018–2027* (PONARS Eurasia Policy Memo 495, 2017), http://www.ponarseurasia. org/sites/default/files/policy-memos-pdf/Pepm495_Gorenburg_Nov201 7.pdf, accessed June 25, 2018.
65. Gorenburg, *Russia's Military Modernization Plans.*
66. Gorenburg, *Russia's Military Modernization Plans.*

67. It is important here to note that Russia has signed a large number of agreements with India in which the two countries are jointly working on defense technology. This could in the future alleviate some of the pain from the Western sanctions.

68. This discrepancy between what the Russian Navy wants and expects from the Russian government and defense industry is a telling story about the divisions that exist within Russia. As I outline in chapter 1, the domestic factors theory of international relations does indeed pertain to Russia. The winners of domestic competitions for authority and control can, and often do, translate their preferences in defense policy.

69. Karen Dawisha, *Putin's Kleptocracy: Who Owns Russia?* (New York, Simon and Schuster, 2014); Gulnaz Sharafutdinova, *Political Conse- quences of Crony Capitalism inside Russia* (South Bend, University of Notre Dame Press, 2010).

70. Julian Cooper, "Can Russia Compete in the Global Economy?" *Eurasian Geography and Economics* 47, no. 4 (2006): 407–425, p. 418.

71. Chris Miller, *Putinomics: Power and Money in Resurgent Russia* (Chapel Hill, University of North Carolina Press, 2018), xiii.

72. Miller, *Putinomics*, xv.

Chapter 4

Russia's Nonconventional Assets

Information and Propaganda Campaigns

If the Russian goal is to destabilize the Western nations, the development of soft power or unconventional assets can provide Russia with a weapon in which it is equal, or even perhaps superior, to its opponents. This chapter traces the development and deployment of nonconventional assets by Russia, primarily since the early 2000s. Russia has built upon its decades-long strength in intelligence agencies and other force ministries (the *siloviki*). Since the end of the USSR, Russia has developed a propaganda machine, a set of cyber assets, and other information and indirect assets to use against his opponents, both in the West and elsewhere. Moreover, Russia has been deploying these units for more than a decade, influencing world politics in many ways, some more obvious than others. When combined with the development of special operations forces and other covert, conventional units, Russia is building the assets that it needs to achieve both its short-term and long-term objectives.

Building Upon Strength: The Russian Intelligence and Force Agencies

Soldatov and Rochlitz summarize the current state of politics in Russia quite succinctly, establishing that Putin and the *siloviki* hold power and make the decisions in contemporary Russia.[1] As listed in the previous chapter, *siloviki* refers both to the "force agencies" in Russia, in other words those agencies that have the authority to use force and violence.[2] The term also is used as a noun to refer to the high-ranking members within Putin's administration who are in control of, or have previously worked in, the force ministries. There is a general consensus that the *siloviki* have entrenched themselves at the heart of Russian politics.[3] The growing presence of the *siloviki* in Putin's administrations does not necessarily imply that it was the product of an intentional process. There is strong evidence that the rise of the *siloviki* was not a coordinated takeover of power, but likely just the result of Putin's personalistic politics.[4] Of course, there is also no assumption that all these important men think alike, as they certainly are not a monolithic force with a single, Cyclopean vision.[5]

Important to the rise of the *siloviki* is the realization that they were strong both before and after the fall of the USSR. After all, most of the current force ministries are the direct descendants of the Soviet force agencies. Yeltsin and his administration sought to reform the force ministries after the downfall of the Soviet Union. Most of the old Soviet agencies were renamed and given a new coat of paint, but for most purposes they were still the same agencies with the same personnel.[6] The KGB was renamed the FSB, the Soviet foreign intelligence directorate was renamed the SVR, and so on. While Yeltsin made honest efforts to reform the force ministries, and he had some initial success in increasing the openness and transparency of these agencies, it became clear quite rapidly that his reforms were only superficial. By 1993 Yeltsin admitted that the *siloviki* were irreformable.

In a development that would pave the way for Putin's autocratic rule, the authority to oversee the *siloviki* slowly moved from the parliament to the president's office. The Official Secrets Act of the Russian Federation,[7] passed on July 21, 1993, limits individuals and organizations from getting information from the force ministries, which can declare any sought information to be a state secret. Since 1993, the number of offices or individuals who can declare information a state secret has grown from 19 to 34, including of course the president. Yeltsin attempted to gain some control over the *siloviki*, mainly by dividing up responsibilities and agencies within the FSB and GRU. Yet, by the end of the 1990s, Yeltsin relied on key *siloviki* as his partners in the Duma. The last three Yeltsin prime ministers (Primakov, Stepashin, and Putin) were all *siloviki*. This was the state of affairs in 2000 when Putin inherited the president's office.

Putin's administration is widely seen as relying on informal, personal networks.[8] Putin placed allies, former associates, and those whom he trusted in key positions all over the Russian government. By 2003, a quarter of all senior bureaucrats in Putin's administration were current or former *siloviki*.[9] This number has since been revised and disputed, but the overall trajectory is relatively clear: Putin placed those whom he trusted into government offices, and those whom he trusted were more likely to be *siloviki* than not. Moreover, Putin appears to have a bias toward the intelligence agencies and a prejudice against the Ministry of Defense. For example, he has placed most of the armed forces under FSB surveillance. Another example is the 2004 purge of military leaders by the civilian Minister of Defense Sergey Ivanov, a former director of the FSB. Despite their increased presence in government, there is also rivalry between the many force ministries, something that Putin has to manage. However, the overall picture is quite clear: the *siloviki* occupy major positions in the government at the request of President Putin.

The importance of this development is tied to the fairly common worldview held by the *siloviki*. Soldatov and Rochlitz summarize the worldview of the *siloviki* into three components: one, the favoring and support of a strong, centralized state; two, the belief that the main threat to Russia comes from the United States and its European allies; and three, that the *siloviki* are the only ones with the information and understanding of the world to counter this threat.[10] As such, they are inherently nationalist and statist. The *siloviki* are also fundamentally motivated to defend the interests of the Russian state, as they define them.

The 2011 Arab Spring confirmed and consolidated the *siloviki's* view of the world in a way very similar to that of Gerasimov's writing, in other words, with much alarm. The popular uprisings were seen as the result of Western manipulation of social media and promotion of pro-democracy groups. From the view of the *siloviki*, the Arab Spring was not an independent, spontaneous uprising of repressed people against corrupt governments. Rather, it was an intentional act by Western intelligence agencies and governments to replace regimes with ones that are more pro-Western. These events proved to the *siloviki* that their worldview was correct, that the West needed to be confronted head-on, and that the *siloviki* were the only ones capable of doing this. The failure of civilian officials to suitably contain the 2012 Russian postelection protests appears to have coincided with then President Medvedev's shift from reliance on civilian officials to the *siloviki*.[11] The crisis in Ukraine starting in late 2013, leading up to the Russian seizure of Crimea and intervention in the Donbass rebellion, further strengthened the position of the *siloviki*. The two takeaways are that the *siloviki* did not take over the Russian government in some sort of *de facto* coup, instead the government over time slowly began to utilize the *siloviki* increasingly as the implementers of policy, and that the force ministries, for all of their rivalries and corruption, are an institutional strength that can be a powerful part of Russian foreign policy.

SOFT POWER AND PUTIN'S BUILDING OF
NONCONVENTIONAL ASSETS

The Russian government viewed the Color Revolutions in the early 2000s in a very unique way. They saw the events as the culmination of Western use of soft power and as a sign that Russian soft power had waned, even to the point of nothingness.[12] Regarding the first point about soft power, Russia was very late to the game in its realization of the concept. Joseph Nye's book *Bound to Lead* was popular in the academic and policy-maker circles in the United States and Europe immediately upon its publication in 1990, and the concept spread further with Nye's later book *Soft Power*.[13] Nye asserted that soft power was the ability to of a nation to attract others to it. In other words, a nation with a great degree of soft power is an exemplary model, a source of inspiration, a paradigm of certain values, a shining example, or perhaps a cultural magnet. To have soft power is not to overcome the resistance of others (because hard power is utilized to accomplish that goal), but rather to eliminate that resistance entirely as other nations willingly move into your orbit. In the early 2000s, it was the Western nations that had the soft power when measured by the attractiveness of their culture, people, and businesses.[14]

But to Russian foreign policy thinkers of the 1990s and early 2000s, Nye's concept of soft power would not resonate strongly. For centuries, power in Russia meant *zhestkaya sila*, or "hard power." Soviet and Russian foreign policy was founded on the projection of hard power. Moreover, internal control of the Russian Empire or Soviet state relied on repressive measures, another function of hard power. Of course, this is not to say that the Soviet Union did not have some soft power, for it certainly did. After the 1917 Revolution, communism and the accomplishments of the Soviet Union did have an attractive force, this certainly cannot be denied.[15] But soft power did not defend the Soviet Union against the Nazi invasion, it was hard power that did. Likewise, it was the Soviet strategic nuclear arsenal that provided deterrence against Western aggression, not any sort of amorphous concept of soft power. To a geographically shrinking, militarily declining, and economically reeling Russia of the 1990s, the concept of soft power was particularly alien.

The Color Revolutions would change that. Russia began to see that soft power was indeed a useful concept, and one that the Western world was using to its advantage. Further, it became apparent in the Color Revolutions that Russia in the early 2000s did not possess much, if any, soft power.[16] This led to a fundamental examination of the concept, and one in which the Russian thinkers would put their own stamp. Soft power was defined as the power to attract others, much along the lines of Nye's definition. Yet, there is one important difference between the Western and Russian conceptualizations of soft power. For Russian thinkers, soft power does not emanate from a civil society through the aggregation of independent, societal actors (such as businesses and cultural icons) but rather through direction of the state. Soft power is a tool, one that the state can mold and use in the same way that the state uses hard power. And much like hard power, having more soft power would lead to a comparative decline in the soft power of rival states. The more attractive your country becomes, the less attractive the rivals become, and vice versa. To Russian thinking, soft power was reconceptualized into the typical Russian thinking about foreign policy. Soft power is warfare by nonconventional means. The battle of soft power is also a war that does not end, as the battle of soft power continues unabated during times of peace.

The Russian state quickly moved to "weaponize" soft power. This is exactly what Putin and Medvedev set out to do in early 2012. Both men used the term soft power in speeches, emphasizing both the use of soft power through agents such as NGOs but also that Western governments direct this soft power, typically through their control of the global media. Moreover, they argued that Western governments used their soft power assets to reduce the cultural attractiveness of Russia, denigrating its government as illiberal, its foreign policy as aggressive, and its leader as autocratic. In short, Putin and Medvedev asserted that the West had been warring with Russia continually both before and after the end of communism. Perhaps of even greater importance, Russia had not been fighting back; instead it had merely been absorbing the damage. The reader may note how this interpretation is similar to two previous Russian realizations of international politics. The first is the rejection of Yeltsin and his reformist supporters in mid-1990s by the more nationalist and/or statist elements in Russian politics. To the statists, Yeltsin's failure was his inability to realize that cooperation with the West gained nothing as the West was fundamentally aligned against Russia. The second instance is Putin's realization after the NATO expansion plans of the early 2000s that the United States and Europe would fundamentally ignore Russian security concerns. The Russian perception of a Western soft power aggression was conditioned by these earlier realizations of aggressive Western foreign policy.

Van Herpen argues that the Russian adoption of soft power warfare has three components: mimesis, rollback, and invention.[17] The first is the early Russian steps to mimic or imitate the soft power information campaigns of the West. Rollback is the plan by which Russia will force out Western soft power incursions of Russian sovereignty, such as the presence of international NGOs in Russia. Invention is the Russian development of new forms of soft power warfare, particularly information warfare.

As Van Herpen rightly argues, Russian "invention" and "innovation" in information warfare is more akin to a mobilization of its traditional intelligence assets. In short, invention is often the use of traditional techniques that have been employed by the *siloviki* for decades, if not centuries, but translated into twenty-first-century politics and technology. As an example, Russian cyber intrusion into the voting process in elections in Western and Eastern Europe (as well as the United States) is justifiably seen as a Russian soft power campaign to undermine the confidence of Western electorates in their governments and democracy in general. This sort of electoral manipulation by Russia is not new—just the technology used is different. The Zinoviev Letter of 1924 caused all kinds of instability in British elections, and in particular led to the blaming of poor Labour electoral performances on Soviet interference rather than inherent problems within the Labour Party and its messaging. Russian use of e-mail spearfishing and social media campaigns are just a new method for an old tactic.

Russia first started with imitation. Russian imitation of Western activities took many initial forms, one group of imitations modeled after NGOs such as the British Council or United States Agency for International Development (USAID). Russian mimics included such organizations as that of the Institute for Democracy and Cooperation, the Russian Cooperation Agency, the Russian International Affairs Council, the Russkiy Mir Foundation, and the Gorchakov Foundation.[18] Typically, the activities of these organizations were in line with the Russian interpretation of soft power: the organizations pushed the Russian government's position on issues. Overall, the effectiveness of these efforts was minimal, mainly due to the transparent nature of their activities. Another set of imitative reforms were upgrades to the Ministry of Defense website, the creation of a Russian cyber command, updates of antivirus software, and other initiatives.[19]

The Russian government had greater success once it began to "roll back" the presence of foreign NGOs inside Russia. Viewing foreign NGOs as merely an arm of a foreign state, Putin and the Russian government moved against them after his return to the presidency in 2012. The Duma passed and Putin signed in July 2012 new legislation that labeled any organization that engaged in political activity or accepted money from outside of Russia to register as a foreign agent (*inostrannyy agent*). Foreign and foreign-funded NGOs would now have to stamp the words "foreign agent" on all their publications and webpages or be under threat of the Russian government fining them or shutting down their activities. Putin turned the threat into reality, as within months he moved against USAID, forcing it to leave Russia in September 2012. In October of the same year, the Duma passed an amendment to the law making it treasonous to pass information or any other assistance to international organizations. As of June 2018, the Russian government has designated more than 150 NGOs as foreign agents and thirty groups have been shut down or voluntarily shuttered.[20] At the time of writing, the government lists seventy-six groups as foreign agents, most of which are domestic Russian social and public NGOs.

It is in the realm of invention that Russia has sought to create its soft power instruments, and where it has been the most successful for as I have said previously, it builds upon a strength in the intelligence services that existed both in Tsarist Russia and the Soviet Union. Initial Russian forays into soft power began after the Color Revolutions in 2003 and 2004. The Kremlin recognized the need for Russia to recreate its image around the globe, or in more modern parlance, rebrand itself. An initial strategy was to employ lobbyists in Western nations to change the perception of Russia in Western circles. For example, there is the 2006 hiring of the the PR firm Ketchum to launder Russia's image. The Russian government's happiness with the results has been evident as more than a decade later the Kremlin still pays Ketchum to work for its interests. Russia also employs GPlus Europe, a sister organization of Ketchum, to lobby on its behalf. Internal documents from these PR firms suggest that both did more than just promotion and marketing, they engaged in direct political lobbying for the Kremlin.[21] As an example, Ketchum is responsible for placing the 2013 op-ed piece by Putin in the New York Times.

The "reset" of US-Russia relations by the Obama administration opened the door for even further Russian government use of PR firms, and the spreading of this tactic to others Russian organizations and political actors. The hiring of Western PR firms quickly caught on with Russian oligarchs and other subnational Russian governmental organizations. As part of their struggle against Georgia, South Ossetia and Abkhazia hired a PR firm in the United States to lobby for their interests and, of course, the interest of the Russian state.[22] Oligarchs, such as Oleg Deripaska, hired PR firms to lobby for both their business and political interests.

Of course, PR firms are not the only organizations capable of helping launder Russia's image, but the use of such firms is illustrative of the types of actions that the Russian government engages in that fall squarely under the category of promoting soft power projection.

RUSSIAN PROPAGANDA

Paying for PR firms to lobby can only do so much. After all, these efforts do not address the underlying problem behind Russia's lack of soft power: its illiberal government and corrupt business practices. Lobbying cannot create a large enough façade to cover up these inherent soft power deficits. What Russia needs is a wider approach that effectively lobbies the masses or, in other words, a public propaganda campaign to reshape Russia's image abroad. Van Herpen does a good job of summarizing the broad methods that Russia employs in its many propaganda campaigns:

- Disseminating official Russian state propaganda directly abroad via foreign-language news channels, making use of TV and the Internet;
- Disseminating official Russian state propaganda indirectly via Western media;
- Takeovers of Western papers;
- Gaining a hold over new social networks and setting up Kremlin-friendly websites;
- An active presence in blogs and discussion forums, as well as the publication of organized posting by "Kremlin trolls" on the website of Western papers;
- Financing Western politicians and/or political parties;
- Reactivating spy rings, which had the task to penetrate influential political circles; and
- Activating the Russian Orthodox Church as a soft-power tool.[23]

Chief among these propaganda efforts has been the success of Russia Today (RT). The state-sponsored television news channel broadcasts globally, both through traditional broadcasts in dozens of nations, but also via a large online presence through social media and streaming services such as YouTube. Van Herpen suggests that for the first few years of its existence, Russia Today was a defensive soft power tool, mainly aimed at promoting a positive image of Russia.[24] He also argues that following the Russia-Georgian War and the success of the Russian propaganda campaign to control the local media reports on the war, Russia turned RT into an offensive soft power weapon. Other scholars agree, saying that Russia is now engaged in information confrontation,[25] that Russia is at war for the hearts and minds of citizens in many countries,[26] and that Russia is involved in full-scale information warfare.[27] In particular during the Obama administration, RT started broadcasting segments that were clearly anti-American and against President Barack Obama, including all manner of conspiracy theory and right-wing rhetoric. Russia Today not only takes advantage of liberal and neutral broadcasting laws in Western nations to pump the airwaves and Internet full of nonsense, it also allows fringe and extremist elements in many nations a platform to disseminate their views and at the same time legitimize themselves as credible pundits. In this way, RT is a vital part of a classic propaganda campaign of influencing the narrative and planting provocateurs/saboteurs in foreign nations.[28] The RT information campaign is also backed by several "news" websites and numerous Russian-supported NGOs that promote the same pro-Russian information.

More and more often in today's connected world, citizens of all countries get their information about politics and government from the Internet. The unfiltered nature of social media and the Internet makes these platforms ripe for coordinated Russian information campaigns. A recent assessment of the overall strategy used by Russia to promote its interests on the Internet suggests that "Russia employs a synchronized mix of media that varies from attributed TV and news website content to far-right blogs and websites (with unclear attribution), as well as non-attributed social media accounts in the form of bots and trolls."[29] The goals of the strategy include "inducing paralysis, strengthening groups that share Russia's objectives or point of view, and creating alternative narratives that match Russia's objectives."[30]

The targets of these coordinated information campaigns include both the Western nations and the "near abroad." Russian goals toward the Western nations are to foment instability, create confusion, and undermine trust in democracy.[31] Still, it is in the "near abroad" where information campaigns can be the most effective due to two factors. First, successful Russian information campaigns in countries in Central Asia or Eastern Europe work towards limiting Western influence in these important buffer states. Thus, the consequences of information campaigns in Ukraine, the Baltic nations, Kazakhstan, or Armenia, for example, provide much more direct and concrete advantages to Russian foreign policy than a campaign in France or some other Western democracy. Second, the presence of a Russian minority population in most of the "near abroad" nations provide a springboard for Russian information campaigns. This creates a favorable base on which to build a pro-Russian narrative and a community that can further disseminate the message. While major Western media focuses on Russian interference in Western elections or with Western political parties, the fundamental truth is that Russian information campaigns aimed at the "near abroad" are more continuous, more effective, and of greater value to Russia.

Russian "active measures" on social media can be very complex. In general, these active measures take a multipronged approach. A RAND Corporation report categorizes a "typical Russian disinformation operation" as a three-layer project. First, Russian or Russian-affiliated agencies create the content. In this step the various themes of the propaganda are developed. Second, a group of "force multipliers," such as trolls and bots, replicate and repost the content. "Troll farms" and "botnets" amplify messages and exploit search optimization algorithms to push Russian-sponsored messages to the top of search lists, trending lists, and other wide-reaching lists. Last, friendly and/or duped outlets acquire the content and push it out even further. This latter group includes blogs of all sorts, media aggregation websites, favorable individuals and groups on social media, and all sorts of agitators.[32]

These information campaigns cannot be conducted without the Russian government investing resources into building, maintaining, and deploying the appropriate assets. Spending by the Russian government on mass media activities now exceeds $1.1 billion and continues to grow.[33] This is a relatively small amount when compared with the defense budget (see chapter 2). It also can be quite cost effective, particularly compared to what is spent on more conventional armaments.[34] Moreover, the extra level of spending by Russia on information and lobbying initiatives cannot be accurately determined. Why? As politics in Western nations becomes more and more expensive, Russia has quietly been providing funding to political parties and candidates. Some of this funding comes in the way of loans through Russian banks, some of whom are partially state owned. Examples include money funneled to the National Front in France and the Green Party in the United States. This sort of backdoor funding does not show up on governmental fiscal ledgers, but one cannot deny that the money ultimately comes from the Russian state. In short, the level of Russian expenditure on its information and lobbying campaigns is certainly much higher than the official number that can be found in the Russian national budget.

OFFENSIVE CYBER ASSETS

Alongside the information and propaganda campaigns is the Russian development of cyber assets that can reliably deliver cyberattacks. The Russian perception of what it terms "information space" is similar to its perception of the global political environment; in other words, a continual state of struggle exists.[35] The Kremlin views cyber warfare under the general framework of information warfare.[36] Thus, cyber warfare is another tool to achieve the aims of the broader information campaign. As I have mentioned already, this conceptualization is similar to how Gerasimov conceptualizes the use of military and nonmilitary measures to achieve regime change. Gerasimov argues that information warfare, including cyberattacks, could indeed reduce the fighting ability of the target. Cyber warfare as part of a broad information campaign could "disorganize governance, organize anti-government protests, delude adversaries, influence public opinion, and reduce an opponent's will to resist."[37]

The Russian development of cyber assets followed a similar trajectory to the rearmament and reorganization of the Russian military: it happened only after a period of neglect in the 1990s and a reexamination due to the 2008 Russia-Georgia War. In the 1990s most cyber assets were headquartered in the Federal Agency for Government Communications (FAPSI). During Putin's first Presidential administration, the FAPSI was disbanded in 2003. Its directives and capabilities were scattered into many agencies, but chief among them were the FSB and SVR. During this period, the Russian military primarily contained cyber assets related to electronic warfare.[38] Just as the poor performance of the military in Georgia in 2008 led to reform of Russian conventional forces, the military also reformed elements of its nonconventional forces. As an example, the Ministry of Defense created a new information operation unit within the armed forces to create and deliver information campaigns. The FSB and other intelligent units pushed back against this move, seeing it as encroaching upon their turf. Despite this domestic clash of agencies, the military moved ahead and created the Foundation for Advanced Military Research in 2013. It is not clear at the time of writing this book how well institutionalized and functioning this unit is.

These days a great deal of the Russian cyber warfare originates from the intelligence *siloviki*. Central to the work of these agencies are the advanced persistent threat groups. The Russian government employees and sponsors groups of hackers drawing upon a vast network of under-employed yet skilled computer experts.[39] Groups such as Fancy Bear (or APT 28), Cozy Bear (APT 29), and the Russian Business Network (RBN) are examples of private groups of hackers who either have interests aligned with the interests of the Russian government, and/or are being employed by the Russian government to carry out the government's wishes. Moreover, the overlapping of business and crime in Russia provides an intersection for government and private citizens to engage in transactional activity. The government pays private citizens to do its dirty work, and the citizens accept the payments as business as usual in Russia.[40]

CONCLUSION

The September 2000 "Doctrine of Information Security of the Russian Federation" outlined three objectives: protect Russian from cyber warfare, protect Russian from harmful foreign information, and promote patriot values in the Russian population (Doctrine of Information Security of the Russian Federation). Since then, the Russian government has actively engaged in developing both propaganda assets and cyber assets. The former has typically been built upon the old Soviet intelligence agencies and have employed very similar tactics to those once employed by the KGB and other Soviet-era operations, albeit with more modern technology. The latter have been developed to exploit the relative openness of the modern Internet. Offensive assets include both government activities through the intelligence agencies as well as the employment of private citizens and groups, mainly hacktivist collectives and other anonymous groups.

But how effective are the propaganda and cyber warfare assets that Russian has developed? When and where have they been deployed? What was the impact of their deployment? In the next chapter, we explore the use of propaganda and cyber assets since 2007 against foreign targets. Both the success of these efforts and the accelerated use of these assets against foreign nations will also be outlined.

NOTES

1. Soldatov and Rochlitz, "Russia as a Great Power," 83–108/

2. Bettina Renz, "Russia's 'Force Structures' and the Study of Civil-Military Relations," *Journal of Slavic Military Studies* 18, no. 4 (2005): 559–585.

3. Dawisha, *Putin's Kleptocracy*; Andrei Illarionov, "The Siloviki in Charge," *Journal of Democracy* 20, no. 2 (2009): 69–72; Olga Kryshtanovskaya and Stephen White, "The Sovietization of Russian Politics," *Post-Soviet Affairs* 25, no. 4 (2009): 283–309.

4. Soldatov and Rochlitz, "Russia as a Great Power"; Bettina Renz, "Putin's Militocracy? An Alternative Interpretation of Siloviki in Contemporary Russian Politics," *Europa-Asia Studies* 58, no. 6 (2006): 903–924.

5. Renz, "Putin's Militocracy?" 904; Howard P. Lovecraft, "Call of Cthulhu" *Weird Tales* 11, no 2 (1928): 159–178.

6. Renz, "Russia's 'Force Structures' and the Study of the Civil-Military Relations."

7. Technically, it is the Law of the Russian Federation NO. 5485-1 of July 21, 1993 ON STATE SECRETS (with the Amendments and Additions of October 6, 1997, June 30, November 11, 2003, June 29, August 2, 2004, December 1, 2007).

8. Soldatov and Rochlitz, "Russia as a Great Power," 12.

9. Kryshtanovskaya and White, "The Sovietization of Russian Politics."

10. Soldatov and Rochlitz, "Russia as a Great Power," 16.

11. Ibid., 20.

12. Anthony Cordesman, *Russia and the "Color Revolution": A Russian Military View of a World Destabilized by the US and the West* (Center for Strategic and International Studies, Full Report, 2014), https://csis-prod.s3.amazonaws.com/s3fs-public/legacy_files/files/publication/1405 29_Russia_Color_Revolution_Full.pdf, accessed 10 May 2019, 2; Van Herpen, *Putin's Propaganda Machine*, 25–26.

13. Nye, *Soft Power*; Joseph S. Nye Jr., *Bound to Lead: The Changing Nature of American Power* (New York, Basic Books, 1990).

14. Van Herpen, *Putin's Propaganda Machine*, 24.

15. One need only look at communist revolutionaries around the globe such as Ho Chi Minh or Che Guevara to see how the ideals of the Soviet revolution were an attractive force akin to the concept of soft power.

16. Van Herpen, *Putin's Propaganda Machine*, 25–26.

17. Ibid., 33–46.

18. Ibid., 34–39.

19. Timothy Thomas, "Russia's Information Warfare Strategy: Can the Nation Cope in Future Conflicts?" *Journal of Slavic Military Studies* 27, no. 1 (2014): 101–130, pp. 116–120.

20. Human Rights Watch, "Russia: Government vs. Rights Groups," https://www.hrw.org/russia-government-against-rights-groups-battle-chronicle, accessed June 30, 2018.

21. Van Herpen, *Putin's Propaganda Machine*, 51–53.

22. Ibid., 54.

23. Ibid., 70.

24. Ibid., 70–72.

25. Todd C. Helmus, Elizabeth Bodine-Baron, Andrew Radin, Madeline Magnuson, Joshua Mendelsohn, William Marcellino, Andriy Bega, and Zeg Winkleman, *Russian Social Media Influence: Understanding Russian Propaganda in Eastern Europe* (Santa Monica, RAND Corporation, 2018), 1.

26. Timothy Thomas, "Russia's 21st Century Information War: Working to Undermine and Destabilize Populations," *Defense Strategic Communications* 1, no. 1 (2015): 11–26, p. 12.

27. Keir Giles, *Russia's 'New' Tools for Confronting the West: Continuity and Innovation in Moscow's Exercise of Power* (Chatham House, Russia and Eurasia Programme, 2016), https://www.chathamhouse.org/sites/default/files/publications/2016-03-russia-new-tools-giles.pdf, accessed July 5, 2018, 27.

28. There are also many instances of Russian Oligarchs buying shares or a controlling position in Western media, mainly newspapers such as the *British Evening Standard* or *Independent,* as well as papers in France and elsewhere. Eastern European media companies also were bought by Russian Oligarchs. It would be presumptuous to conclude that all of these purchases were part of a large, state-directed propaganda campaign, although some connection between state and business interests might exist in some cases.

29. Helmus et. al., *Russian Social Media Influence*, x.

30. Ibid., 2.

31. Ibid., 11.

32. Ibid., 11–13.

33. Ibid., 8.

34. Goure, "Mosxcow's Visions of Future War," 99.

35. Michael Connell and Sarah Vogler, *Russia's Approach to Cyber Warfare* (CNA Analysis and Solutions., 2017), https://www.cna.org/cna_files/pdf/DOP-2016-U-014231-1Rev.pdf, assessed July 6, 2018, p. i; James J. Wirtz, "Cyber War and Strategic Culture: The Russian Integration of Cyber Power into Grand Strategy," In *Cyber War in Perspective: Russian Aggression Against Ukraine* edited by Kenneth Geers (Tallinn, NATO CCD COE Publication, 2015), 31.

36. Gerasimov, "The Value of Science is in the Foresight."

37. Connell and Vogler, *Russia's Approach to Cyber Warfare*, 4.

38. Connell and Vogler, *Russia's Approach to Cyber Warfare*, 8.

39. David Smith, "How Russia Harnesses Cyber Warfare," *Defense Dossier*, American Foreign Policy Council, no. 4 (2012): 7–11, p. 9.

40. An important advantage of using private groups in cyber warfare is the plausible deniability it gives to the Russian government. Cyberattacks are almost never traced back to any government agencies or computers. If the attack serves the Russian government's interests, this is merely coincidental due to the hacking group's similar interests. This is a similar argument made by Putin regarding the "little green men" in Ukraine: they are merely private citizens exercising their right to support their interests. Dawisha, *Putin's Kleptocracy*; Marie Mendras, *Russian Politics: The Paradox of a Weak State* (New York, Columbia University Press, 2012).

CHAPTER 5

CYBER WARFARE

RUSSIA TESTS ITS USEFULNESS
AS A FOREIGN POLICY TOOL

Three key questions about the Russian development of nonconventional weapons (e.g., propaganda campaigns, information campaigns, cyberattacks) are why, when, and where are they used? This chapter outlines the Russian use of these weapons, focusing first on defining the form of warfare in which they are employed and then looking at their actual use.

ASYMMETRICAL (OR HYBRID) WARFARE

The concept of hybrid warfare is not new, but it has gained in importance recently with the widespread use of the Internet. At its most basic level, hybrid warfare is the blending of conventional forces engaged in traditional war (i.e., armed forces acting on behalf of a nation and/or state against a similar opponent) and irregular forces which may include state or non-state actors.[1] Hybrid warfare is, of course, not a twenty-first-century invention; it has been a regular part of world politics since the dawn of history.[2] Though the concept has come back into vogue in the last two decades due to the rise of cyber warfare. Therefore, when most scholars and analysts talk about hybrid or asymmetrical warfare, they really are talking about "modern" hybrid warfare.[3]

One definition of modern hybrid warfare is aggressive action that "remains below the threshold of the clear use of armed force."[4] Along with this threshold idea is the underlying concept of what war is and who participates in it. Such definitions range from a direct state versus state conflict with conventional forces, to non-state actors versus a state, to indirect state versus state conflict involving proxies and nonconventional assets, to intrastate conflict with any combination of state and non-state actors.[5] Asymmetrical warfare is a subset of war where typically one side has a preponderance of power, particularly in conventional assets. In such situations, the weaker side often turns to nonconventional assets in order to fight the conflict. This is why the terms "asymmetrical" and "hybrid" have often been confounded in the literature: weaker sides in war/conflict often turn toward a mix of conventional and nonconventional assets; in other words, they engage in hybrid warfare.[6] The terms have further gotten mixed together because of the very nature of Russian Post-Soviet wars: the Russians have always had the preponderance of power versus their opponents, and thus every war is asymmetrical (often to a large degree). What is unusual is the use of hybrid warfare by the side that has the preponderance of power!

Now we see why the hybrid warfare/asymmetrical warfare craze began in the early 2000s. The United States was dealing with hybrid warfare from jihadists, international terrorists, and insurgents in Iraq and Afghanistan. The American response was to develop counterinsurgency (COIN) strategies to bring its advantage in conventional forces to bear against a scattered, weaker opponent utilizing hybrid warfare.[7] This is basically the common approach used by the stronger side during an asymmetrical conflict and has been employed for centuries.[8] Analysts in the United States only began to think about hybrid warfare as distinct from counterinsurgency after Frank Hoffman's paper in 2007 and his reconceptualization of the concept in 2009.[9] Yet, American theorists still viewed hybrid warfare as something in which only the inferior side in asymmetrical warfare typically engaged.[10]

The Russian response to a similar array of non-state actors (e.g., Chechen rebels, Islamic terrorists) initially was the same, particularly in Russia's wars in Chechnya in the 1990s. Russia responded to the Chechen independence movement as an insurgency and employed traditional conventional forces and counterinsurgency tactics (see chapter 2). However, it was in the wake of the Chechen wars that Russia began to adopt more hybrid strategies. The question as to "why" was answered in the previous chapter: Russian leaders felt that throughout the 1990s the United States and its allies had secretly been waging war against Russia—a war that was not being fought via conventional means—and that Russia was losing that war because it was the "weaker" side in the nonconventional combat. Further, Russian conventional strength was insufficient to engage directly in state-to-state combat with NATO. Thus, shortly after the year 2000 and Putin's directive to develop such assets, Russia began to develop nonconventional assets, mainly piggy backing off the strength of the post-Soviet intelligence communities and *siloviki.*

It is important to note that the Russians do not have the same conceptualization of hybrid warfare as that in the West.[11] This arises from two fundamental issues. The first relates to the previous discussion that the West seems to only view hybrid warfare as something in which the weaker side in an asymmetrical conflict engages. Second, and related to my analysis in chapter 4, the Russian conceptualization of warfare, both before and after Gerasimov's writings, is more holistic than in the West. Even though Russian strategists draw a distinction between military and nonmilitary force, war is thought of as encompassing all aspects of conflict, both conventional and nonconventional. One important article by Chekinov and Bogdanov illustrates this point. They place the idea of "future warfare" squarely into concepts that have been a part of conventional warfare for decades.[12] Another author notes that Russian interest specifically in cyber war as "an integral component of information war" grew after an influential article by Andrey Kokoshin, a former Deputy Minister of Defense and former Secretary of the Security Council.[13] Thus, new forms of technology based warfare were placed into Russian conceptual thinking of warfare that is not new.

In short, the Russian view is that all warfare is warfare. The idea that hybrid warfare is somehow different, mainly because it does not primarily rely on conventional warfare, is alien to Russian strategic thinking.[14] Monaghan argues that the Western over-examination of hybrid warfare leads to Western analysts missing the conventional parts of Russian foreign policy, particularly their actions in Ukraine.[15] Kofman argues that a better term for what Russia is doing is "raiding." He states that Russia is not necessarily engaging in hybrid warfare, but rather using conventional and unconventional assets to take strategic operations with firm objectives.[16] Whether Monaghan and Kofman are correct or not, the Western conceptualization of hybrid warfare is useful to the degree that it helps Western thinkers and strategists get a better understanding of what Russian foreign policy is doing, whether or not Russia conceptualizes it in exactly the same way. Of interest, too, is that the Russian use of hybrid warfare mainly came to the attention of Western scholars and analysts after the 2008 Russian-Georgia War. Yet, Russia had already been employing such tactics prior to that war. Thus, it appears that Western thinkers are playing "catch-up" to Russian military strategy.

RUSSIAN CYBER WARFARE: RUSSIA TESTS THE USEFULNESS OF ASYMMETRICAL HYBRID ATTACKS

Connell and Vogler rightly point out that the 2007 Russian cyberattack on Estonia was a "milestone."[17] In April 2007, the Estonian government planned to relocate the Soviet-era Bronze Soldier memorial away from a public square to a military cemetery. Native Estonians viewed the memorial as a reminder of their nation's oppression under the Soviet Union.[18] This angered the ethnic Russians in Estonia, who make up around 26 percent of the Estonian population.[19] Protests against the removal of the statue resulted in violence, leading to over 1,000 arrests and one death. At the same time as the protests, a series of DoS and DDoS attacks targeted Estonian websites, as well as a coordinated e-mail spam attack and some SQL injection attacks.[20] Targets included the Estonian parliament, other government sites, most banks, media publishers, ISP providers, and the servers via which they communicated. Estonia quickly blamed Russia for the attack, but the attacks were, of course, coming in from all over the world in what is now a classic botnet tactic to obscure the original source of the attack.[21] As Estonia was the most wired country in the world at that time, the attack effectively brought government services, business, and even telephone lines to a complete halt. From late April to early May, Estonia worked with other nations to combat the attacks and restore services. Service was being restored when another wave of attacks hit on May 8–9, and a week later another wave of botnet activity crippled Estonian sites. By the end of May, the attack had ended.[22]

As Connell and Vogler point out, Russian culpability in the attack has not been established without a doubt, but assuming that Russia at the least encouraged (if not coordinated) the attacks seems reasonable. Of importance for foreign policy discussions is the knowledge that Russia was willing to launch a cyber offensive against a Baltic nation when so very little was at stake. Russian security was never threatened by Estonia, and in the long run the movement of the memorial has not changed Russian-Estonian relations in any significant way from what they were before the incident. What is clear is that Russia is willing to intervene in countries that it considers part of its hegemonic sphere of influence. Why does it do this? As I argued in an earlier chapter, Russia initiates aggressive action for two reasons. First, it feels not only that it has a right to intervene in such countries, including the Baltic nations, but that it has a responsibility to do so. Second, Russia considers defense of Russian minorities in such countries to be a worthy foreign policy, and domestic policy, objective. Defense of Russians abroad is popular inside Russia, and it also has the intended effect of reminding foreign governments of the Russian presence in their nation. While the latter reason may be a convenient smokescreen for the underlying realist objective of dominating the region, it builds on popular support in Russia for the Kremlin to protect Russian minorities abroad.

As observers point out, the long-term impact of the attack was significant. Russia demonstrated to the entire world its ability to deploy cyber assets and effectively shut down a target's Internet service as well as the government, business, media, and other services that rely on it. In response, "NATO adopted a uniform policy on cyber defense and formed the Cyber Defense Management Agency to coordinate and centralize cyber defenses in all member states" and placed in Tallinn the headquarters of its defenses, there Cooperative Cyber Defense Center of Excellence.[23] To NATO, the threat was obvious: what Russia did to Estonia it most certainly could do to other NATO members unless a suitable defense was established.

In 2008 and 2009 Russia launched two more cyber-attacks on nations. In July 2008, just three days after the Lithuanian government passed a law making it illegal to use communist and Soviet symbols, Lithuanian websites were attacked. A series of DoS and other attacks shut down hundreds of Lithuanian sites, and many more were disrupted or vandalized. On January 18, 2009, the very day that the Russian government was pressing Kyrgyzstan to end its commitment allowing the United States access to the Bishkek airbase, a number of DoS attacks on Kyrgyzstan's main Internet servers occurred. DDoS attacks also targeted websites of groups and organizations that supported a continuation of the American presence. The attacks on Lithuania and Kyrgyzstan were not very disruptive, or at least not as disruptive as the attack on Estonia. However, both signaled the exact same message as the attack on Estonia: Russia will use its cyber assets to demonstrate its displeasure with the domestic politics in neighboring countries.

The why, when, and where of Russian attacks prior to the 2008 Georgian war are simple to see. The "why" involved Russia's desire to penalize neighboring governments that took actions that the Kremlin opposed.

If the offending government's actions could be painted as targeting a Russian minority in that country, it added another layer to Russian motivation, a layer that fits with our theories of domestic politics and social constructivism driving foreign policy. When these two factors align with a realist desire to influence neighbor's policies, even if the policy is not directly related to security, it is a strong motivator of Russian action. The "when" is also quite clear. Russian cyberattacks were immediate responses to actions by the target state. The rapidity of the Russian action following an instigation demonstrates that Russia planning was already in place as were the capabilities. The "where" is typically Russia's neighboring nations. As detailed in earlier chapters, Russia has a keen interest in establishing friendly governments on its borders. It is precisely in these countries that Russia feels it can meddle.

RUSSIAN CYBER WARFARE COMBINED WITH CONVENTIONAL WAR: GEORGIA

In 2008 Russia would launch a new form of hybrid warfare: combining cyberattacks with conventional military operations. As detailed in chapter 2, the Russia-Georgian War of 2008 was indeed a conventional war, but Russia also launched a series of cyberattacks against Georgia.[24] Russian troops supporting the independence-minded territories of South Ossetia and Abkhazia invaded Georgia and swept aside the more lightly armored and lightly armed Georgian units. Russia air, land, and sea power were brought to bear in what appeared to be a very traditional military operation. Yet, there was another dimension to the war. For the first time in history, a massive cyberattack preceded the conventional war and continued throughout the course of the conflict.[25] In short, Georgia would be Russia's test of its new hybrid capabilities and how effective integration of nonconventional and conventional war could be.

Russian cyber intrusion into Georgia began weeks before the August 7 invasion. Discussions on Russian chat rooms and networks about cyberattacks on Georgia coincided with actual DDoS attacks starting around July 20.[26] Instructions, targets, malware, and other information was available on Russian "hacktivist" websites, providing a blueprint by which Russian-aligned hackers could contribute to the cyber campaign against Georgia.[27] For a number of weeks, a series of attacks on Georgian Internet servers shut down Georgian government web sites (including the Georgian president's website) and Internet service providers. Georgia was especially vulnerable to Russian cyberattack for two reasons: first, most of the external connections for Georgian sites ran through Russia, and second, Georgia lacked sufficient internal Internet exchange points by which to reroute connections.[28] While these early DDoS attacks did no lasting damage, they did demonstrate the ability of the Russian hackers to bypass Georgian Internet security measures. Russia relies on a well-educated and active pool of hackers that rival those available in the United States or China.[29]

Cyberattacks during the military campaign had the appearance of coordination with ground and air operations. Most cyberattacks sought to cripple national and local websites associated with official Georgian military and political units that could potentially resist Russian conventional intrusion, such as the Georgian Ministry of Defense, Ministry of Foreign Affairs, military websites, and local policy force websites.[30] Other more targeted cyberattacks also displayed coordination. For example, attacks on government and media sites in Gori preceded the aerial bombing of the city by a few hours.[31] There was also a larger tactical sense of the cyber operations. Initial Russian intrusions into Georgia cyberspace were aimed at disrupting a popular Georgian hacker forum. This appears to be a clear attempt to shut down any countermeasures by Georgian hackers before the war started. In this way, Russian gained sovereignty over Georgian cyberspace as a way of assuring Russian dominance over Georgian Internet networks. This sort of violation of sovereignty now sits in a grey area in international relations: whether a violation of cyberspace sovereignty should be regarded as gravely as the more traditional violation of physical/geographical space and sovereignty that leads to conventional warfare.[32]

Russian cyberattacks also displayed a sort of restraint similar to that of the conventional campaign. Russian aerial attacks purposely avoided destroying the key energy infrastructure of Georgia, including the vital Baku-Ceyhan oil pipeline. Russian cyberattacks similarly avoided shutting down key energy and power networks.[33] Russian attacks were clearly disruptive of communications systems in Georgia, including those used by the government and military. Yet, Russian cyberattacks did not give the appearance that they were seeking to damage or destroy key physical Georgian infrastructure. Therefore, while Russian cyberattacks coincided and reinforced the Russian conventional operations, unlike the battle in physical space, the battle in cyberspace was not destructive. This is not say that media organizations and businesses, especially banking, that were targets of Russian cyberattacks did not suffer financial loss; they most certainly did. This sort of loss, while important to the individual businesses involved, is not the degree of violation of sovereignty or aggression that destruction of energy production or infrastructure would represent.

Overall, the Russian message to Georgia, and most likely to other neighbors of Russia, was clear: in both physical space and cyberspace Russia could disable or destroy key national infrastructure if it chose to do so. Ronald J. Deibert, et. al, summarize the overall dominance of the Russian cyber efforts and their coordination with events on the ground.[34] Moreover, they highlight "the importance of control over the physical infrastructure of cyberspace, [and] the strategic and tactical importance of information denial."[35]

RUSSIAN CYBER WARFARE GETS DESTRUCTIVE: UKRAINE

Russian cyberattacks in Ukraine accomplished both information denial and control over cyberspace. But the Russian hybrid actions in Ukraine went a step further than Russian actions against Georgia. In the case of Ukraine, for the first time Russian cyberattacks were used to damage and/or destroy key energy networks, control physical infrastructure, and enlist a host of non-state cyber privateers. As one assessment puts it, Russian cyber warfare produced "kinetic" effects.[36] This would be a new escalation of Russian cyber warfare, demonstrating the sort of destruction that operations in the cyber or information space could accomplish. This change toward a more offensive cyberattack coincided with the previous forms of cyber intrusion and information campaigns aimed at the target population. Thus, Russia would bring all of its capabilities to bear against Ukraine.

The exact start of Russian cyber intrusion into Ukrainian politics cannot be determined. It is fairly certain that a Russian disinformation campaign was active prior to the start of the crisis in 2014. The presence of Russian and pro-Russian television channels (e.g., Pervyi Kanal, Rossija 1, NTV, RT), radio networks (e.g., Radio Mayak), and Internet sources (e.g., TV Zvezda, Tass, RIA Novosti) along with print media and a large Russian population in Ukraine proved a fertile ground for Russian propaganda.[37] The basic thrust of the information campaign was to establish Russian sources of information as viable alternatives to Ukrainian or Western sources. This would prove useful in the upcoming conflict.

Two studies point to the year 2013 as the beginning of a persistent Russian cyber campaign against Ukraine.[38] The studies state that in 2013 pro-Russian hackers launched attacks on Ukrainian government and military websites, defacing some and gaining access to information contained in others. As relations between Ukraine and Russia deteriorated in January and February 2014 due to protests against the Ukrainian President Viktor Yanukovich, Russian cyber intrusion increased. The attacks were too numerous to chronicle here, but Connell and Vogler summarize the attacks as "Russian hackers...utilized spear phishing, malware, DDoS attacks, telephone denial of service (TDoS), and other forms of cyber disruption and espionage to conduct a steady drumbeat of cyberattacks targeting Ukraine's government, military, telecommunications, and private-sector information technology infrastructure."[39]

The combination of the information campaign and cyberattacks against Ukraine played a role in the Russian seizure of Crimea. Western media became silent when confronted with a coordinated Russian attempt to hide the truth behind its operations.[40] As the little green men poured into Crimea, and local media began to report that the invaders were indeed Russian units, the Russian disinformation campaign ramped up to obscure the truth. Cyberattacks against pro-Ukrainian media incapacitated reporting of alternative versions of events. Pro-Russian media broadcasting Russian denials of involvement were repeated in Western media and remained unchallenged for up to a year in some instances.[41] Given the speed with which Russian special operations units seized Crimea (see chapter 2), the Russian cyber and information campaigns were successful in obfuscating Russian involvement long enough for Russia to secure Crimea using conventional means.

Russian cyber intrusions in Ukraine were not only about helping Russian special operations units secure Crimea, Russia targeted other elements of the Ukrainian state. One example is the intrusion into the Ukrainian Central Election Commission information system by the pro-Russian hacktivists CyberBerkut just three days before the 2014 Ukrainian presidential election. This intrusion was a minor attack compared to the December 2015 attack on the Ukrainian power grid. Hackers were able to gain access remotely to power distribution centers in Western Ukraine and shut off power to more than 220,000 Ukrainians.[42] Planning for the attack certainly took months as post-event analysis suggests that spearfishing e-mails, the placement of malware, and trial runs all preceded the actual attack. This was the first time that pro-Russian hackers were able to translate their control of cyberspace into kinetic events in the physical space.

A more serious attack on Ukraine happened in late June 2017. The NotPetya variant of the Petya ransomware virus spread rapidly across Ukraine as computers performed a routine scheduled update of a tax-accounting program. The attack is estimated to have spread to over one million computers in Ukraine (and also across portions of Europe) within the first day. The attack had physical impact as radiation monitoring equipment at Chernobyl went offline due to disruption of the computer software. Banks, government offices, transportation hubs, and other businesses in Ukraine were also incapacitated. Within two days the Ukrainian government effectively countered the attack. Afterwards, Ukrainian government officials seized equipment used in the attack and said that these were owned by Russian agents. In January 2018 the American Central Intelligence Agency (CIA) linked the development of NotPetya to Russian Military Intelligence (GRU) and suggested that Russia was responsible for the attack. In February 2018 the British government concurred, saying that their intelligence showed that Russia was responsible.

The purpose of these and other Russian cyberattacks on Ukraine appears to serve three Russian goals. First, it serves to disrupt the Ukrainian government and society. The attacks limited the effectiveness of Ukrainian government services, private business, and the Ukrainian defense forces. As such, it helped Russia in seizing Crimea and serving the interests of the pro-Russian separatists in the Donbass region in their struggle against the government of the western portion of Ukraine. Second, these attacks are a way for Russia to remind the Ukrainian government of the power that Russia wields. It is a not-so-subtle reminder that Russia will use all available resources at its disposal to shape politics in Eastern Europe. Cyberattacks are a crude but effective way to send the signal that any Ukrainian policy that Russia perceives as anti-Russian could provoke Russian retaliation—and that Ukraine is incapable of stopping the Russian attack, at least initially. Third, the Ukrainian information space provides Russia with a laboratory for its cyber-warfare capabilities. It does not take a far stretch of the imagination to consider that Russian intrusion into the Ukrainian power grid, presidential elections, or business software could be replicated elsewhere in the world.[43]

In summary, Russian cyberattacks and hybrid warfare against Georgia and Ukraine fits the same pattern of "why, when, and where" as Russian action against the Baltic republics. Russia attacks when it feels its influence or interests in a neighboring country are threatened. The presence of a Russian minority and/or pro-Russian populations makes Russian action even more likely and provides a local base of support for Russian aggression.

RUSSIAN PROPAGANDA, INFORMATION, AND CYBER INTRUSION CAMPAIGNS IN WESTERN COUNTRIES

Russia has been engaged for years in using cyberattacks to support its propaganda and information campaigns against Western nations. I shall use two examples: first, the Russian campaign of turning the Internet of Things (IoT) into a botnet army of zombie computers aimed at the West and second, the Russian cyber interference into the 2016 American Presidential election. The first example illustrates the Russian tactic of compromising devices in foreign countries to use as part of future attacks; the second example illustrates how Russian cyber resources can be utilized to both support an information campaign and help achieve a very specific foreign-policy goal.

In April 2018 both the United States and United Kingdom issued a joint alert about Russian cyber activities to compromise millions of devices connected to the Internet.[44] The joint alert stated that Russian hackers had targeted mainly home-operated routers and other fairly mundane Internet devices in order to compromise their security. The hackers also targeted the IoT, typically comprised of smart devices that are continually connected to the Internet but have very little security, such as baby monitors, refrigerators, security camera systems, and such devices. It is common for such devices to have factory-set passwords and security that the normal user either does not know about or does not change. The routers and the IoT devices, if comprised through external control, can provide an army of zombie computers to use in DDoS attacks. These sorts of attacks make it difficult for the target to determine exactly who is directing the attack. This masking of the true attacker gives Russia or Pro-Russian hackers plausible deniability.

It is also been suggested that control over routers and the IoT provides the Russian troll-farms and bots another tool by which to spread disinformation. It is possible for hackers who control routers to either modify or replace information. Russia did exactly this in Ukraine, although Ukrainian cyber experts were able to spot it and counter it quite quickly.[45] Manipulation of information through control over routers is a common technique of criminals, and perhaps the Russian intelligence community hackers have taken a page from their playbook. There is evidence that the Russian government has not only turned a blind eye to cyber criminals but has even weaponized the criminal community when its interests align with those of the government's. Thus, the Russian cyber compromising of routers and IoT poses a threat not so much to the individuals who own the devices, but rather at to whomever Russia points all those devices.

Russian cyber intrusion into the 2016 American presidential election campaign shows how many different parts of an information campaign can all come together. At the time of writing this in the Spring of 2019, not everything is yet known about the Russian attacks on the American democracy, yet certain elements have taken enough shape to talk about them. First, like most Russian information operations, the broad goal of the operation followed from fundamental Russian foreign policy: to destabilize opposing states and to challenge American hegemony. In this instance, the broad Russian goal was to weaken the American public's support for their government. A secondary goal appears now to be to drive a wedge between the United States and its NATO allies. If Russia were to be successful in such a plan, it would go a very long way in increasing Russian control and influence in Eastern Europe, as well as make it easier for Russia to assert itself on the global stage. A more narrow and targeted goal appears to be the desire of Russian intelligence agents, and most likely President Putin himself, to support the defeat of Democratic Party candidate Hilary Clinton. Animus between Putin and former Secretary of State Clinton is the result of Putin's perception of American interference into the 2011 Russian parliamentary elections and 2012 Russian presidential election, as cited in the indictments of July 2018 by US Special Counsel Robert Mueller.[46]

Russian cyber activities to achieve these goals seems to have centered on the actions of Russian Military Intelligence officers in the GRU. At least twelve officers of the Russian military working in two units (Unit 26165 and Unit 74455) began around March 2016 to target e-mail accounts of the Democratic Congressional Campaign Committee (DCCC), the Democratic National Committee (DNC), and individuals associated with the Clinton campaign with spearfishing attacks (i.e., e-mails that spoof legitimate e-mail traffic in order to get a targeted individual to reveal password information or other personal information). These efforts were successful and by April 2016 the Russian hackers were able to compromise hundreds of e-mail accounts, computers, and servers belonging to the DCCC and DNC, stealing tens of thousands of individual e-mail messages and an unknown quantity of other information and documents. In June 2016 the hackers began releasing information, primarily the e-mails of candidate Clinton, via fake accounts under their control (such as DCLeaks and Guccifer 2.0) as well through third-parties such as Wikileaks (referred to as "Organization 1" in the Mueller indictments).[47] The Russian agents hid the origin of their activities by using compromised computers in many countries and making any online purchases using cryptocurrencies. The release of the information was spread via the Pro-Russian botnet army and troll-farms on social media, as well as being distributed directly to (unnamed in the indictment) pro-Trump media outlets.[48]

The precise fallout from this Russian information campaign is still not known. The embarrassing information released about candidate Clinton and some of the DNC members certainly had some impact upon the Clinton's defeat, but whether it was the deciding factor in the loss will probably never be known. The destabilization of American domestic politics that has occurred after the election of Republican presidential candidate Donald Trump is, however, undeniable. The events of summer 2018 in which President Trump continued his tirade against his NATO allies at an alliance meeting in Brussels while heaping praise on Vladimir Putin at an impromptu meeting in Helsinki give us a clue as to the degree to which the Russian information campaign may have paid off handsomely for Russian foreign policy.

CONCLUSION: AN AGGRESSIVE RUSSIAN PRESENCE IN CYBERSPACE AND HYBRID WARFARE

As the examples in this chapter illustrate, Russia has been acting more and more aggressively in cyberspace over the past decade. It has used cyberattacks in targeted attacks against its neighbors in Eastern Europe and Central Asia. In Georgia it displayed a new type of hybrid warfare, combining cyber operations with conventional military operations, in which the superior conventional power also established control over cyberspace. In Ukraine, Russia would bring all of its weapons to bear: a persistent information campaign, the use of conventional special operations forces, cyberattacks, and for the first time a cyberattack to bring down portions of the Ukrainian power grid. Russian cyber activities have also targeted elections and political parties around the globe. Specifically, in what at the time of writing this book appears to be Russia's most spectacular success—officers in Russian military intelligence hacked into computers in the United States and interfered in the 2016 American presidential election. There is every reason to believe that given this pattern of overall successful results, that Russia will continue its aggressive use of cyberattacks, information, and propaganda campaigns against target nations.

Notes

1. Peter R. Mansoor, "Introduction: Hybrid Warfare in History," In *Hybrid Warfare: Fighting Complex Opponents from the Ancient World to the Present* edited by Williamson Murray and Peter R. Mansoor (New York, Cambridge University Press, 2012), 1–17, p. 2.
2. Williamson Murray and Peter R. Mansoor, editors, *Hybrid Warfare: Fighting Complex Opponents from the Ancient World to the Present* (New York, Cambridge University Press, 2012).
3. It should be noted here that there is still some disagreement about the term "hybrid warfare" and its variants "hybrid threat" and "hybrid conflict." Max G. Manwaring, *The Complexity of Modern Asymmetric Warfare* (Norman, University of Oklahoma Press, 2012); Russell W. Glenn, "Thought on 'Hybrid' Conflict," *Small Wars Journal,* 2009, http://smallwarsjournal.com/blog/journal/docs-temp/188-glenn.pdf, accessed June 25, 2018.
4. Monaghan, "Putin's Way of War," 66–67.
5. Manwaring, *The Complexity of Modern Asymmetric Warfare,* 7.
6. For a short discussion on why the term hybrid is not really that useful and that the terms "irregular force" or "comprehensive approach" would be better, see Glenn, "Thought on 'Hybrid' Conflict."
7. Michael Evans, "From Kadesh to Kandahar: Military Theory and the Future of War," *Naval War College Review* 56, no. 3 (2003): 133–150; Douglas Porch, *Counterinsurgency: Exposing the Myths of the New Way of War* (New York, Cambridge University Press, 2013).
8. Murray and Mansoor, *Hybrid Warfare;* Daniel Marston and Carter Malkasian, editors, *Counterinsurgency in Modern Warfare* (New York, Osprey Publishing, 2008).
9. Frank Hoffman, *Conflict in the 21st Century: The Rise of Hybrid Wars* (Arlington, Potomac Institute for Policy Studies. 2007); Frank Hoffman, "Hybrid Threats: Reconceptualizing the Evolving Character of Modern Conflict," *Strategic Forum,* no. 240 (2009): 1–8.
10. For example see Michael J. Mazarr, "The Folly of 'Asymmetric' War," *The Washington Quarterly* 31, no. 3 (2008): 33–53; Josef Schroefl and Stuart J. Kaufman, "Hybrid Actors, Tactical Variety: Rethinking Asymmetric and Hybrid War," *Studies in Conflict and Terrorism* 37, no. 10 (2014): 862–880.

11. Bettina Renz, "Russia and 'Hybrid Warfare'," *Contemporary Politics* 22, no. 3 (2016): 283–300; Giles, "Russia's 'New' Tools for Confronting the West."

12. Examples of such phrasing are their statements such as "the role of mobile joint forces operating in an integrated reconnaissance and information environment is rising" and "asymmetric actions too, will be used to level off the enemy's superiority in armed struggle." Thus, they squarely plant hybrid warfare squarely into the more general concept of warfare. Col. S. G. Chekinov and Lt. Gen. S.A. Bodanov, "The Nature and Content of a New-Generation War," *Military Thought* 22, no. 4 (2013): 12–22.

13. Thomas, "Russia's Information Warfare Strategy," 103.

14. Monaghan, "Putin's Way of War," 67–68.

15. Ibid., 68.

16. It is interesting to note here that Kofman's assertion of raiding, and its assumptions of clear strategic objectives, runs counter to Monaghan who asserts that Russian actions often lack strategic forethought. Charap and Coltan also fundamentally disagree with Kofman's assumption. Monaghan, *Power in Modern Russia*; Charap and Colton, *Everyone Loses*; Kofman, "Raiding and International Brigandry,"

17. Connell and Vogler, "Russia's Approach to Cyber Warfare," 13.

18. Stephen Herzog, "Revisiting the Estonian Cyber Attacks: Digital Threats and Multinational Responses," *Journal of Strategic Security* 4, no. 2 (2011): 49–60, p. 51.

19. Connell and Vogler, "Russia's Approach to Cyber Warfare," 13.

20. The list of possible cyberattacks is as large as one's imagination. The most typical are Denial of Service (DoS), Distributed Denial of Service (DDoS), Permanent Denial of Service (PDoS), defacement of websites, injection of viruses other malicious programming, IP spoofing, and SQL injection. The DDoS attacks, in which a horde of zombie computers and/ or devices are used to attack a single network are increasingly common, and effective. Taking advantage of the Internet of Things (IoT) in which many common devices (think refrigerators, printers, baby monitors, etc) are all connected to the internet, a DDoS attack captures these seemingly innocuous devices and turns them into automated bots that relentlessly ping the target network. This collection of zombie devices, often referred to as a "botnet," can effectively and without much cost to the hackers, shut down target networks. Phillip Pool, "War of the Cyber World: The Law of Cyber Warfare," *International Lawyer*, 47, no. 2 (2013): 299–325.

21. Connell and Vogler, "Russia's Approach to Cyber Warfare," 14.
22. Connell and Vogler, "Russia's Approach to Cyber Warfare," 14.
23. McNabb, *Vladimir Putin and Russia's Imperial Revival*, 115–116.
24. For the course of this discussion, I will drop the word "alleged" before all mentions of Russian cyberattack and intrusion into Georgia. While the Georgian government has never been able to prove that Russia committed or directed the cyberattacks, the accumulation of coincidental evidence is so great as to make the denials by Russian implausible. Most of the botnet attacks were eventually traced to servers in Russia and Turkey, but not directly to the Russian government. For the sake of brevity, as well as clarity, I am not going to maintain the charade that Russian involvement is merely "alleged." For a list of statements and sources about the "alleged" nature of the attack and Georgia's attempts to prove Russian involvement see Hollis, *Cyberwar Case Study*.
25. Connell and Vogler, "Russia's Approach to Cyber Warfare," 18.
26. McNabb lists the first attack as taking place on July 19, while both Hollis, as well as, Connell and Vogler (2017) list the attack as July 20. McNabb, *Vladimir Putin and Russia's Imperial Revival*, 119; Hollis, *Cyberwar Case Study*; Connell and Vogler, "Russia's Approach to Cyber Warfare,"
27. Connell and Vogler, "Russia's Approach to Cyber Warfare," 17.
28. Hollis, *Cyberwar Case Study*, 2.
29. Thomas, "Russia's Information Warfare Strategy," 107.
30. McNabb, *Vladimir Putin and Russia's Imperial Revival*, 119.
31. Connell and Vogler, "Russia's Approach to Cyber Warfare," 18; Hollis, *Cyberwar Case Study*, 3–5.
32. Hacker wars, as they are known, in which hackers and others patriotic to rival nations fight over cyber space has become an increasing part of modern international relations. Kay Hearn, Patricia A. H. Williams, and Rachel J. Mahncke, *International Relations and Cyber Attacks: Official and Unofficial Discourse* (Australian information Warfare and Security Conference, 2010), http://ro.ecu.edu.au/isw/32, accessed July 15, 2018.
33. Hollis, *Cyberwar Case Study*, 4–5.
34. Ronald J. Deibert, Rafal Rohozinski, and Masashi Crete-Nishihata, "Cyclones in Cyberspace: Information Shaping and Denial in the 2008 Russia-Georgia War," *Security Dialogue* 43, no. 1 (2012): 3–24.
35. Deibert et. al., "Cyclones in Cyberspace," 3.
36. Connell and Vogler, "Russia's Approach to Cyber Warfare" 19.

37. NATO Strategic Communications Centre of Excellence (NATO Strat-com). *Russian Information Campaign Against Ukranian State and Defense Forces* (Latvia. 2016), www.stratcomcoe.org.
38. Connell and Vogler, "Russia's Approach to Cyber Warfare"; McNabb, *Vladimir Putin and Russia's Imperial Revival.*
39. Connell and Vogler, "Russia's Approach to Cyber Warfare," 19.
40. Giles, *Russia's "New" Tools for Confronting the West,* 31.
41. Ibid., 31–32.
42. Connell and Vogler, "Russia's Approach to Cyber Warfare," 20.
43. As a side note, I am not arguing that the Russian use of hybrid war-fare in Ukraine validates the "hybrid war" proponents or those who might argue that Russian warfare has fundamentally changed to a hybrid model. Rather, I agree with Renz that circumstances in Ukraine, particu-larly Crimea, were conducive to Russian hybrid attacks. Moreover, I am not arguing that because Russia's hybrid attacks went well that Russia is now forever more going to show a superiority in such forms of warfare. I am instead illustrating how Russia's actions have changed over time and how they have been employed. See Renz, "Russia and 'Hybrid Warfare'".
44. Nicole Kobie, "Nobody is Safe from Russia's Colossal Hacking Operation," *Wired,* April 21, 2018, http://www.wired.co.uk/article/russia-hacking-russian-hackers-routers-ncsc-uk-us-2018-syria, accessed July 16, 2018
45. Kobie, "Nobody is Safe from Russia's Colossal Hacking Operation."
46. Mark Mazzetti and Katie Benner, "12 Russian Agents Indicted in Mueller Investigation," *New York Times,* July 13, 2018, available (subscription) athttps://www.nytimes.com/2018/07/13/us/politics/mueller-indictment-russian-intelligence-hacking.html, accessed September 30, 2019.
47. Ibid.
48. Ibid.

CHAPTER 6

THE CONTINUING RUSSIAN THREAT TO THE BALTIC NATIONS AND EASTERN EUROPE

REPEATING THE PAST IN THE NEAR FUTURE?

Russian desire to dominate its neighbors to its west is a credible threat to those countries. In this chapter, we explore the why, when, and where of Russian actions in the Baltic nations and Eastern Europe.

RUSSIA AND THE BALTIC NATIONS

The backdrop for the current tensions in the Baltic region is one that combines a long history with recent events. The long history of Russian aggression against its Baltic neighbors of Estonia, Latvia, and Lithuania has made an indelible imprint on the foreign policies of all the involved countries. After gaining independence, all three nations hurriedly sought to join NATO in an effort to deter any future Russian military actions against them. Russia viewed their joining NATO as an inherent threat to

Russian security because NATO troops would now be stationed directly across the Russian border. The rational fears of the smaller Baltic nations surrounding their giant Russian neighbor have led to a tense NATO-versus-Russia standoff in the region that resembles to some degree the Cold War standoff of forces across the West German and East German borders.

The Historical Relationship of the Baltic Nations to Russia

Historically, the Baltic nation populations have been on the receiving end of Russian aggression for centuries, dating back to the Livonian War of 1558–1583. Following the Russian success against Sweden in the Great Northern War (1700–1721), most of the modern-day Baltic nations fell under the control of the emerging Russian Empire. In the Treaty of Nystad, the Russian tsars allowed for local nobility (mostly of German-Baltic origin) to rule in the Baltic nations of Estonia and Livonia.[1] As the Russian Empire fell into turmoil at the start of the twentieth century, nationalist movements arose in the Baltics, particularly in Estonia and Latvia. All three countries became independent after the Russian Revolution, although the independence movements in each nation played out very differently and often with a great deal of violence. During the interwar period, all three nations succumbed to home grown versions of authoritarian/proto-fascist governments.

During World War II, the Baltic Nations were divided into the Soviet sphere of influence in the infamous Molotov-Ribbentrop Pact of 1939. As the USSR invaded Poland in September 1939, it intimidated the Baltic Nations into allowing Soviet troops onto their territories. Subsequently in 1940, the USSR declared the three Baltic nations to be Soviet Socialist Republics and integrated all three into the Soviet Union. From 1940 to 1941, the Soviet leadership purged perceived enemies in the Baltic nations, sending most into work camps. The Nazi invasion of the Soviet Union in June 1941 (Operation Barbarossa) led to German domination and the establishment of the *Reichskommissariat Ostland* to maintain civil control over the subjugated Baltic nations. Under German direction, the Jewish populations of the Baltic nations were largely exterminated, with almost the entire Jewish population of Lithuania killed in the Holocaust. The Soviet Red Army rolled back through the Baltics in 1944 and reincorporated the Baltic nations back into the USSR.

A consequence of Russian invasions of the Baltic nations, the Russification of the Baltic tnations over the last century or so also has a long history. After World War II, Soviet Russification of the Baltic republics intensified. Russian citizens were encouraged to relocate to the Baltic republics, typically to contribute to state-directed industrialization of the region. Due to ethnic Russian migration, all three contemporary Baltic nations host a minority Russian population. The largest Russian minority as a share of the total national population is in Latvia, where almost one-third of the population is ethnically Russian. Estonia also has a large Russian population (roughly 27 percent) while Lithuania's Russian population is only about 12 percent of the entire Lithuanian population. These Russian communities are a perfect target for Russian information and propaganda campaigns, as well as a willing source of pro-Russian hacktivists. Russia uses the pretense of discrimination against these Russian minorities as a rationale for Russian intrusion into the politics and foreign policies of the Baltic nations.

More recently, a source of tension has been Russian aggression in Ukraine. The Baltic nations were alarmed by the Russian seizure of Crimea in 2014, as well as the continued Russian support of the Donbass rebellion in the Eastern Ukraine Oblasts of Donetsk and Luhansk. The Baltic nations consider the Russian actions in Ukraine to be a blueprint for how Russia might act against them. The threat against the Baltic nations is, of course, quite real. Russia has been increasing its asymmetrical attacks, both propaganda and cyber, against the Baltic nations since the first cyberattack in 2007 (see chapter 4). Moreover, Russian military drills in the region have increased over the same time period and taken on a more and more aggressive tone, even simulating the use of tactical nuclear weapons against NATO countries during Russian attacks in the Baltic region.[2]

Russian Foreign Policy Goals in the Baltic Nations

Russian foreign policy goals in the Baltic region range from those of large geostrategic, great power consideration, to the those of more direct concern to Russian domestic and identity politics. Starting at the level of the international system, the larger goal of Russian foreign policy is the reestablishment of Russia as a great power. This goal requires Russia to accomplish two geostrategic objectives: establishing dominance over Eastern Europe and gaining greater access to the Baltic Sea to enhance Russian naval capabilities. Regarding the former, one analyst considers the Russian need for dominance of the region as the greatest motivator of Russian foreign policy toward its smaller Baltic neighbors.[3] This goal faded when Russian influence over Eastern Europe waned post-1991 and eventually culminated in the Baltic Nations joining NATO and the European Union in 2004. It made perfect sense for the Baltic nations to seek a security alliance to balance against their large, and historically belligerent, Russian neighbor.

But of course, the small Baltic nations cannot balance Russia by themselves. In the early 2000s the armed forces of each nation numbered about 3,000–5,000 each and thus were neither adequate in defending their territory nor deterring Russian aggression.[4] From the Russian perspective, the Baltic nations joining NATO was a betrayal of Russia. To the Kremlin, the Baltic nations appeared ungrateful for all the efforts that Russian and Soviet societies had put in to develop the Baltic region for two centuries. Russia also perceived a betrayal from the Western powers who reneged on commitments not to extend a Western security alliance into the region. Given the position of the Baltic nations as protected nations under Article 5 of the NATO Treaty, Russia is now confronted with an armed security alliance on its border. Unlike the Cold War period where the Warsaw Pact nations kept NATO troops far away from Russia, since 2004 NATO troops could conceivably shake hands with Russian soldiers. In fact, the Russian Foreign Policy Concept lists "the geopolitical expansion pursued by the North Atlantic Treaty Organization and the European Union" as creating "a serious crisis in the relations between Russia and the Western States."[5] Such language highlights the degree to which Russia is dissatisfied with the status quo in the Baltic region.

Of course, Russian actions have contributed to the NATO perception that Russia will act aggressively toward its smaller neighbors. After the 2014 Russian seizure of Crimea and interference in Eastern Ukraine, NATO members met in Wales. There the NATO nations committed to the Readiness Action Plan (RAP), part of which is the Very-High Readiness Joint Task Force (VRJTF) that has deployed more than 5,000 NATO troops into the Baltics.[6] In the 2016 Warsaw Summit meeting, NATO members agreed to an Enhanced Forward Presence in which NATO would field a multinational battalion in each of the three Baltic nations as well as Poland. These battalions were deployed in 2017. Moreover, NATO has ramped up its military exercises in the region, including the June 2018 "Saber Strike 18" exercises involving 19 NATO members and more than 18,000 troops throughout Poland and all three Baltic nations.

The deployment of the NATO troops and the commitment of NATO under Article 5 to defend the Baltic nations has interfered with Russia's goal of creating friendly and compliant neighbors. David E. McNabb argues that the inherent Russian goal in the region is to "bring the former [Baltic] republics politically, militarily, and economically into the Russian orbit."[7] The most direct method would be for Russia to regain the ability and/or the right to provide military security for the Baltic nations. NATO actions have made that impossible, at least in the near term. As long as Russia believes that NATO members will indeed act in the case of any violation of Baltic national sovereignty, Russian actions to gain control over the Baltic nations are limited to nonmilitary methods.

The second geostrategic goal of Russian foreign policy is greater access to the Baltic Sea. With the end of the Soviet Union, Russia's access to the Baltic Sea is now essentially limited to its base in Kaliningrad. From the

Russian perspective, this base is vulnerable to having any Russian land connection to it being cut off by NATO states, a concern that Russian military strategists rate as a critical vulnerability.[8] For the last few years, Russia has spent significant resources trying to upgrade its radar, missile batteries, and submarine fleet at Kaliningrad. The Russian Baltic Sea Fleet at Kaliningrad now includes roughly 75 surface ships, two *Kilo*-class submarines, one *Lada*-class submarine, a naval aviation unit, and a coastal Army corps. An important element of the Russian buildup in Kaliningrad is the ability of the Russian forces, especially the submarine and coastal missile units, to effectively choke off the Baltic Sea and deny NATO naval units any direct sea access to the Baltic nations.[9] Potentially key to NATO defense of the Baltic Sea is the use of the seaport at Gdansk, Poland, as a resupply point that could be used to overwhelm the defenses at Kaliningrad.[10] In response to this obvious NATO strategy, Russia has deployed *Iskander-M* ballistic missiles to Kaliningrad.[11] With a range of around 400 kilometers, the *Iskander-M* missiles can target all Polish coastal bases, as well as all bases in the Baltic nations. In sum, the Russian units at Kaliningrad form a significant Anti-Access/Area Denial (A2/AD) capability that most likely exceeds the NATO forces in the region (i.e., Poland and the Baltics) and also the neutral Scandinavian units of Sweden and Finland. Thus, while Russia could not assure itself of using the Baltic Sea to gain access to the Atlantic, it most likely can deny NATO use of the Baltic Sea to reach the Baltic nations.

Included in the Russian foreign policy goals for the Baltic nations is support for the Russian minorities who live there. Protection of the Russian minorities bridges the gap between foreign policy and domestic politics for President Putin. In early 2014, and roughly coinciding with Russian aggression in Ukraine, Putin announced on Russian television that the Russian state is at the center of the Russian-speaking world and that Russia guarantees the safety of all Russians in Europe. This guarantee supposedly would extend to the roughly 7 million Russian speakers currently residing in NATO countries, with more than one million in the Baltic nations (with more than 50 percent of those in Latvia). Putin has not missed an opportunity to complain about human rights violations of Russian minorities (particularly in Estonia) and to speak on behalf of the Russian diaspora. Russia has pushed for pro-Russian language laws and referendums in the Baltic nations and generally has sought to paint Baltic citizenship laws as discriminatory toward the Russian minorities.[12]

Protection of Russian speakers is the nominal rationale for Russian dominance over Crimea and support for the independence movement in Eastern Ukraine. The aggressive actions taken by Putin in Crimea were very popular in Russia.[13] Not coincidentally, Russian foreign policy actions to support a Russian minority in Ukraine also coincided with the need for Russian security forces to maintain control over the Russian naval base at Sevastopol and the continued Russian presence in the Black Sea. This happy congruence of Russian foreign policy and domestic politics is not lost on the governments in the Baltic nations who could reasonably see Kaliningrad as their Sevastopol. Therefore, the presence of the sizable and vocal Russian minorities in the Baltic nations poses a structural security risk.[14] Moreover, these Russian minority communities are a willing target of Russian propaganda efforts and a source of pro-Russian hacktivists. Thus, the Russian threat to the Baltic nations is quite real, given how Russia has motivations for aggressive behavior stemming from realist, domestic, and social constructivist forces.

Russian Methods of Influence and Control over the Baltic Nations

Russia attempts to achieve its foreign policy goals in the Baltic region mainly through a combination of military posturing and nonmilitary actions. The combination of these techniques corresponds with the overall thrust of the Gerasimov doctrine but predates Gerasimov's writings in many instances, demonstrating that Russian use of multiple sources of influence is not something that began in 2013.[15] Generally, Russia combines militaristic displays of force with economic pressure (mainly in energy policy), information and propaganda campaigns, diplomatic pressure, and cyber warfare in order to influence the foreign policies of the Baltic nations.

Russian Force Posturing Toward the Baltic Nations

Over the past decade, or roughly since the end of the Russia-Georgia War of 2008 and growing in intensity after the seizure of Crimea in 2014, Russian military behavior in the Baltic region has become more provocative. Russian military maneuvers as far back as 2009 (i.e., the *Zapad* 2009 military exercise) have mocked threatening behavior to NATO and non-NATO nations in the region, including a simulated Russian nuclear attack on Warsaw.[16] In September 2017, Russian military units, mainly deployed in Belarus and Kaliningrad near Lithuania and Poland, held the largest military exercises near a NATO border since the Cold War. These exercises comprised more than 65,000 troops and included the test launch of two RS-24 ICBMs just before the exercise began.[17] Russian bombers have also simulated attacks on targets in non-aligned Sweden and NATO member Denmark. Similarly, Russian air units have violated the airspace over the Baltic nations routinely, with an increasing number of occurrences since 2014. Russian naval units, particularly the submarines of its Baltic Sea fleet, have made incursions into the territorial waters of all the nations on the Baltic Sea. On April 4–6, 2018, Russian naval units held a military exercise closer to the Latvian coast than at any time since the independence of the Latvian nation.

The intent behind the Russian aggression is three-fold. First, these maneuvers do actually increase the readiness and capability of Russian military units. As discussed in chapter 3, Russian military commanders drew the conclusion from the 2008 Russia-Georgia War that the modernization and preparedness of Russian military units needed to be improved and exercises of this sort would help. Second, simulated Russian attacks on NATO and non-NATO nations can help Russian gauge the response of Russia's opponents. These first two objectives can reasonably be seen as part of Russian defense policy and perhaps not inherently aggressive. The third intent of the exercises fits squarely into an aggressive foreign policy. The provocative Russian military actions are meant to intimidate the Baltic nations. Russian ground exercises, simulated air strikes, and naval incursions remind the Baltic nations that Russia could attack them without a great deal of advance notice. This threat is credible as Russia massed more than 150,000 troops for a "training exercise" on the Ukrainian border before it seized Crimea in 2014.

Nations along the Baltic Sea have heard the Russian message loud and clear. Poland was the first to react. Since 2008, Poland has increased its defense spending, modernized its forces, procured air and missile defense systems, upgraded its navy, created a national defense force, and sought more integration with NATO defense. Since 2014, Latvia and Lithuania also have increased their defense spending at the highest rates of any of the NATO members. All three Baltic republics have modernized their defense forces, including increasing the size of their armed forces, both regular and reserves. And as mentioned previously in this chapter, NATO has increased its commitment to these nations by both establishing a rapid force that can be inserted into the region and committing more permanent troops in the Baltic nations, including four battalion-sized battlegroups from the United States, Germany, Canada, and the United Kingdom. In addition to the response of the smaller Baltic nations, Sweden and Finland have positioned more of their air and missile defense forces closer to the Baltic Sea, including the Swedish reinforcement of Gotland Island.

Russian Economic Pressure on the Baltic Nations

Since 1991 the presence of ethnic Russian minorities has made Baltic-Russian relations quite contentious, but there is another element of the tension, one that revolves around economics. While a good portion of the post-independence issues about citizenship and discrimination are slowly being dealt with, one larger issue not only transcends the decades from 1991 to today but has also remained fairly constant across time and the three Baltic nations: energy dependence on Russia.[18] The Baltic nations are dependent on Russia for the overwhelming majority of their oil and import 100 percent of their natural gas from Russia.[19] This makes these nations particularly vulnerable to proactive energy diplomacy emanating from Moscow. Russia has used pipeline shutoffs and interruptions of energy flows to put pressure on the Baltic nations and their domestic policy choices. Two examples are the 2003 stopping of oil shipments to Latvia and the 2006 interruption of the oil pipeline into Lithuania. An example of Russian coordination of energy policy with other methods of foreign policy would be the stopping of Russian oil deliveries to Estonia in May 2007, which coincided with Russian-friendly cyberattacks on Estonia that began on April 27, 2007.

Complicating the matter is that Russian leverage of energy deliveries over the Baltic nations is not solely based on being the source of the energy. Among the many reasons for this, two stand out. First, there exists a tangled web of connections between the businesses and individuals in Russia and the Baltic nations. The end of the Soviet Union did not mean that former Soviet bureaucrats living in the Baltic nations suddenly forgot their connections to Russia. The dynamic among individual businessmen and oligarchs, as well as the corporations and businesses that they represent, is the same as for the Russian *siloviki*. The flow of money and connections between Russia and the Baltic nations allows for the powerful in Russia to pursue their interests via legitimate and corrupt uses of money in the domestic politics of the Baltic nations, particular in campaign politics.[20] Second, Russian energy companies often have a direct stake in Baltic energy firms. For example, in 2012 Gazprom owned shares of large energy producers/distributors in the Baltic nations, such as 37 percent of *East Gass* in Estonia, 34 percent of *Latvijas Gaze* in Latvia, 30 percent of *Stella Vitae*, 37 percent of *Lietuvos Dujos*, and 99.5 percent of the Kaunas Heat and Power Plant in Lithuania.[21]

Russian Information and Propaganda Campaigns to Undermine the Baltic Nations

Russian propaganda campaigns toward the Baltic nations tend to take two forms: positive messages about Russian society and critiques of the

Baltic nations' governments.[22] Most of the Russian messages targets the sizable Russian minority communities. However, Russian information campaigns are more complicated than just ginning up its most likely supporters. Russia has increased its presence in the physical space, typically through support for pro-Russian NGOs. The Alexander Gorchakov Public Diplomacy Foundation organizes and supports NGOs, including those operating in the Baltic nations. The foundation presents a positive depiction of Russian society, culture, and politics. In particular, it promotes a series of youth gatherings centered around dialogue between Russian and Baltic youth titled the *Baltic Dialogue*.[23] As mentioned in chapter 4, Russia established the Russkiy Mir Foundation in 2007 specifically to extend the Russian soft-power reach, primarily into Europe. Along with its sister organization Rossotrudnichestvo, Russkiy Mir promotes Russian culture and has a physical presence in the Baltic nations. At a broader level, Russian media—both traditional media such as radio and television, as well as social media via Internet channels and streams— flows into the Baltic nations. One scholar suggests that the Russian-speaking minority communities tend to get their news from these sources while the Baltic ethnicities choose local sources. The pervasiveness of pro-Russian information creates a strong propaganda campaign that has been described by leaders of the Baltic nations as "war" and a "parallel reality" in their own countries.[24]

It thus appears that Russian information campaigns in the Baltic nations typically follow Nye's basic idea of soft power: that it is the power of attraction. Importantly, the success of such campaigns may be limited. Typically, the ability of Russian information campaigns to present a positive image of Russia gets contradicted by the more forceful "hard power" actions of the Russian government.[25] A survey of the Baltic populations shows evidence that while there is an appreciation of the Russian people and some of their traits and/or values, there is a general distrust of the Russian government and its interests.[26] Moreover, Russian use of hard power instruments (such as cyberattacks, threats, and energy shutoffs) reinforce negatives views of Russia.

Russian Cyber Warfare Against the Baltic Nations

The Baltic nations have been some of the earliest and most targeted nations by Russian cyber intrusions. In many ways, Russia appears to test its cyber techniques on the Baltic nations. As mentioned in chapter 5, Russia launched cyberattacks on Estonia in 2007 and Lithuania in 2008 in response to domestic politics in both of those nations. These attacks seemed to pave the way for the Russian cyberattacks in the Russia-Georgia war of 2008. But Russian cyber intrusion does not have to be direct cyberattack. Increasingly, Russian control over cyberspace involves actions that complement their information warfare campaigns. In particular, there is the Russian use of bots and trolls on social media. After the Russian intervention in Ukraine, pro-Russian comments on Latvian online news outlets spiked, with some stories having a majority of posts made by trolls and/or bots.[27]

Russia continues to test ways in which to use cyber intrusions and disruptions against its opponents, often deploying them against the Baltic nations first. On August 30, 2017, the mobile network in Latvia went down just hours before Russian military exercises started across the border. Latvian officials believe that the jamming effect originated in Kaliningrad. There is evidence that one or more of the Baltic nations' energy grids were targeted with largely unsuccessful cyberattacks in late 2015 that have been attributed (although not proven) to Russian hackers.[28] Thus, Russian cyberattacks on the Baltic nations remains a real and constant threat.

In response to these threats NATO formed the Cyber Defense Management Agency in 2008 to create a single counter-cyber policy and to coordinate defenses.[29] That same year, NATO established the Cooperative Cyber Defense Center of Excellence in Tallinn.[30] In 2012 NATO created the NATO Energy Security Centre of Excellence in Vilnius, and in 2014 the NATO Strategic Communications (STRATCOM) Centre of Excellence opened in Riga. Thus, NATO has responded to the Russian cyber activities by strengthening its monitoring and defense of cyber intrusions.

RUSSIA AND ITS EASTERN EUROPEAN NEIGHBORS: UKRAINE, POLAND, AND BELARUS

In what a number of Russian authors call "the Polish question," Russia is fearful of continued and further NATO expansion and consolidation in the former Soviet republics and satellite states of North-Central Europe. Russia views the increasing nationalism in Poland warily but sees an opportunity for Russian influence as Poland clashes with its European Union partners. Likewise, Putin has sensed an opportunity in Belarus to place a Russian military base there, as Lukashenko's multivector foreign policy of remaining equidistant between the West and Russia is put under increasing strain. "Strategic cooperation with the Republic of Belarus" is the second listed priority in the Russian Foreign Policy Concept.[31] As a very different type of foreign policy, the conflict in Ukraine depicts the utility to Russian foreign policy of well-timed intervention in Eastern Europe as well as its potential pitfalls. Initially, it appeared that Russian asymmetrical warfare had indeed produced considerable material gains. Yet, the Ukrainian government's stabilization of the situation has frustrated Russia. In the continuing conflict, Russian cyber and communications attacks against the Ukrainian government occur with regularity, destabilizing the Ukrainian ability to fight. Yet despite all the Russian efforts, they have not produced noticeable improvements of the pro-Russian position in Ukraine so far.[32]

Russian Foreign Policy Goals in Eastern Europe

By a reasonable extension of logic, any attempt by Russia to restore itself to great power status must necessarily seek to compromise the independent foreign policies of Ukraine, Belarus, and Poland. As President Putin has himself stated, Russia believes that Russian hegemony over half of Europe is what is needed to bring stability to the region.[33] And similar to the Baltic nations, Russian initiatives to create a hegemonic influence over Eastern Europe can take many forms. In the most limited form, Russia uses its economic ties, energy resources, and military threats to force a "Finlandization" of the target nations' foreign policies, making each nation more compliant with Russian wishes. At the most extreme and interventionist form, Russia can forcibly integrate the East European nations into either an alliance with Russia or directly into union with the Russian Federation. Put simply, the goals of Russian foreign policy toward Poland, Belarus, and Ukraine are not different from that of Russia toward the Baltic nations.

There is also a similarity: the presence of ethnic Russian minority groups in each nation. Both Belarus and Ukraine have large ethnically Russian populations. Around 785,000 ethnic Russians live in Belarus, making up about 8 percent of the Belarusian population and the third largest group of Russians in former Soviet republics (behind Ukraine and Kazakhstan). While Russification of Belarus during the Soviet period saw large numbers of ethnic Russians relocating to Belarus, the opposite has occurred since 1991. Following the separation of Belarus from Russia, an undetermined number of ethnic Russians moved, and are still choosing to move, from Belarus to the Russian Federation. In 2006 President Putin encouraged ethnic Russians to migrate back to Russia, and there is some evidence that the number of ethnic Russians in Belarus has continued to decline partly due to this encouragement. Importantly, ethnic Russians were instrumental during the Soviet era in dominating the politics of the Belarusian SSR and continue to this today to play an outsized role in the government of President Alexsandr Lukashenko.

Ukraine is home to the largest ethnically Russian community outside of Russia. Roughly 8.3 million ethnic Russians live in Ukraine. While this is only around 17 percent of the Ukrainian population, this number is misleading as most of the ethnic Russians live in the Eastern districts of Ukraine. There is a sharp divide in Ukraine between the western half in which most of the citizens are ethnically Ukrainian and the eastern half in which the majority of citizens are ethnically Russian. For example, the share of ethnic Russians in most western Ukrainian regions is in the single digits while ethnic Russians in Crimea, Luhansk, and Donetsk number 58.3 percent, 39 percent, and 38.2 percent respectively. In the Black Sea port of Sevastopol which hosts the Russian Black Sea fleet, over 71 percent of the city's population is ethnically Russian. The clear ethnic segregation in Ukraine also plays into their electoral politics, with the Russian population being the largest source of support for pro-Russian candidates such as Viktor Yanukovich.

Poland is the exception. The number of ethnic Russians in Poland is quite small, only about 13,000 (roughly .03 percent of the population) or at most around 20,000 for those with both Russian and Polish ethnic identity (Polish National Census of Population and Housing, 2011).[34] Moreover, there are other larger ethnic groups (such as the Silesians) within Poland that play a larger role in Polish politics than the small Russian community.

Thus, there are clear distinctions between the impact of ethnic Russians in the three nations. The Russian community in Poland is both small and of little political significance. They are neither an independent source of domestic political power nor a large enough group to be a true target of support for Russian information campaigns. The Russian community in Belarus is small but powerful politically. Moreover, President Lukashenko is quite pro-Russian[35] as is the majority of the Belarusian population. Therefore, Russian foreign policy will rely more on direct diplomacy between Putin and Lukashenko than on information campaigns.

It is in Ukraine where the presence of a large concentrated Russian minority creates an atmosphere for Russian foreign policy to be similar to that towards the Baltic nations. The presence of a Russian community in Ukraine, as well as accusations of discrimination against them by an ethnically Ukrainian–dominated government, provides the pretext for Russian interference into the affairs of Ukraine. Where such a large Russian minority community exits, there is a congruence between the macro-level Russian foreign policy goal of extending its influence into Eastern Europe, the domestic policy goal in Russia of protecting Russians abroad, and the ideational need for Russia to protect, nurture, and sustain a sense of a Russian national identity and national pride. It is the combination of these factors that can so easily drive the Russian government to take aggressive action.

Russian Methods of Influence and Control over its East European Neighbors

Russia attempts to achieve its foreign policy goals in neighboring East European nations in a similar fashion to that of its policies toward the Baltic nations: typically via a combination of military posturing and nonmilitary actions. Russia combines militaristic displays of force, economic pressure (most typically through energy policy), information and propaganda campaigns, diplomatic pressure, and cyber warfare to influence the foreign policies of the East European nations.

Russian Force Posturing Toward the East European Nations

Russian force posturing toward Eastern Europe takes many forms, of which three come to the fore: provocative posturing, direct deployment, and insertion of nonmilitary forces. Regarding posturing, Russian military force is projected into the region through military exercises close to the East European nations, the placement of permanent Russian forces near borders, and provocative actions such as flybys, airspace intrusions, mock attacks, intrusion into coastal waters, and other such aggressive behaviors. In the past decade, and increasingly the last few years, Russia has increased its pressure toward Eastern Europe by stepping up military operations not only near its neighbors but also by expanding military operations around the globe. In March 2014, shortly after the seizure of Crimea and the start of the Donbass rebellion, Russian bombers increased their flights over the Atlantic.[36] This was a clear signal from Russia to NATO that it should not interfere in the expanding conflict in Eastern Ukraine. In the same time period, Russia announced a series of unexpected inspection exercises of Russian strategic nuclear forces.

Force posturing plays a key role in the Russian domination of force escalation in the region. A few days after pro-Russian militias and

Russian special operations forces began to operate in Crimea, Russian announced a massive, and previously unanticipated, inspection exercise of two of its commands near the Ukrainian border. This surprise exercise mobilized more than 150,000 Russian regular troops near Crimea.[37] Artillery and air defense units were also put on alert. Through these actions, Russia signaled to Ukraine that any Ukrainian resistance to Russia's seizure of Crimea would be met with a greater Russian escalation of the conflict. Similarly, more than 90,000 Russian troops mobilized near the northeastern Ukrainian border in the Spring of 2014, shortly after the start of the Donbass rebellion. Likewise, in the spring of 2015, Putin announced a surprise inspection exercise of units in western Russia near the Ukrainian border.

Direct deployment of Russian troops and bases is another way that Russia extends its control and influence over its neighbors. In the 1995 intergovernmental agreement between Belarus and Russia, the former agreed to lease to the latter two "immovable" military properties for twenty-five years. The first is the radio technical station in the Brest region and the second the home of the 43rd Russian Navy Signal Station near Minsk. Importantly, both installations allow for the armies of each nation to use the firing ranges that are present. It should be noted that Belarus has thus far resisted Russian overtures toward establishing a full-fledged Russian military base in Belarus. Recently however, Belarus has been rethinking the need for a Russian base as a balancing response to the proposed new NATO base in Poland.[38]

The Russian insertion of nonmilitary forces comprises the bulk of Russian policy toward Ukraine since 2014 (as already detailed in this book). Using nonmilitary forces, such as special forces, private contractors, and the arming of local militias, allows for plausible deniability about any Russian involvement. Yet, at the same time, Russia maintains some control over such units and the actions that they take, allowing Russia to determine the extent to which they are engaged in conflict.[39] Further, the use of nonmilitary units enforces the impression of a domestic civil war, and not an international conflict.[40] Consequentially, Russia continues the narrative that the rebellion in Ukraine is a civil war between a fascist, unrepresentative and repressive government and a legitimate set of rebels with serious and substantial concerns. In short, Russian insertion of nonmilitary forces allows them to have their cake and eat it too: Russia can shape the combat in the region while also denying that they are involved at all.

Russian use of militias, both local and those arriving from Russia, combined with special operations forces had little difficulty in changing the leadership in Crimea. A regiment of the Russian Airborne Forces arrived in Crimea on February 22, 2014, and quickly led the storming of the Crimean parliament on February 27 that resulted in the change of local government to a pro-Russian faction.[41] While the cohesion and effectiveness of the militias, both local and arriving, were questionable, the Russian use of well-trained, equipped, and ready special forces provided the key backbone to the action. Among the assets that the Russian operation possessed that contributed to its success were deception at both the tactical and strategic levels, effective air and sea logistics to transport troops and material, mobility and speed of land units to seize objectives without much use of firepower, and the use of training exercises to covertly mass units for the invasion.[42]

Russian nonmilitary forces also were, and still are, employed in the Donbass rebellion. Evidence exists that Russia had intelligence operations afoot in the Donbass Oblasts before the start of the rebellion.[43] Russia also encouraged, or directly enabled, militias from the Russian Federation to transit into the Donbass. There is evidence of Russian militias coming from Chechnya, South Ossetia, and other regions of Russia. And as in Crimea, Russian special forces and advisors supported these militias, helping them seize government buildings and key facilities, including transportation and energy production/distribution. The major difference between the Russian operations in Crimea and Donbass is that Ukrainian forces, including local militias and local governments, fought back in Donbass.

A clear indication that Ukrainian forces were able to stabilize the situation in the Donbass is the introduction of Russian regular military forces in the Summer of 2014 into the conflict. In August 2014, Russian artillery units began to fire from the Russian side of the border at targets in Ukraine. Moreover, Russian regular units began to train and equip the militias in Ukraine, including the arming of the militias with fairly sophisticated multiple-rocket launch systems and air defense systems.[44] Interestingly, Russia often did very little to conceal the use of these regular, military forces while still denying that Russia employed these units.[45]

Russian Economic Pressure on the East European Nations: The Example of Ukraine

One of Russia's greatest assets in foreign policy is its energy reserves. In short, Russian transfers of oil and natural gas provide energy security for many nations in Europe. Russian exports of energy to Eastern Europe solidified the loose network of old *nomenklatura* in the former Soviet client states that comprised the Commonwealth of Independent States.[46] The theory, as espoused in particular by Sergei Ivanov, was that cheap energy supplied to loyal comrades in Eastern Europe would have benefits to Russia. First, the beneficiaries of the Russian largess would be more powerful in their domestic political arenas and thus be able to obtain positions of power and influence. Second, these same individuals and/or businesses would be beholden to Russia for their wealth and power. Last, these fellow travelers would be likely or ready upon Russian demand to help curtail democratic progress and reforms.[47]

Chief among the Russian aims for its energy policy is domination of Ukraine. Russia used the shutoff of gas supplies to Ukraine in both 2006 and 2009 as a tool to show its displeasure at the decisions of the Ukrainian government (as it also did to Belarus in 2007). Importantly, the West interpreted the Russian actions not as some economic dispute over prices, but rather "as part of Russia's allegedly neo-imperial foreign policy" aimed at Ukraine but also at the downstream economies of Western Europe.[48] Part of the problem, according to the West, was the ability of the crony-led Russian energy firm Gazprom to act on the whims of the Russian government, and also that there was an oil monopoly in Ukraine (*Naftohaz Ukrainy*) that was susceptible to Russian extortion. The reader should note that it was leverage over gas exports to Ukraine that gained Russia the 32-year lease on Sevastopol in 2010 from Ukrainian President Viktor Yanukovych. Specifically, Yanukovych sought the removal of the 30-percent export duty on Russian supplies to Ukraine and in return he extended the Russian lease on its naval base in Crimea on the Black Sea.[49]

Russian Information, Propaganda and Cyber Warfare Campaigns to Undermine the East European Nations: Ukraine as an Example

Russian information and propaganda campaigns toward Ukraine are too numerous for complete enumeration here. Thus, we will concentrate on the Russian information campaigns during the seizure of Crimea and the ongoing rebellion in the Donbass region. In general, Russian information campaigns effectively revolve around information warfare seeking to control or condition the reflexive actions of the opponent.[50] In particular, Russian information campaigns aimed at Ukraine seek to deliberately mislead Ukrainian officials, both national and local, about the true intentions and actions of pro-Russian units. This concept was first utilized during the Russian Empire, became functionally operationalized during the Soviet era, and is called *maskirovka*.[51] The thrust of *maskirovka* is to deliberately mislead the opposition so that they are either paralyzed or make wrong decisions based on faulty or misinformation. One of the largest Russian *maskirovka* information campaigns focused on the continual Russian denials of any state-led intervention in Crimea and eastern Ukraine.[52]

Concurrently, Russian information campaigns were also used to condition pro-Russian populations. The framing of the conflict in Ukraine as between the *Russkiy Mir* (the concept of the Russian world or a common international nation of Russians) and an evil, fascist Ukrainian government was an effective narrative aimed at pro-Russian populations.[53] This narrative was put forth not only by President Putin but also Russian "diplomats, print and broadcast media to the Kremlin troll army...RT (Russia Today) played the most visible and vital role in spreading the message."[54]

Of course, Russia's information and propaganda campaigns w more varied than just these examples. The overall sources of the messaging for the campaign were numerous. These included (but are not exclusive to):

- Russian-controlled television, radio, and other media,
- Internet sites, both news sites and other media sites,
- Social blogs and other online communities,
- Printed material distributed in the physical space,
- The leasing of billboards and other advertising in the physical space,
- The engagement of elite speakers (such as Russian and Ukrainian politicians, business leaders, social influencers, protest leaders, professionals, celebrities, and others), and
- Troll farms and other cyber participants.[55]

These and other sources of Russian information emphasized a common set of themes. Chief among these were Crimea-specific messaging about the historical connection of Crimea to Russia. This included both the story about the Russian Empire's acquisition of Crimea and its placement at the heart of the Russian Empire, but also the "mistake" of allowing the Ukrainian Soviet Socialist Republic to acquire Crimea in 1954.[56] Overall, the Russian messaging emphasized the fascist nature of the post-Maiden Ukrainian government (even going so far as alleging that members of the current government were direct or ideological descendants of Nazi supporters), the violent ultra-nationalist mobs that put it into power, and the connections of the new government to the West, the European Union, and the United States. Russian propaganda and information campaigns also highlighted the economic weakness of Ukraine, particularly if the Ukrainian economy became divorced from Russian aid.[57]

Russia also launched a similar propaganda and information campaign in Eastern Ukraine. One unique aspect of the Russian campaign aimed at the Donbass region was Putin's invocation of the term *Novorossiya*, an old Russian imperial term used to denote portions of southern and eastern Ukraine and their unity with the greater Russian Empire.[58] The concept of *Novorossiya* provided a unifying rallying cry for a disparate set of separatist and nationalist groups in Eastern Ukraine. While the use of the term by the Russian government has been abandoned (mainly because it has led to the interpretation by rebels that Russia supports the integration of the Luhansk and Donetsk Oblasts into the Russian Federation, something that Russia wishes to avoid as a dangerous escalation of the conflict), the concept of *Novorossiya* is still important to rebels in the breakaway republics as a unifying force.[59]

Much as Russia has retreated from its use of *Novorossiya*, Russia has assessed the effectiveness of some of its campaigns in Eastern Ukraine and backtracked from them. Many of the propaganda and information campaigns used to destabilize Ukraine that were under the initial control of Russian operatives quickly became usurped by others, such as the separatists. Russia found itself struggling to manage and control the various "groups, their leaders, and competing agendas" that were self-generating in Eastern Ukraine.[60] A recurring problem was the belief of the separatists that if they seized control of a city or territory, as they did in Slovyansk, that Russian would then put a "Crimea-style" operation into action that would effectively grab the territory away from Ukraine. When Russia did not do so, again mainly because of the fear of conflict escalation, the separatists would begin to distrust Russian help.[61] On the other side of the coin, the Russian trust in the separatists was eroded after the downing of Malaysian Air Flight 17 over separatist territory. Russia began to realize that its low-cost bid to influence events could spiral out of control given the irresponsible use of weapons by ill-trained separatists. For some of these reasons and more, Russia now finds itself with few good alternatives on how to advance its interests in the Donbass region.[62]

What is also interesting about the conflict is the haphazard Russian application of hybrid warfare. Kofman et al. argue that initial Russian actions in Eastern Ukraine did not display the type of hybrid warfare that was present in the 2008 Russia-Georgian War or the Russian seizure of Crimea.[63] This argument emphasizes that Russia was not prepared for the events as they unfolded; instead, Russia was reacting to events. Russia also misjudged the resilience of the Ukrainian people, the actions of non-state actors that supported the nascent Ukrainian post-Maiden government, the danger in supporting myriad separatists with competing objectives, a lack of general control, and the response of the West. This juxtaposition of a well-prepared and orchestrated campaign to seize Crimea versus the *ad hoc* nature of Russian participation in Eastern Ukraine leads to a conclusion: Russia had intended to seize Crimea for some time and was prepared to do so when an opportunity arose but had no such plan for Eastern Ukraine. The lack of a clear objective or planning has contributed to a conflict in perpetual stalemate.

THE CURRENT THREAT OF RUSSIAN FOREIGN POLICY TO THE BALTIC NATIONS AND EASTERN EUROPE: WHY, WHEN, AND WHERE

The current Russian threat to the Baltic nations and Eastern Europe cannot be precisely determined but the why and where of the general threat are obvious: Russia seeks to create friendly neighbors as a general strategy to enhance Russian defense. This goal is so obvious that Russian actions in the region are only thinly veiled and very direct. As an example, the seizure of Crimea appeared to be a pre-planned and well-orchestrated campaign. It exposed that Russia still has designs on portions of Eastern Europe and if given an opportunity will act. At the very least, the Russian threat to Eastern Europe remains persistent, as the Russian attempts to extend hegemony over the region can be felt daily through the Russian military presence, cyber warfare, and pro-Russian media. In the Baltic nations and Poland, Russian military exercises and other provocations serve to remind the NATO allies that Russia is ever-present and nearby. In Belarus, Lukashenko has taken the posture of voluntary Finlandization and acquiescence to the Kremlin's wishes in order to bandwagon with his stronger neighbor. Moreover, a fairly pro-Russian population in Belarus makes Russia a "natural" ally for Lukashenko, a man who is fairly pro-Russian himself. Given Russia's history of replacing governments on its borders and in Eastern Europe with which it disagrees (e.g., Afghanistan 1979, Czechoslovakia 1968), Lukashenko clearly understands that trying to balance against Russia is not feasible if he wishes to remain as leader of Belarus.

The Russian military possesses a dramatic asymmetrical advantage over the militaries of its East European neighbors. This imbalance ensures that short of a massive NATO presence in the East European nations, something that is extremely unlikely to happen, the Baltic nations, Poland and Ukraine will never have a sufficient conventional defensive force to stop a Russian invasion. This asymmetry of conventional power allows Russia to intimidate its neighboring former communist nations. Combining the imbalance in the physical space with the Russian attempt to dominate the cyberspace, Russian hybrid warfare threatens to force all the East European nations to acquiesce to Russian demands time and time again. Poland is perhaps the exception because its lack of any sizeable Russian minority, combined with Polish incorporation into the European Union and NATO, creates some degree of deterrence against Russian aggression.

The Russian threat to Ukraine is the most obvious and the most constant. The "when" in this instance is contemporary and continuous. Douglas Mastriano characterizes the Russian continued intervention in Ukraine as relying on the following six factors, all of which are predicted on the use of hybrid warfare and a mix of regular and irregular forces, and operations in the more conventional sense:

- The use of subversive activity to foment instability among pro-Russian and Russian speaking populations in Ukraine.
- The use of movement, deployment, and activity of regular units along the border with Ukraine to dissuade aggressive action by Ukraine against the Donbass rebellion.
- The use of information campaigns, particularly disinformation and plausible denial, to increase obscure Putin's strategy toward Ukraine among his opponents.
- The violation of international borders by Russian irregular and regular troops to support the pro-Russian rebels.
- The seizure of territory that adds to the strategic security of Russia if the opportunity arises, as it did in Crimea.
- The use of the Russian strategic arsenal as nuclear blackmail against the NATO nations to prevent any coordinated NATO responses in Ukraine.[64]

The impressive efforts that Ukraine has made to defend itself have blunted the Russian threat. The Ukrainian Armed Forces (UAF) have increased in size by more than 200,000 personnel since 2014. Simultaneously, the UAF have been improving its command, control and communications (C3) structure, special forces, intelligence and counter-intelligence capabilities, and overall logics support.[65] Ukraine also has one of the world's largest and most productive defense industries. Cooperation between the Ukrainian defense industry and NATO has been increasing, particularly as a product of the 2015 signing of the "Roadmap of Military-Technical Cooperation between Ukraine and NATO."[66]

Returning to the region in general to answer the "when" question, at the most extreme, Russia could invade any of the Baltic nations, Belarus or Ukraine and subdue them by putting in place a proxy government or by incorporating them directly into the Russian Federation. This is least likely for Ukraine and Belarus but a possibility for the Baltic nations.

Russian policy toward Belarus is more about cooperation and using its support of the Lukashenko regime as a means to have Belarus balance against NATO. Regarding Ukraine, Russia seems to have received the signal from the United States and NATO that any overt aggression by Russia would be met with a response. Exactly what that response might be is not exactly clear, but at this point Putin does not appear ready to expend a greater effort on behalf of the Donbass rebels if the cost of such action is borne by Russia. Therefore, the Russian threat to Ukraine is more likely to be continual probing and destabilization through Russian propaganda, information, and cyber campaigns. The Russian goal is to weaken the Ukrainian government. If Putin cannot subdue the Ukrainian government or force them to ally with Russia, he will try to keep them weakened so that they are of little use to the NATO and EU nations.

Regarding Poland, Russia is not directly threatening invasion or any serious violation of Polish sovereignty. Putin understands that the European Union and the United States firmly support Poland's independence and that any Russian aggression toward Poland would more than certainly be met with a strong military response by NATO. At this time, Putin appears to be taking a cautious approach to the right-wing Duda Presidency and his Law and Justice Party. To the degree that Duda's government clashes with its European Union partners, it furthers the Russian foreign policy goal of weakening the political and economic institutions in Western Europe. The more troublesome issue is that the Polish government is staunchly supportive of NATO and is requesting a greater NATO presence in both Poland.

Thus, the question of when Russia has acted aggressively in Eastern Europe appears to be complicated. It appears from Russian interference in the Baltic nations that Russia is most likely to act when it perceives the rights of Russian minorities in these nations to be under attack. Russian action in Ukraine also seems to fit this pattern. Yet, the two are different in another aspect: the more aggressive seizure of Crimea shows how the realist background in which Russian foreign policy is made. When realist interests come into play, as they did in Crimea due to the naval base at Sevastapol, Russia acted with greater force projection. Thus, while it seems all three theoretical approaches (realist, domestic, and ideational) to explain Russian action indeed seem to be motivators, realist interests appear to create stronger force application by the Kremlin.

NOTES

1. The historical territory of Livonia is now mostly contemporary Latvia and Lithuania.
2. McNabb, *Vladimir Putin and Russia's Imperial Revival*, 161.
3. Ari Puheloinen, *Russia's Geopolitical Interests in the Baltic Area*, Finnish Defense Studies 12 (Helsinki, National Defense College, 1999), 57–58.
4. Gvosdev and Marsh, *Russian Foreign Policy*, 215.
5. Foreign Policy Concept of the Russian Federation.
6. Eoin Michael McNamara, "Securing the Nordic-Baltic Region," *NATO Review Magazine*, 2016, https://www.nato.int/docu/review/2016/also-in-2 016/security-baltic-defense-nato/EN/index.htm, accessed August 8, 2018.
7. McNabb, *Vladimir Putin and Russia's Imperial Revival*, 170.
8. Mastriano, *A U.S. Army War College Assessment on Russian Strategy in Eastern Europe and Recommendations on How to Leverage Landpower to Maintain the Peace*, 31.
9. Justyne Gotkowska and Piotr Szymanski, *Russia and the Security in the Baltic Sea Region: Some Recommendations for Policy-Makers* (Centrum Balticum Foundation. 2017), http://www.centrumbalticum.org/files/2157 /BSR_Policy_Briefing_1_2017.pdf, accessed August 8, 2018; Tobias Oder, "The Dimensions of Russian Sea Denial in the Baltic Sea," January 4, 2018 (Center for International Maritime Security, 2018), http://cimsec.org/ dimensions-russian-sea-denial-baltic-sea/35157, accessed August 8, 2018.
10. Jerry Hendrix, "When Putin Invades the Baltics," February 5, 2018, *National Review*, 2018, https://www.nationalreview.com/magazine/2018 /02/05/vladimir-putin-invade-baltics/, accessed August 8, 2018.
11. Charlie Gao, "NATO's Worst Nightmare: Russia's Kaliningrad is Armed to the Teeth," May 25, 2018, *The National Interest*, 2018, https:// nationalinterest.org/blog/the-buzz/natos-worst-nightmare-russias-kaliningrad-armed-the-teeth-25958, accessed August 8, 2018.
12. Gvosdev and Marsh, *Russian Foreign Policy*, 217.
13. The popular support of the Russian people for their undemocratic regime has been increasing since the early 2000s. Foreign policy that supports Russian minorities outside of Russia is one leg of that support. Richard Rose, William Mushler, and Neil Munro, *Popular Support for an Undemocratic Regime: The Changing Views of Russians* (Cambridge, Cambridge University Press, 2011).

14. Gvosdev and Marsh, *Russian Foreign Policy,* 218.

15. Mastriano, *A U.S. Army War College Assessment on Russian Strategy in Eastern Europe and Recommendations on How to Leverage Landpower to Maintain the Peace,* 33–34.

16. Gotkowska and Szymanski, *Russia and the Security in the Baltic Sea Region,* 4.

17. Michael Birnbaum and David Filipov, "Russia Held a Big Military Exercise This Week. Here's Why the U.S. is Paying Attention," September 23, 2017, *Washington Post,* 2017, https://www.washingtonpost.com/world/europe/russia-held-a-big-military-exercise-this-week-heres-why-the-us-is-paying-attention/2017/09/23/3a0d37ea-9a36-11e7-af6a-6555caaeb8dc_story.html?noredirect=on&utm_term=.4c202e4c4d28, accessed August 9, 2018.

18. Grigas, *The Politics of Energy and Memory between the Baltic States and Russia.*

19. McNabb, *Vladimir Putin and Russia's Imperial Revival,* 165.

20. Keith C. Smith, *Russian Energy Politics in the Baltics, Poland, and Ukraine: A New Stealth Imperialism?* (New York, Rowman & Littlefield/Center for Strategic and International Studies (CSIS), 2004).

21. Grigas, *The Politics of Energy and Memory between the Baltic States and Russia,* 35.

22. Greg Simons, "Perception of Russia's Soft Power and Influence in the Baltic States," *Public Relations Review* 41, no.1 (2015): 1–13, p. 4–7.

23. Simons, "Perception of Russia's Soft Power and Influence in the Baltic States," 5.

24. Rod Thornton and Manos Karagiannis, "The Russian Threat to the Baltic States: The Problems Shaping Local Defense Mechanisms," *Journal of Slavic Military Studies* 29, no. 3 (2016): 331–351, pp. 343–344.

25. Simons, "Perception of Russia's Soft Power and Influence in the Baltic States," 11.

26. Ibid., 10–11.

27. Helmus et. al., *Russian Social Media Influence,* 15–16.

28. Latvian Public Broadcasting (LPR), "Russia-backed Hackers Targeted Baltic Energy Grid - Claim," May 12, 2017, https://eng.lsm.lv/article/society/defense/russia-backed-hackers-targeted-baltic-energy-grid-claim.a236228/, accessed August 15, 2018.

29. McNabb, *Vladimir Putin and Russia's Imperial Revival,* 115.

30. Ibid., 116.

31. Foreign Policy Concept of the Russian Federation.

32. Charap and Colton, *Everyone Loses.*

33. President of Russia, 70th Session of the UN General Assembly, September 28, 2015 (Official Internet Resources of the President of Russia. 2015), http://en.kremlin.ru/events/president/news/50385, accessed August 9, 2018.

34. As a side note and to add some comparison and clarity, there are roughly 12,000 Polish citizens who describe themselves as ethnically American. Polish National Census of Population and Housing (*Ludność: Stan i Struktura Demograficzno-Społeczna: Narodowy Spis Powszechny Ludności i Mieszkań 2011*) (Warszawa, Glowny Urzad, 2013).

35. As a member of the Belarusian Supreme Soviet, Lukashenko was the only member to vote against Belarus leaving the Soviet Union.

36. Fredrik Westerlund and Johan Norberg, "Military Means for Non-Military Measures: The Russian Approach to the Use of Armed Force as Seen in Ukraine," *Journal of Slavic Military Studies* 29, no. 4 (2016): 576–601, pp. 595–596.

37. Ibid., 591.

38. Siarhei Bohdan, "Belarus's Balancing Between NATO and Russia: Squaring the Circle?" June 13, 2018, *Belarus Digest,* 2018, https://belarusdigest.com/story/belaruss-balancing-between-nato-and-russia-squaring-the-circle/, accessed September 3, 2018.

39. Westerlund and Norberg, "Military Means for Non-Military Measures," 585–587.

40. Ibid., 588–589.

41. Westerlund and Norberg, "Military Means for Non-Military Measures," 590.

42. Michael Kofman, Katya Migacheva, Brian Nichiporuk, Andrew Radin, Olesya Tkacheva, and Jenny Oberholtzer, *Lessons from Russia's Operations in Crimea and Eastern Ukraine* (Santa Monica, RAND, 2017), 22–26.

43. Westerlund and Norberg, "Military Means for Non-Military Measures," 593.

44. Ibid., 596–597.

45. Ibid., 597.

46. Baev, *Russian Energy Policy and Military Power,* 69.

47. Ibid., 69.

48. Mankoff, *Russian Foreign Policy,* 147.

49. Ibid., 234.

50. Han Bouwmeester, "Lo and Behold: Let the Truth Be Told—Russian Deception Warfare in Crimea and Ukraine and the Return of

'Maskirovka' and "Reflexive Control Theory,'" In *Netherlands Annual Review of Military Studies* edited by P.A.L. Ducheine and F. P. B. Oshina (Breda, Asser Press, 2017), 125–153, p. 125; Timothy Thomas, "Russia's Military Strategy and Ukraine: Indirect, Asymmetric—and Putin-Led," *Journal of Slavic Military Studies* 28, no. 4 (2015): 445–461, p. 456.

51. Bouwmeester, "Lo and Behold," 136–140.

52. Ibid., 146.

53. Ibid., 144.

54. Ibid., 144–145.

55. Kofman et. al., *Lessons from Russia's Operations in Crimea and Eastern Ukraine*, 82–83.

56. Ibid., 79.

57. Ibid., 79–81.

58. Ibid., 51.

59. Ibid., 51.

60. Ibid., 67.

61. Ibid., 67.

62. Charap and Colton, *Everyone Loses.*

63. Kofman et. al., *Lessons from Russia's Operations in Crimea and Eastern Ukraine*, 69.

64. Mastriano, *A U.S. Army War College Assessment on Russian Strategy in Eastern Europe and Recommendations on how to Leverage Landpower to Maintain the Peace*, 5–6.

65. Ibid., 24.

66. Ibid., 27.

CHAPTER 7

RUSSIAN ACTIONS
IN CENTRAL ASIA
AND THE MIDDLE EAST

AVOIDING NEW COLOR REVOLUTIONS
BY RUSSIAN INFLUENCE

Russian foreign policy towards the former Soviet Socialist Republics to its south boil down to two goals: maintaining a friendly set of neighbors and extending Russian influence into the region. The first goal is similar to the one Russia pursues for its East European neighbor. In this regard, Russia seeks to prevent any further "color" revolutions in Central Asia and the Caucasus, or in other words, any regime changes that could lead to the establish of any anti-Russian governments. While Russia is not necessarily promoting autocratic governments in the region, its attempts to counteract the promotion of democracy, particularly from Western sources, is an attempt to maintain its regional influence.[1]

The second goal is part of the larger competition between the leading powers of the China, the United States, and Russia for influence. To some degree, this competition resembles the "Great Game" played by Imperial

Russia and the United Kingdom in the nineteenth century. Russia seeks to counter Chinese influence, which mainly relies on economic initiatives, with Russian economic aid and programs, particularly energy and increased trade. The American presence in Afghanistan, and the resulting radicalization, including religious and political, of Muslim populations in Central Asia, is of concern to Russia. In particular, radicalization in Central Asia spills over into the South Caucuses, a region already destabilized by terrorism and separatism. To increase Russian security, Russia maintains diplomatic and security ties with Central Asian states such as Kazakhstan as a buffer against both Chinese and American influence in the region.

Unlike its approach to Eastern Europe, Russia uses a more cooperative set of policies toward Central Asia. The Foreign Policy Concept explicitly states that "Russia views as a key objective strengthening and expanding integration" in the region.[2] Russia bundles its ability to provide trade opportunities, energy resources, and military aid into an attractive package. Illustrative of the cooperation between Russia and the former Central Asian Soviet Republics, is the Russian-Tajikistan relationship. More than a million Tajiks work in Russia and send to Tajikistan remittances that are a significant source of its overall wealth. In return for the relatively free movement of Tajik labor and capital across the Russian border, Tajikistan has allowed Russia to maintain roughly 6,000 to 7,000 troops (201st Motor Rifle division) in Tajikistan as a rapid reaction force to guard the Tajik border with Afghanistan.

Thus, Russian efforts in the "near abroad" to keep former Soviet satellites in the Russian orbit are part of the larger Russian foreign policy effort to blunt other great powers from making inroads into former Russian imperial space. The asymmetry in power and influence between Russia and the Central Asian republics makes the latter naturally reliant on good relations with Russia, and thus they are receptive to most Russian overtures of cooperation. Yet, Russia also has to deal with the legacy of Soviet actions in the region, and specifically, the 1979 Soviet invasion of

Afghanistan. A general level of distrust from suspicions about Russian motives, but also the anti-Muslim nature of Soviet and Russian wars since the 1970s. This does not preclude Russia from making significant inroads into Muslim countries. Russian intervention in the Syrian conflict on the side of President Bashar Al-Assad has been largely successful in two ways: prevention of any color revolution in Syria and also an extension of Russian influence into the region. It does, however, make Russia's attempt to maintain its influence in Central Asia a bit harder.

THE HISTORICAL LEGACY OF THE SOVIET INVASION OF AFGHANISTAN

During the Cold War, the contemporary Central Asian Republics were Soviet Socialist Republics inside the USSR. As such, Soviet foreign policy after the end of World War II was mainly concerned with maintaining positive relations with India, Pakistan, and the People's Republic of China. The nonalignment of India sat well with the Soviets as the former British colony would have been a major security concern if it had been firmly in the Western camp. Soviet relations with China were tense; there were mainly border skirmishes, but the two communist powers were never seriously threatening to invade each other.[3]

Soviet relations with neighboring Afghanistan were slated to improve after the 1973 coup in Afghanistan by Mohammed Daoud Khan, who was supported by the communist People's Democratic Party of Afghanistan (PDA). But the ruling PDA split into rival factions and Afghan domestic politics dissolved into a violent power struggle. Eventually Khan was overthrown by other elements of the PDA in the 1978 Saur Revolution. Nur Muhammad Taraki took over and after a few months purged the main leaders of the revolution. In September 1979, Taraki's foreign minister Hafizullah Amin overthrew Taraki and executed him. Citing the Brezhnev Doctrine that allowed socialist states to intervene in other socialist states, formulated by the USSR after the 1968 Czechoslovakian uprising to justify retroactively their invasion of that country, Soviet leader Leonid Brezhnev ordered his nation to invade Afghanistan in order to stop the governmental turmoil.[4]

The Soviet invasion of Afghanistan soured relations in the region greatly. Pakistan cut ties with the USSR and soon would be a conduit for American aid and arms to the Muslim Afghan resistance (i.e., the Mujahideen). The Soviet invasion also alarmed India and infuriated the Muslim population in the region. While mainly occupied with matters surrounding Vietnam and the South China Sea, China too reacted to the Soviet action by increasing its security on the border of the USSR. In short, the invasion of Afghanistan did not improve a single bilateral relation of the USSR in the region and dramatically worsened it with Pakistan and the greater Muslim community. Before the end of the war, Soviet Premier Mikhail Gorbachev would mend fences with India (in particular, resuming Soviet arms sales to India), but Pakistan still remained a key ally of the United States.

Without a doubt, the Soviet war in Afghanistan was a key factor in the fall of the Soviet Union, along with the weak Soviet economy and troubles in Eastern Europe. The immediate effect on Russian foreign policy post-1991 was a withdrawal from the region. In the 1993 Russian Foreign Policy Concept, the importance of Asia was ranked at seventh out of ten policy priorities. Further, the breakup of the USSR created a host of new nations comprised of the former Soviet Socialist Republics in the area. Russia's foreign policy toward Central Asia would now have to consider this increase in the number of nations and the resulting increase in bilateral relations that would have to be negotiated. And as mentioned in an earlier chapter, the precipitous decline of the Russian arms industry post-1991 meant that Russian arms sales to India fell to near nothing.

RUSSIA, THE NEAR ABROAD, AND THE COLOR REVOLUTIONS

It is in the context of both the breakup of the Soviet Union and the war in Afghanistan that Russian relations with the "near abroad" began.

Quite quickly, Russia asserted its prerogative to protect ethnic Russians in the region.[5] Foreign Minister Andrei Kozyrev expressed Russia's intention to defend its interests, including through the deployment of Russian troops.[6] Russia quickly sought to stabilize the region through inclusion of a number of the new Central Asian Republics into both the Commonwealth of Independent States and a Collective Security Treaty (CST) in 1992. The CST came into effect in 1994 with Armenia, Azerbaijan, Belarus, Georgia, Kazakhstan, Kyrgyzstan, Russia, Tajikistan, and Uzbekistan as members.[7] The agreement was reorganized in 2002 as the Collective Security Treaty Organization (CSTO) and continues today to be the main organization managing stability in the region.[8] The Russian Foreign Policy Concept lists the CSTO as "one of the key elements of the current security framework in the post-Soviet space," highlighting its importance in Central Asia.[9]

At the same time as Russia under the new presidency of Vladimir Putin was reasserting itself in the "near abroad," the color revolutions began. While there is no direct causation or correlation between the two phenomenon, each impacted the other.[10] The term "color revolutions" in regard to the post-Soviet sphere refers specifically to uprisings in Georgia (2003 Rose Revolution), Ukraine (2004 Orange Revolution), and Kyrgyzstan (2005 Tulip/Pink Revolution).[11] In all three instances, popular movements removed authoritarian or autocratic leaders. In a limited sense, they were pro-democratic revolutions without any direct impact on foreign policy. However, in all three instances pro-Russian leaders were removed. From the Russian viewpoint, the color revolutions were not benign regime changes nor political development or modernization. Instead, Russia viewed them as anti-Russian movements that were likely to install pro-Western governments. As I mentioned earlier in this book, Russia also saw in the events of the color revolution the clear imprint of Western promotion of the events, as comments at the time by Foreign Minister Sergei Lavrov made clear. Even in 2014 at the Moscow Conference on International Security, comments by Lavrov, Chief of the General Staff Valery Gerasimov, and the Defense Minister of Belarus

Yury Zhadobin all continued the line that the color revolutions were not actually internal movements, were not free from Western sponsorship or interference, and have led to a decline of stability in the regions in which they occurred.[12]

Important to a discussion of Russian foreign policy in the "near abroad" is the sense that, geographically speaking, this is "post-Soviet space" and perhaps post-imperial space.[13] This was true of regions inside of Russia (e.g., Chechnya) as well as new nation-states (e.g., Armenia, Azerbaijan, Georgia, Kazakhstan). Both types of polities would now engage in a struggle to define their post-imperial/Soviet identities. Other scholars use the term "in-between" to highlight how these new nations form two regions[14] that "are neither formally aligned with the 'collective West'...nor Russia."[15] Part of the struggle in these regions is the truth that the collapse of the Soviet Union "laid bare a series of fragile, unsettled territorial disputes between competing power centers."[16] These disputes, put into historical perspective, are "the latest in an apparently unending centuries-long set of struggles over imperial 'space' in and around Russia."[17] Importantly, Russia defines its interests in the "near abroad" in a way similar to that of the United States' Monroe Doctrine.[18] President Yeltsin, in 1992, and Foreign Minister Kozyrev, in both 1992 and 1993, made declarations about Russia's "special role and influence" in the region, its need to intervene so that Russia did not lose "geographical positions that took centuries to conquer," and "Russia's special responsibility" to maintain stability on its borders.[19] The New Russian Military Concept of 1993 institutionalized these ideas into an understanding that the region contained vital interests to Russia and that a Russian military presence would be necessary to secure those interests.

The war in Georgia in 2008 fits this pattern. The seeds for the war began in the 2003 Rose Revolution. Russia saw the revolution as evidence of a Western policy of regime change in the region and an event that destabilized the regional order.[20] The Georgian revolution that replaced Eduard Shevardnadze with Mikhail Saakashvili fits into the general pattern:

a pro-Western government replaced a more pro-Russian government. Russia reacted to the regime change by securing its interests in the area. (Detailed in chapter 2 are the events leading up to the war.) In summary, separatist movements, a new and aggressive government in Georgia, developments in NATO that Russia perceived as threatening, and cycles of escalating violence all combined to create tension in the region.

To return to our theories of foreign policy, in the context of the Russian vision of the "near abroad" in a realist perspective, Russia action to defend pro-Russian territory and separatists, oppose nationalist aggression, and bring stability to Georgia look less like pre-planned Russian aggression and more like a sensible, policy from a major power to problems on its borders.[21] From a social constructivist perspective, one could argue that Russia's attempt to maintain influence in Georgia stems from its imperial identity and the concept of *Russkiy Mir*.[22] And from a domestic politics perspective, survey data from 1993 to 2016 shows a strong uptick since 2010 in the percentage of Russians who equate Russia's national interests as "for the most part, extend[ing] beyond its existing territory."[23]

Closer even than the nations of the Caucasus to Russia's desired sphere of influence are the five post-Soviet Central Asian republics.[24] These nations have established themselves as separate from Russia but have all maintained a close relationship with their much larger neighbor.[25] As stated in earlier chapters, Russian foreign policy toward the newly independent states post-1991 began with little Russian interest in them. Foreign Minister Primakov in the mid-1990s began to turn Russian attention to Central Asia, but i was with the ascendency of Putin to the Russian presidency in 2000 that Russian foreign policy focused on Central Asia. Fundamentally, Russian policy is to maintain influence in the region "in the face of rising engagement from powers like China and especially the United States."[26] This Russian desire to maintain a dominance over the region "survives regime change and state collapse—most recently in 1917 and 1991," precisely because it is rooted in a realist need to protect Russia's southern border.[27] But Russian foreign policy is more complex than just the strategic balance of power, as Russia has economic and security interests in Central Asia related to countering Islamic terrorism, maintaining the transit of energy, and defending common boundaries against other foreign powers, such as Iran and Pakistan.[28]

In an August 29, 2014, speech, Putin declared Kazakhstan to be Russia's "closet strategic ally and partner" and that the "vast majority of the citizens of Kazakhstan favor stronger ties with Russia."[29] Such a statement reflects the centrality of Kazakhstan in the region to Russia's interests. Kazakhstan is the largest Central Asian republic in terms of population, territory, and economic activity. Kazakhstan hosts several important installations related to Russian space exploration; it supplies Russia with uranium and engages with Russia in collaborative efforts in agriculture, transportation, science, and industry. Likewise, Russia is important to Kazakhstan, specifically as the transporter of Kazakh oil and gas exports to pipelines for wider distribution.[30] Uzbekistan and Turkmenistan also sit on large natural gas reserves (as well as some oil) and have a similar symbiotic relationship with Russia: earning money through energy sales that rely on Russian energy transportation systems. Turkmenistan has also completed the opening of an energy transport route through and to China, a country that accounts for roughly 70 percent of Turkmen gas exports.[31]

Since 1994, Russia has sought to transform its economic relations with Central Asia into a more permanent, institutionalized organization. As a culmination of negotiations that began with a customs union in 1995, the Eurasian Economic Union (EAEU) came into existence in 2015 between Russia, Armenia, Belarus, Kazakhstan, and Kyrgyzstan. A single, economic union between Russia and "near abroad" states was the brainchild of Kazakhstan's first President, Nursultan Nazarbayev, but it was Putin's support of the idea that transformed it into a reality.[32] This union works for all nations, but in slightly different ways. The smaller nations get greater access to Russian trade and gain a greater bargaining position vis-à-vis regional trade partners such as China, India,

Iran, and others. Russian business interests, such as Lukoil, Transneft, and RusAl, gain more latitude to operate in countries such as Kazakhstan and Kyrgyzstan and to purchase greater ownership of local companies.[33]

Closer cooperation has also facilitated a greater Russian military presence in Central Asia. Russia has permanent bases in both Tajikistan and Kyrgyzstan. As mentioned previously in this book, the Russian 201st Motor Rifle Division participated in the 2003 Tajik Civil War. This division transformed the next year into the 201st Military Base, stationed at three facilities in Dushanbe and Bokhtar with around 6,500 troops, 100 tanks, 300 APCs, and a handful of helicopters and aircraft. Foreign Minister Lavrov has stated in early 2019 that the Russian presence is "an important factor for Tajikistan's security" by "strengthening the state border" and countering "existing threats that continue to be imposed from the territory of Afghanistan."[34] Russia also maintains air bases in Armenia and Kyrgyzstan, as well as a military base in Armenia that ostensibly provides defense against Azerbaijan.

While I have painted the thrust of Russian foreign policy toward Central Asia as primarily cooperative, this does not imply that Russia has not resorted to force when it suits their needs. Obviously, the 2008 war in Georgia is a reminder of Russia's ability to act aggressively toward its smaller neighbors, but this is the exception not the rule. In line with Russian nonconventional actions in Eastern Europe and against the Baltic Nations, Russia has employed information and cyber assets against the nations of Central Asia. Typically, Russian information campaigns are more about the projection of soft power, typically through the large Russian-language media presence in these nations (due to the common use of Russian in Central Asia).[35] Thus, perceptions of Russia and its foreign policies are looked upon favorably by most Central Asian populations.[36] But Russia is not hesitant to employ more aggressive forms of information and cyber campaigns when necessary. There is evidence that Russia utilized its media and cyber assets against former Kyrgyz President Kurmanbek Bakiyev in 2009–2010 to drive him out of power.[37]

CHINA: A NEW RIVAL BUT ALSO A FRIEND IN CENTRAL ASIA

Arguably, Russia's most important foreign policy relationship in the region is with the People's Republic of China. China is not only a great power with a global economic footprint but also a potential suitor of countries in Central Asia. Because of China's power, Russia typically has maintained a rather complicated relationship with its massive neighbor. The 1949 Chinese Revolution led to a potential friendship between the two communist nations. However, distrust between the two nations, owing to centuries of conflict in the region, continued despite the commonality of their political regimes. Disagreement between Stalin and Mao over the Korean War, along with border disputes, kept the two communist nations from effectively cooperating. Ideological differences between Moscow and Beijing, particularly the de-Stalinization of Khrushchev, as well as Mao's dislike for the new detente between the USSR and United States, led to the 1961 Sino-Soviet split. Mao effectively moved the People's Republic of China (PRC) out of the Soviet camp, leading to China acting as a truly independent nation in global politics. This generated the realization in the West that communism was not monolithic and that the PRC could be played off against the USSR. The Russian reaction to the split was to recognize China not only as a potential ally but also as a potential enemy and/or rival.[38]

For the remainder of the Cold War, the Soviet Union kept a watchful eye on its Chinese neighbor. The opening of relations by Mao to the United States in 1972 was seen by Moscow as a particularly disturbing move. With Mao's death in 1976 and the subsequent turn of the Chinese Communist Party (CCP) toward a more pragmatic, bureaucratic authoritarian rule, relations between the Soviet Union and China stabilized. The Soviet invasion of Afghanistan in 1979 was opposed by China, and the aggressive Soviet action led to relations turning frosty again. Gorbachev tried to reset relations during the late 1980s, but it really was the fall of the Soviet Union that changed the bilateral relationship.

As Russia was rebuilding and reorganizing during the early 1990s, relations with China, and the entire Asian vector in Russian foreign policy, were now on the back burner. It was not until Russian Foreign Minister Yevgeny Primakov in 1998 proposed a Russia-India-China (RIC) trilateral framework to promote stability in Asia that relations would improve. Negotiations among the three nations led to the start of RIC informal meetings in 2002. The first formal meeting of the group was in 2005 at Vladivostok. Now, the RIC meets annually, usually during the annual BRIC meetings. The RIC mainly operates as platform for the three large nations to keep open communication among themselves and to iron out differences. The three nations have more in common than may be apparent at a quick glance. First, all three support the supremacy of state sovereignty. Russia, China, and India all have rebellious groups or populations that they wish to dominate, such as the Chechens, Uyghurs, and Muslims in Kashmir, respectively. Second, all three support the territorial integrity of states and the preservation of current borders. All three nations have separatist or irredentist territories over which they are attempting to retain control (e.g., Chechnya, Tibet, and Kashmir, respectively). Third, all three nations have a distrust of humanitarian interventionism, although the Indian distrust is more muted than that of the two others.

Since the late 1990s, Sino-Russian relations appear to be bolstered by the shared idea that each is resisting the international liberal order in their own way. As an example, both Russia and China viewed the NATO bombing of Serbia in 1999 as a clear sign of the American belief that they can intervene anytime and anywhere that they want. Moreover, Russia and China perceived that the liberal order is more likely to use its military might against nondemocratic nations. After 1999, both Russia and China began to use their vetos on the UN Security Council to block proposed US interventions. In 2001 the two nations cooperated by launching the Shanghai Cooperation Organization (SCO), along with Kazakhstan, Kyrgyzstan, Tajikistan, and Uzbekistan.[39] The SCO is a diplomatic and economic council that seeks to sponsor social and economic development in Asia. Importantly, the SCO also recognizes the sovereignty of each of its member nations and has pledged to the principle of noninterference in domestic affairs. Communication between the CSTO and the SCO allows Russia and China to better maintain stability and order in Central Asia. Much as the CSTO is central to the Russian Foreign Policy Concept, so is the SCO and Russia's desire to further strengthen "the SCO's role in regional and global affairs."[40] Neither country desires instability, radicalism, or regime change in the region, and the two overarching organizations allow them to monitor and encourage Central Asian countries toward friendly relations with China and Russia. The key goal is to maintain Russian and Chinese influence, while keeping Western influences out. As an example of this type of thinking, the Russian Political Scientist Alexei Arbatov said in 2014 that solving the problems in Afghanistan might best be done through a joint venture of the CSTO and SCO.[41]

As an example, both Russia and China viewed the 2003 American-led invasion of Afghanistan as part of a continuing trend of Western interventionism. In response, the two nations agreed in 2004 to sign a bilateral treaty ending a number of conflicts over their shared border. The number of bilateral treaties between Russia and China boomed after this initial agreement. Since 2005, China has become Russia's leading trade partner. The two nations cooperate in the energy sector as well as in energy-development projects. There is also a lively arms trade flowing from Russia to China, with China typically being the second or third most likely destination for Russian arms, with China accounting for about 40 percent of Russian arms sales from 1992 to 2007.

But of course, Russian perceptions of China have been changing.[42] Russia sees the PRC as a potential ally or at least a fellow traveler, but it also fears China and treats China as a potential enemy. Russia is cognizant of two factors that limit how close Russia can and should get to China: the massive size of the Chinese economy and the military potential of China. While partnering with China on the energy trade, Russia is quite mindful of the vast differences in the size of the two nations' economies. Russia views the vast Chinese domination of the overall level of trade in Asia as a potential threat to the Russian economy. Second, the increasing militarization of China, particularly the expansion of the Chinese navy and the Chinese territorial demands in the South China Sea, alarms Moscow. Since 2007, Russia has lessened its rate of arms sales to China and has expanded its weapons sales to countries that ring China, such as Vietnam, India, Malaysia, and Indonesia.

An example of the complex love-hate relationship between Russia and China is the "Vostok 2018" military exercises that took place in August 2018. The Russian Vostok military exercises in the Eastern and Central Military District historically have focused on preparing for a large ground war with China. The massive 2018 exercises were not only the largest since the fall of the Soviet Union (with Russia claiming that up to 300,000 military personnel spread across ground, naval and airborne units participated) but also included 3,200 Chinese troops. The new focus of the Vostok exercises as a defense against an aggressive and unfriendly, yet unnamed, foreign power most likely is more a display of the two nations' disdain for the current international order than a true defensive exercise against some sort of massive invasion from the Pacific Ocean. Cooperation between Russia and China in Vostok 2018 also comes on the heels of earlier cooperation in military exercises organized by the SCO.[43] Yet, these exercises do not herald some new defensive alliance between the two nations. This point was clear from the Chinese description of the exercises not as cooperation, but as mainly "enhancing both sides capabilities to jointly respond to various security threats."[44]

That Russia may be trying to draw Chinese closer to Russian defense than the other way around speaks to the growing strength of China in the bilateral relationship between the two titans. In fact, this asymmetry has been growing for a while, a fact that is not lost on Russian policy-makers. There is also evidence that China has not abused its growing position of strength against Russia.[45] Thus, while "Russia and China neither offer unconditional support of each other's positions [they] do not directly criticize each other."[46] This tacit arrangement has left Russia as the *de facto* influencer over the former Soviet Republics in Central Asia.

Syria: Russia's Gamble for Influence in the Middle East

Russian support of Syria started during the Soviet era. At the end of the Second World War, the Soviets supported Syrian independence form French occupation and the development of a Syrian Arab army. Relations between the two nations improved in the 1950s through bilateral agreements in which Syria bought Soviet weapons and the USSR built infrastructure projects inside of Syria. This relationship fit into the Cold War at the time as a balance to the more Western-leaning powers in the Middle East and their creation of the Baghdad Pact. In this sense, Soviet support for Syria was inherently realist: the USSR could court an ally in the region to counter American- and British-led alliances and do so at a very low cost.

Russian-Syrian relations strengthened further in the early 1960s due to internal events in Syria. In 1963 the Ba'athist Party staged a coup d'état and overthrew the Syrian government. A young fighter pilot by the name of Hafez al-Assad was a member of the party and would in 1966 be one of two men to seize power in an internal Ba'athist coup.[47] Assad had been trained on MIG fighter planes by Soviet trainers and his views on the Cold War were certainly pro-Soviet. In 1970 Assad launched a silent coup against his political rival Salah Jadid, resulting in Assad being the *de facto* dictator of Syria. In 1971 Assad concluded a bilateral agreement with the Soviet Union to build a Russian naval facility at Tartus. This facility was at the time, and still is currently, Russia's only naval facility on the Mediterranean Sea.

During the Cold War, Syria could not directly pay for all the weapons that it purchased from the USSR, and Syria slowly fell into debt with its

Soviet creditors. In 1991 after the fall of the Soviet Union, arms exports from Russia to Syria ended with Syria also reneging on debt payments. The exact extent of the Syrian debt is not clear, but it numbered roughly about $12 to $15 billion in the mid-2000s. After the American-led invasion of Iraq in 2003, Syria asked Russia to once again sell weapons to them. Putin sensed that not only an opportunity existed for Russia to capitalize on Syria's needs but also that Russia possessed a position of strength in the negotiating because of the outstanding Syrian debt. Putin agreed to forgive around three-quarters of the Syria debt and restart weapons sales to the country if in exchange Russia could upgrade its naval base at Tartus to accommodate larger Russian naval vessels, including nuclear-powered ships. This led to the Russians renovating Tartus and the eventual 2017 agreement for Russia to maintain its base there permanently.

As mentioned previously, the events of the 2011 Arab Spring had a transformative effect on Russian foreign policy. In general, Russian military and political thinkers realized that unexpected regime change could occur quickly through mass protests organized via social media. One of the results was the new thinking in military strategy that Russia could take advantage of the social media techniques to further Russian aims. The other—and diametrically opposed—conclusion was that Western-sponsored regime change could damage Russian interests. The effect of this thinking in Syria was to enhance Russian determination to bolster its Syrian ally in the region lest it too fall due to the rebellious forces of the Arab Spring. When protests against Syrian President Bashar al-Assad (the second son of Hafez al-Assad and ruler of Syria since 2000) began in 2011, Russia used its diplomatic power to back the Assad regime against the emerging Syrian rebellion. Putin feared that any change of government in Syria would most likely result in a less pro-Russian government, whether they be Muslim extremists or Western-backed rebels. As Assad turned all the weapons of the Syrian state, including chemical weapons, on the rebels and even against his own citizens, Russia used its permanent position on the United Nations Security Council to veto UN resolutions condemning Assad.

From 2012 to 2015 the region encompassing Syria and Iraq began to deteriorate into chaos and anarchy. The ineffectiveness of the American-backed Iraqi government to maintain sovereignty over the north and west of Iraq, combined with Assad's inability to extend Syrian government control over eastern Syria, created a power vacuum in that area. While the Kurdish forces maintained some control over Northern Iraq, vast territories of both nations were lost to a radical, Islamic movement: the Islamic State (a.k.a. IS, ISIS, or ISIL). The mainly Sunni ISIS was a strange mixture of former Ba'athist party supporters who had been removed from power by the United States and Islamic extremists inspired by the success of Al-Qaeda and other international Islamic terrorist organizations. Thus, the region now saw Syria government forces, Iraqi government forces, Kurdish units, ISIS, and Syrian rebel units all vying for territory, control, resources, and power across Iraq and Syria. In 2014, Vladimir Zarudnitsky, the Chief General of the Main Operational Directorate of the General Staff of the Russian Armed Forces, explained that to Russia the Western destabilization of Libya and Syria had paved the way for the weakening of these nations, creating the conditions for the chaos that followed.[48] To be specific, he labelled the Western action in these events as "aggression in the form of a 'colour revolution'."[49]

While the United States clearly had staked a claim, both recognized and not resisted by the international community, in helping the Iraqi government and the Kurds remove ISIS from Iraq, the situation in Syria was not so straightforward. The United States and other European powers supported the pro-Western rebels in Syria, but they would not supply them with weapons. Kurdish forces, supported and armed by the United States, operated in the northeast of Syria, which alarmed Turkey. Pro-Kurdish terrorist attacks in Turkey inflamed tensions between the Turkish government and its minority Kurdish community. President Recep Tayyip Erdoğan claimed that the Kurdish terrorists could only carry out their attacks in Turkey with support of the local Kurdish political party and the more militant Kurdistan Workers' Party (PKK) that operated in both Turkey and Iraq. Similarly, Assad's regime in Syria made no distinction between pro-Western rebels and pro-Islamic rebels, declaring that all of them were both rebels and terrorists. By 2015 very little progress was being made and ISIS had extended its control over vast territory in both countries. Moreover, ISIS had not only drawn in fighters from traditionally Muslim nations but also from European nations. This radicalization of Western youth by ISIS led to numerous ISIS-directed or ISIS-inspired terrorist attacks in West European nations and the United States. Thus by 2015 the Western powers stepped up their fight against ISIS while still supporting the pro-Western rebels against Assad. This was a clear signal that the West wanted to defeat ISIS and stabilize Iraq, while still seeking the eventual overthrow of Assad.

At this time Russia decided to intervene directly in the conflict on the side of Assad. This made sense from a Russian foreign policy perspective in many ways. First, Russia's help to prop up Assad would prevent another color revolution. Second, stopping regime change would preserve Russia's historical investment in the region. Third, Russian intervention to weaken the Islamic State would also further Russia's counterterrorism operations. Fourth, Russia could strengthen its argument as an important player on the world stage. Last, uncompromising Russian support for Assad would help to consolidate domestic support for Putin.[50]

In September 2015, Assad requested assistance from Russia in dealing with the rebels and ISIS. By the end of the month the Russian Federal Council (the upper house of the Russian parliament) approved Putin's request to move Russian air units to the Khmeimim base in Syria. In a sign that Russian units had already been based in Syria, one hour after the approval Russian aircraft began to bomb rebel positions in Syria. Backed by the new Russian air coverage, Syrian forces started numerous offenses against rebel positions. Within days, Iranian forces launched ground offensives coordinated with Russian air strikes against ISIS forces near Raqqa.

From October 2015 to February 2016, Russia used numerous military assets to help the Assad regime against its opponents. This included *Kilo-*

class submarines launching cruise missiles from the Mediterranean Sea, *Kalibr*-class cruise missiles launched from naval forces on the Caspian Sea, long range Tu-22M3 strategic bombers, Su-35S fighter jets, and other advanced Russian units. In order to carry out these attacks, Russia began to develop ground assets in Syria, including upgrading the Hamedan Airbase and the Khmeimim Air Base near Latakia to accommodate more fixed-wing aircraft and the installation of helicopter pads. It is also been documented that Russia installed two signal intelligence spy bases in Syria at this time. In order to deter Western airstrikes on any of the Syrian government positions, Russia sold to Syria a wide array of air defense systems, including Anti-Aircraft guns and the S-300 Anti-Aircraft missile system.[51]

The results of Russian intervention paid off. By early 2016 the Syrian government was gaining the upper hand against the Syrian rebels. Russian attacks on ISIS positions were also contributing to stopping the expansion of ISIS, as were Western and Kurdish attacks on ISIS. In August 2016, Russia also briefly flew air missions from Shahid Nojeh, an airbase in Western Iran. The Iranian airbase was closer to the Russian targets and could accommodate the larger Russian Tu-22M3 and Sukhoi-34 bombers.[52] Russia was forced to abandon use of the airbase after the "secret" agreement with Iran became known.[53] In March 2016, Putin announced that Russia would bring some of its units home while also normalizing its security relationship with Syria.[54] By 2017, ISIS was slowly being defeated by all of the combined forces against it, including a Turkish offensive that crossed the Syrian border and joint Russian-Turkish airstrikes against ISIS. Russian and Syrian forces were so successful in defeating ISIS that in September 2017 the Russian Ministry of Defense declared that most of Syria had been cleared of ISIS forces. In December, President Putin said that Syria had been completely liberated.

Table 3. Russian Bases and Russian Use of Other Installations in Syria

Base or Installation	Nature of the Base	Purpose
Tartus Naval Base	Logistics Facility; upgrades in progress to transform into full-scale naval base	Access to Mediterranean Sea and beyond
Khmeimim Air Base	Adaptation of a civilian airport; upgrades in progress to transform into full-scale air base	Provide air presence over Syria; cover naval units
Latakia Listening Station	Old Syrian listening post, now converted to Russian use and coordinated with listening abilities at air and naval bases	Intelligence and signal gathering
Tiyas Military Airbase (T-4)	Converted civilian airstrip	Backup airstrip; extend air control
Palmyra Airport	Shared airbase with Iranian units	Support of air operations in eastern Syria
Hama Military Airport	Shared use with Syrian Air Force	Extend Russian air presence in Syria
Shayrat Airbase	Shared use with Syrian Air Force; Russia expanded its capacity in 2015	Base for attack helicopters; transit and transport hub

Sources: Mercouris, "Russia's Military Bases in Syria"; DEBKAfile, "Russia Builds Four New Air Bases in Syria, Deploys Another 6,000 Troops."[55]

Without a doubt, the Russian military intervention in the Syria Civil War not only led to the defeat of ISIS but also saved the Assad regime.

With Russian airpower behind them, the Syrian government forces were able to get off the defensive and move to the offensive against both the Syrian rebels and ISIS. In return for this help, Russia has made its bases at Tartus and Khmeimim permanent, and Russia has plans to upgrade both to accommodate further Russian forces. Russia also operates air units out of a number of air bases spread through western Syria (see Table 9-1). In October 2018, Defense Minister Shoigu announced that Russia had flown more than 40,000 combat sorties in Syria, more than three times that of the US-led international coalition.[56]

At the time of writing in December 2019, most of the Syrian rebel positions have collapsed and the Assad regime has reasserted control over the major population centers of the nation, with the exception of the last major rebel stronghold in Idlib.[57] Kurdish forces still occupy and control vast portions of territory in the northeast of Syria, roughly one-fourth of all of Syria. The American-backed Syrian Defense Forces (SDF) have entered into negotiations with the Assad regime over some sort of decentralized control of the territories occupied by the SDF. American troops still occupy the American base at Tanf in southeastern Syria, an internationally recognized zone from which America directs efforts against the remnants of ISIS in the region. Yet, it is clear that Russia's interventionist policy on the side of Assad has been victorious, successfully accomplishing three goals: preventing regime in Syria, "forcing Washington to deal with Russia as an equal," and strengthening support for Putin's foreign policy inside Russia.[58]

THE CURRENT THREAT OF RUSSIAN FOREIGN POLICY IN CENTRAL ASIA

Russia's actions to achieve its goals in the "near abroad," particularly to the south of its borders, rely more on support and cooperation than direct intimidation (which is used more by Russia in its relations with Eastern Europe). As such, there is no direct Russian threat to the area. As long as most of the Central Asian governments are autocratic, the overriding

Russian goal of maintaining friendly governments on its southern border does not require Russian to be aggressive. It is only when regime change occurs that Russia might act, as it did in Georgia (although Georgian actions contributed greatly to the conflict). Strong nationalist or Islamic movements in one of more countries in Central Asia could lead to Russian action. At the time of writing, such radical changes do not appear to be on the near horizon. Moreover, Russian hegemony in the region is not challenged by China.

Russian intervention in the Syrian Civil War illustrates how a renewed Russia under Putin is willing to gamble on extending its foreign policy into the Middle East. But we should not make too much of it or think it likely to recur any time soon. Russia's historical connection to Syria is fairly idiosyncratic and not replicated throughout the wider region. While Russian intervention in Syria was perhaps as surprising as its intervention in Ukraine, the two are very different.[59] While technically Russia and the West were opposed in both conflicts, in Syria all participants were fighting to eliminate the Islamic State. Thus, in Syria the United States and Russia could cooperate, even if begrudgingly and to a limited extent; cooperation in Ukraine is not possible unless Russia fundamentally changes its support for the Donbass rebellion, which is unlikely.

NOTES

1. Nelli Babayan, "The Return of Empire? Russia's Counteraction to Transatlantic Democracy Promotion in its Near Abroad," *Democratization* 22, no. 3 (2015): 438–458.
2. Foreign Policy Concept of the Russian Federation.
3. Adam B. Ulam, *Expansion and Coexistence: The History of Soviet Foreign Policy, 1917–1967* (New York, Praeger, 1968).
4. I assume that the reader is most likely familiar with the basic outlines of the Soviet war in Afghanistan and thus I shall omit a history of events here.
5. Oliker et. al., *Russian Foreign Policy in Historical and Current Context*, 5.
6. The reader should note this congruence between realist ambitions and a stated motivation based on identity. A similar pattern was observed in Russian intentions toward Eastern Europe. See Oliker et. al., *Russian Foreign Policy in Historical and Current Context*, 5.
7. Azerbaijan, Georgia and Uzbekistan withdrew from the CST in 1999.
8. Goure, "Moscow's Visions of Future War," 95.
9. Foreign Policy Concept of the Russian Federation.
10. Lincoln A. Mitchell, *The Color Revolutions* (Philadelphia, University of Pennsylvania Press, 2014), 114.
11. The term "color revolution" has a broader connotation that encompasses many revolutionary movements from Portugal to Lebanon to the events of the 2011 Arab Spring. In all instances, the term implies a popular uprising against a centralized, authoritarian government or autocratic leader.
12. Cordesman, *Russia and the 'Color Revolution.'*
13. Gerard Toal, *Near Abroad: Putin, the West, and the Contest over Ukraine and the Caucasus* (New York, Oxford University Press, 2017), 36.
14. One region of "in-betweens" is in Eastern Europe (Ukraine, Belarus and Moldova) and the other in the Caucasus (Georgia, Armenia, and Azerbaijan) (Charap et al, 2018: 1).
15. Chayli, "Approaches to Resolving the Conflict over the States In-Between," 33.
16. Toal, *Near Abroad*, 58.
17. Stephen Blank and Younkyoo Kim, "The North Caucasus: Russia's Other War," *Journal of Slavic Military Studies* 29, no. 2 (206): 185–202, p. 186.
18. Toal, *Near Abroad*, 80–87.

19. As quoted in Toal, *Near Abroad,* 83–84.
20. James Dobbins and Andrei Zagorski, "Lessons Learned from Russia-West Interactions on European Security," In Samuel Charap, et al., *Getting Out from "In-Between": Perspectives on the Regional Order in Post-Soviet Europe and Eurasia* (Santa Monica, RAND Corporation, 2018), 5–15, p. 9.
21. Toal, *Near Abroad,* 128.
22. Radin and Reach, *Russian Views of the International Order,* 12–13.
23. As cited in Radin and Reach, *Russian Views of the International Order,* 14.
24. Kazakhstan, Kyrgyzstan, Tajikistan, Turkmenistan and Uzbekistan. Radin and Reach, *Russian Views of the International Order,* 10–11.
25. Agnia Grigas, *Beyond Crimea: The New Russian Empire* (New Haven, Yale University Press. 2016), 173.
26. Ibid., 184.
27. Giles, *The Turning Point for Russian Foreign Policy,* 24.
28. McNabb, *Vladimir Putin and Russia's Imperial Revival,* 82–83.
29. Vladimir Putin, Speech August 29, 2014, http://en.kremlin.ru/events/president/news/46507, accessed May 28, 2019.
30. Since 2009 Kazakhstan has reduced its dependency on Russia's transportation pipelines by opening a new route through China. Grigas, *Beyond Crimea,* 187.
31. Grigas, *Beyond Crimea,* 187.
32. Izvestia (in Russian), "New Integration Project for Eurasia--The Future that is Born Today." (Новый интеграционный проект для Евразии — будущее, которое рождается сегодня.) October 3, 2011, https://iz.ru/news/502761, accessed May 29, 2019.
33. Grigas, *Beyond Crimea,* 191.
34. RFE/RL-Tajik Service, "Lavrov Calls Russian Military Base in Tajikistan 'Important Security Factor'," February 5, 2019, Radio Free Europe/Radio Liberty, https://www.rferl.org/a/lavrov-calls-russian-military-base-in-tajikistan-important-security-factor-/29752743.html, accessed May 29, 2019.
35. Grigas, *Beyond Crimea,* 200–201.
36. Ibid., 201.
37. Ibid., 203–204.
38. Rensselaer Lee and Artyom Lukin, *Russia's Far East: New Dynamics in Asia Pacific and Beyond* (Boulder, Lynne Rienner, 2016), 39–44.

39. India, Pakistan, Afghanistan, Iran and Mongolia are official "observers" to SCO meetings, while Turkey, Belarus, and Sri Lanka are official "dialogue partners."
40. Foreign Policy Concept of the Russian Federation.
41. Cordesman, *Russia and the "Color Revolution,"* 109.
42. Lee and Lukin, *Russia's Far East*, 99–116.
43. Sebastien Roblin, "Russia's Massive Vostok Military Exercise was Intended to Prepare for War with China. So What Happened?" September 2, 2018, *The National Interest,* https://nationalinterest.org/blog/buzz/russia's-massive-vostok-military-exercise-was-intended-prepare-war-china-so-what-happened, accessed September 2, 2018.
44. Roblin, "Russia's Massive Vostok Military Exercise was Intended to Prepare for War with China."
45. Charap and Colton, *Everyone Loses.*
46. Samuel Charap, John Drennan, and Pierre Noël, "Russia and China: A New Model of Great-Power Relations," *Survival* 59, no. 1 (2017): 25–42, p. 39.
47. The 1966 Ba'athist Coup in Syria is what effectively separated the Ba'athist Party into two parties: one in Syria and a separate party in Iraq.
48. Cordesman, *Russia and the "Color Revolution."*
49. Ibid., 56.
50. Hanna Notte, "Russia in Chechnya and Syria: Pursuit of Strategic Goals," *Middle East Policy* 23, no. 1 (2016): 59–74, p. 64–69.
51. It is interesting to note that Russia has not yet deployed the S-300 system to Syria. At the time of writing, the downing of a Russian aircraft by Syrian anti-aircraft fire in the Fall of 2018 might make the transfer of the S-300 system even more doubtful.
52. Brian Glyn Williams and Robert Souza, "Operation 'Retribution': Putin's Military Campaign in Syria, 2015–2016," *Middle East Policy* 23, no. 4 (2016): 42–60, p. 54.
53. Williams and Souza, "Operation 'Retribution'," 55.
54. Michael Kofman and Matthew Rojansky, JD, "What Kind of Victory for Russia in Syria?" *Military Review*, March–April 2018 (2018): 4–23, p. 20.
55. Alexander, Mercouris, "Russia's Military Bases in Syria," February 9, 2017, *The Duran,* http://theduran.com/russias-bases-syria/, accessed November 5, 2018; DEBKAfile, "Russia Builds Four New Air Bases in Syria, Deploys Another 6,000 Troops," February 1, 2018, https://www.debka.com/russia-builds-four-new-air-bases-syriafffffffdeploys-another-6000-troops/, accessed November 5, 2018.

56. Nikolai Novichkov, "Russia Details Counter-Terror Operation in Syria," *Military Technology*, December 2018, 42–43.
57. At the time of writing at the end of 2019, Syrian government forces continued to press an offensive on the last rebel stronghold of Idlib.
58. Kofman and Rojansky, "What Kind of Victory for Russia in Syria?" 10.
59. Stent, "Putin's Power Play in Syria."

CHAPTER 8

CONCLUSION

RECOMMENDATIONS FOR RESISTING
FUTURE RUSSIAN AGGRESSION

When Russia decided to intervene in Syria, it caught the United States and its allies off guard. Russia had surprised the West, just as Russia had done so with the 2014 annexation of Crimea.[1] Two related sets of questions must now be answered. The first has been the main concern of this book: *where, when, and why will Russia act again?* The second set of questions revolves around what the United States and NATO can do about the Russian threat to democratic states in Eastern Europe and elsewhere.

WHERE, WHEN, AND WHY RUSSIA WILL ACT AGAIN?

In chapter 1, the major international relations theories and their predictions about foreign policy behavior were outlined. To briefly summarize the three theories and their predictions:

> **Realism**: States act to increase their security, mainly through assuring self-preservation; a state's interests are generated by the state itself; assessments of power and capability determine actions; states seek to protect themselves in an anarchical, self-help international environment by balancing opponents and bandwagoning

with those whom they cannot balance; status in this system is determined by power and the ability to project it into a region and/or the world.

Domestic Politics: States act in the interests of the domestic actors who "capture" the state; different actors can have different interests and as they rotate into and out of power, the state's interests change; foreign policy decisions may be driven by considerations of domestic politics.

Social Constructivism: Identity and a nation's sense of their identity drive foreign policy; a nation's people develop norms of behavior that may differ from other state's norms; norms and identity do not change rapidly, leading to a continuity in foreign policy despite a changing international environment and/or changing domestic actors.

Each of these theories can be applied to Russian foreign policy to help us answer the question of where, when and why. An example of a realist impulse was the shift in foreign policy that occurred with the fall of the Soviet Union. The change from the aggressive, balancing behavior of the USSR to the bandwagon behavior of the early Yeltsin years was dramatic and unmistakable. Domestic politics theory predicts stability under a single administration, but change occurring when administrations change. A clear example is the change from Yeltsin's policies in the 1990s to Putin's more assertive policies in the 2000s. Social constructivism predicts policy will follow the interests and needs of the dominant identity. In early chapters, we established that Russians consider themselves exceptional and the natural hegemonic leaders of Eurasia. In this way, Russian identity supports a foreign policy that seeks to expand Russian influence, control and domination of its neighbors, especially in the "near abroad."

It is important to note that at times all three theories might predict the same behavior. In other words, it is possible for realist considerations, the interests of the dominant political actors, and the national identity to all point in the same direction. *In fact, I argue that Russian foreign policy is currently in such a position.* The need to increase Russian security (primarily by rebuilding the armed forces), the desire of the Kremlin and the *siloviki* to reestablish Russian dominance of neighbors, and the resurgence of Russian nationalism among the Russian population (although not among all elements of the Russian people) all encourage an aggressive foreign policy. In short, Russian foreign policy is in a period of aggressive expansionist behavior supported by rational realist arguments, the interests of key domestic actors, and a supportive base in the domestic population.

The answer as to *why* Russia will again act assertively is straightforward: Russia is most likely to act to achieve its fundamental security interests when all three theories align. In other words, Russia is most likely to act if its security is jeopardized or an opportunity to extend its security presents itself, if domestic actors support aggression for political and economic gain, and if Russian identity or Russian minorities are threatened, thus mobilizing Russian public opinion that supports action. Of course, my statement is not deterministic, but rather probabilistic. The more that all three factors are present, the greater the likelihood that Russia will act; when only a single factor exists, Russia is less likely to act. Moreover, the more the theories all align, the greater the level of force that Russia will employ. As Kofman argues, Russia will seek to obtain its foreign policy goals by selective "raiding." These raids (such as in the seizure of Crimea) are both strategic in that they represent the key motivations of security and national identity, and they are also limited because they have very specific operational goals that can be achieved with limited forms of warfare.

The answer as to *when* Russia will be aggressive is a bit trickier. Russian action is not consistently aggressive nor is it looking for any and all opportunities on a daily basis to strike a blow against the West. Efforts to paint Russian foreign policy as such mistakenly translate *when* as *always* are thus are misguided.[2] Of course, arguments that Western provocation is to blame for times of Russian aggression (e.g., because of NATO expansion, support for Georgia) are also mistaken. Rather, a more sophisticated and accurate answer, even if less satisfying, is that Russia acts aggressively when it is in its interests to do so. Russia does tend to act when triggering events occur that prod the government to respond.[3] As an example, Russian intrusion into Ukraine was spurred by the destabilization of that country in early 2014. Another example is Russian cyber intrusion into the Baltic nations tended to follow specific events and governmental actions in those nations. Likewise, the 2008 Russian invasion of Georgia followed multiple Russian efforts to diffuse the emerging crisis and came directly on the heels of the Georgian escalation of the conflict.

The answer as to *where* is the most obvious: Russia acts along its borders. The nations of the "near abroad" typically possess a congruence of realist, domestic, and ideational factors that support Russian aggressive action. Russian foreign policy fundamental aims to secure Russia's borders and maintain friendly relations with its neighbors. It also seeks to protect Russian minorities in other states. The nations of the "near abroad," whether in Eastern Europe or the Caucasus, fall within Russia's designated sphere of influence, have friendly or pro-Russian governments and elite, and often possess a sizeable Russian minority.

Ukraine as an Example of Why, When, and Where
Throughout this book, I have placed a well-founded emphasis on Russian actions in Ukraine. Russian interference in Ukraine illuminates the fundamental realist nature of Russia's goal to maintain influence on its borders. It also displays Russia's attempts to influence Ukraine, short of direct military intervention. Russia has inserted itself in Ukrainian politics pretty much on a continual basis since 1991, mainly due to the need to maintain the flow of Russian natural gas to Western Europe. What changed in the early 2000s was the gradual movement of Ukrainian foreign policy toward accommodation with the European Union and perhaps in the future with NATO. Covert Russian interference in the 2004 Ukrainian presidential election not only failed to produce a pro-

Russian outcome, it contributed to the further movement of the Ukrainian government towards the West. When in 2014 pro-Russian President Viktor Yanukovich's cancellation of the association agreement with the European Union led to protests against his rule, Putin and the Russian government decided to take more aggressive action. Thus, Russian intervention in 2014, ostensibly to protect a threatened Russian minority, was the more a last resort than a first step. Russian aggression followed decades of failed foreign policy to create a compliant Ukraine.

It also can be argued that Russia exercised a good deal of restraint in Ukraine. After all, Russia did not choose a conventional war with Ukraine, like its actions in Georgia in 2008. Rather, Putin chose a more limited set of actions that involved covert action, deception, and plausible deniability. Russian actions in Ukraine highlight both the potential of nonconventional campaigns to further Russian goals as well as the limitations of such an approach. The use of disguised military units, combined with private contractors, cyber assaults, information, and propaganda campaigns, worked very well in both seizing Crimea and fomenting rebellion in Eastern Ukraine. Russia not only succeeded in keeping control of its valuable naval base at Sevastopol and the ability to project power into the Black Sea but also adding territory to the Russian Federation. The Russian incursion into Ukraine also has been very low cost, at least in terms of material and manpower.

On the flip side, the Ukrainian government remains fiercely anti-Russian and the Donbass Rebellion is at best stuck in a stalemate. The two Donbass oblasts now rely on Russian contributions and support to maintain themselves. Further, the actions of the rebels and their Russian advisors/supporters—such as the downing of Malaysian Air Flight 17 on July 17, 2014, by a Russian *Buk* surface-to-air missile launcher (NATO codename SA-11 "Gadfly") operating out of a region occupied by the Donbass rebels—are directly attributed to Russia by Western powers. Moreover, Russian covert actions in Crimea did not fool the West into thinking that the "little green men" were somehow local Crimean separatists. Western sanctions against Russia in the aftermath of the Crimean seizure have not only dented the Russian economy, they have also signaled to Russia that the West is more resolute in its defense of Eastern Europe than Russia believed. The Russian insertion into Eastern Ukraine is also the largest motivating factor behind the demand by Poland and the Baltic nations for greater NATO involvement in their defense. In short, Russian aggression in Ukraine has led to exactly the opposite of what Russia desired: the NATO presence in Eastern Europe and its resolve to defend East European nations has increased rather than decreased; Russian security has not been enhanced but perhaps it has even been compromised further; and Russia has not gained greater influence over Ukrainian politics. Thus, Russia remains locked into a foreign policy commitment that neither provides it with a clear victory nor a clear path to disengagement.[4]

WHAT CAN THE UNITED STATES AND THE WEST DO ABOUT RUSSIAN AGGRESSION?

The ascension of Putin to the Russian presidency in 2000 coincided with a large structural development: the end of the decline of the Russian economy in the 1990s. As Russia slowly began to regain its economic strength, and thus the capability to further its interests, Russian foreign policy began to shift toward a more assertive stance. Putin secured an unchecked authority in domestic politics through his successful corralling of the Oligarchs and his organization of party politics, particularly his control of the Duma through the founding of and dominance of the United Russia party. His constitutional reforms to limit the power of the federal units, regional governors, and any challenge to his rule or dissent, effectively checked any opposition. The stoking of Russian nationalism tied to a resurgent Russian identity provided enough popular support to solidify Putin's grasp on power.[5] By roughly 2008, Putin (and Medvedev too, given their collaboration) was not only free to engage in a more aggressive foreign policy, his actions also were met with general approval from Russian elites, the *siloviki*, and the general population (although of course, not the entire population). The Russian acquisition of Crimea in 2014 and Russian intervention in Syria are signs of how Putin can reassert Russian interests on the world stage. Wegren asserts that Putin has created a personalistic and autocratic system of rule (which Stephen L. Wegren calls "Putinism") that allows Russia more initiative in foreign policy.[6]

Thus, with Putin winning a new six-year presidential term in 2018, the West should operate on the idea that Russian assertion in pursuit of great power status is not going to stop anytime soon. The three driving factors of realist ambitions, domestic actors pushing for action, and support for Russian and pro-Russian ethnic groups will stand line up to create an impetus for Russian action. As Oliker et al. put it "Russia's foreign policy is rooted in long-standing beliefs about its rights within its region, beliefs that are rooted in Russian history and geopolitical circumstance. These are exacerbated by a consistent post-Soviet view of a continued competition with the United States."[7] If Kofman is indeed right with his raiding analogy, Russia will indeed keep trying to take small bites whenever the opportunity presents itself.[8]

As outlined in earlier chapters, Russian aggression is not as blatant as direct military intervention in the affairs of its neighbors. Despite how obvious this may sound, Russian foreign policy is nuanced, calculated and sophisticated. On a daily basis, Russian foreign policy takes two forms: one, a traditional use of economic cooperation/coercion and military posturing; and two, the presence of information and propaganda campaigns as part of asymmetrical means to assert soft power and gain influence. If the West is going to resist Russian aggression that fundamentally seeks to erode Western power and the American-led liberal world order, Western nations must blunt both aspects of Russian foreign policy.

The United States and its allies, particularly its NATO allies in Western and Eastern Europe, have traditionally done a good job of resisting Russia's conventional threat. The expansion of the NATO alliance after the end of the Cold War has prevented any conventional Russian intrusions into its foreign, Soviet-era satellite states that have joined NATO. Putting nations such as Poland, the Czech Republic, and the Baltic nations (among others) under the collective security of NATO has insured that Russia is not the *de facto* hegemonic leader of Eastern Europe. Moreover, it has extended the Western liberal and democratic order to nations and populations that were denied political and economic freedoms for more than four decades due to Soviet domination. The roughly concurrent expansion of the European Union eastward has accomplished similar effects. Aligning the trade and economics of East European nations with the Western European nations reduces the reliance of former communist states on the legacy and continuities of Cold War–era trade relationships between satellite states and Russia. The European Union also seeks to preserve and development democratic political and social norms in its member-states.

It should be clear that the Russian realist aspirations of great power status place Russia at odds with the pro-American world order, particularly in Eastern Europe. Any Russian hegemony will not be liberal: it will neither enshrine nor promote democratic ideals over any nations the fall under its influence. Rather, Russian foreign policy seeks to create compliant, friendly, and pro-Russian governments on its borders. Such governments typically are more autocratic than democratic. Thus, if the Western nations truly support liberal democratic norms they must continue to defend their allies in Eastern Europe, particularly the Baltic nations and Poland, while also bolstering non-allies, such as Ukraine, that are actively defending against Russian action. As Oliker et al points out, the best possible strategy would be to "rebuild the stability that has been lost in Ukraine and in Europe more broadly."[9] Yet, this is much easier said than done. It requires maintaining the strength of the security and military alliances backed by Western powers (e.g., NATO) and also the health and integrity of political and economic alliances (such as the EU).

Along these lines, and of great concern to the defense of the Western international order, is the threat from Russia's asymmetrical warfare. As established in chapters 4 and 5, Russia's development of nonconventional assets and cyber warfare poses a continuous and credible threat to the stability of Western security and economic alliances. Resisting the Russian propaganda and information offensive requires that Western powers recognize the threat (which it appears they are finally starting to do) and fight back against it. In 2016 Van Herpen succinctly offered seven measures by which the West could resist:

1. Spend more money.
2. Create an alternative Russian-language TV station.
3. Analyze the facts [of Russian information and propaganda campaigns].
4. Raise public awareness.
5. Tell the truth [i.e. do not create false counter-propaganda].
6. Don't be too tolerant.
7. Fight trolls.[10]

It is not clear that Western governments have done enough along these lines, particularly given the direct threat of Russian asymmetrical actions against the Baltic nations.[11] As Western nations have slowly gained an awareness of this threat, they must now turn toward an active plan to counter it. The response thus far has been fairly piecemeal, rather than a coordinated effort. For example, the government and media in both the United States and the United Kingdom have made it clear to their publics that there was Russian interference in the Brexit vote and the 2016 US presidential election. However, there is still disagreement and mixed messages about both the extent of the Russian interference and its impact. Clearly more needs to be done.

Fighting cyber warfare and cyber terrorism requires three efforts. First, the West needs to properly determine the source of threats. Second, it must recognize all the various types of threats. Last, the West needs to develop methods by which to counter those threats.[12] While the US government (and other Western governments) are getting much more sophisticated at the two first efforts, it is the third that remains underdeveloped. According to one analysis, improvement in defensive or counter measures require Western governments to do more of the following:

- Design and implement cybersecurity programs at national agencies,
- Address cybersecurity for access control systems,
- Enhance oversight of all IT contractors,
- Improved security incident response activities,
- Limit the risk to and respond quicker to breaches of personally identifiable information, and
- Implement security programs at smaller agencies of government.[13]

The great difficulty with these recommendations is that they are very costly and require a large amount of coordination among multiple governmental agencies. To some degree, the US Department of Defense has led the way in developing effective counter force. The US Cyber Command has developed three types of Cyber Mission Forces:

- National mission forces to protect critical national and economic security infrastructure, such as electrical grids and computer systems,
- Combat mission forces to launch offensive operations as either retaliation against attacks or to preempt attacks, and
- Cyber protection forces to enhance, defend, and fortify the DOD's networks.[14]

The placement of counter-cyberattack forces into the Department of Defense is indicative of the blossoming realization of the United States (and similarly in other Western nations) of the true nature of Russian (and other countries) cyber intrusions. In other words, Russian propaganda, information, and cyber campaigns are a form of continuous warfare similar to traditional espionage between antagonistic nations. All nations have developed counterespionage measures to protect themselves against this low-grade and constant threat. In the modern age, asymmetrical warfare is an extension of the concept of international espionage and must be countered accordingly.

Some Region-Specific Recommendations to Resist Russian Aggression

Russia uses a mix of foreign policy tools to try and extend its influence into nations, and this mix varies by regions. Toward Eastern Europe, Russia is mainly belligerent, using threat, intimidation, and a mix of hybrid warfare to subdue governments, policies, and actions with which it disagrees. Russia has been even more aggressive in the Caucasus, using military intervention as a weapon against nations that will not fall into line behind Russian foreign policy. Toward the Central Asia, Russian foreign policy is more cooperative, employing its economic might, military support, and diplomacy to further Russian goals. The number-one weapon in the Russian arsenal in Central Asia typically is control over the transportation of energy exports (although, not in all cases).

As I have been arguing, Russian foreign policy is not just based on realist concerns. Where a significant Russian minority exists, Russian foreign policy is also driven by Russian domestic politics and issues around Russian identity. Large Russian minorities exist in the Baltic nations, Ukraine, and Belarus. This combination of three different sources for foreign policy makes Russian policy toward these nations more complex, more likely to be assertive, and sometimes counterproductive (as in the case of the Russian participation in the Ukrainian conflict where it might be domestically popular but it has exposed Russia to a long-term commitment in Ukraine and sanctions from the West).

Given the difference between the Russian foreign policy vectors that are mainly realist (e.g., Syria) and the vector (i.e., Eastern Europe) that contains realist, domestic, and ideational factors, the Western response to each vector must take into account this difference. In general, where

Russian foreign policy is driven almost strictly by realist factors, the Western response should be proportional balancing. Where the Russian foreign policy is driven by three different sets of factors, and particularly when all three drive Russian foreign policy to be more assertive, the Western response must be more forceful and address all three factors driving Russian foreign policy.

Moreover, Western nations must consider that Russian foreign policy relies a great deal on hybrid tactics and less on overt military action. Russia does not immediately go to the greatest level of escalation to achieve its goals. Rather, Russia tends to try low-cost methods first. As such, relatively low-cost Russian intelligence, propaganda, and information campaigns are the face of Russian foreign policy on a daily basis and pose a threat to Western security. Russian information campaigns seek to undermine the short-term support for Western and pro-Western governments and leaders. They also seek to erode the long-term support for democracy in these same nations. The end goal of both type of attacks is to destabilize Western nations, thereby diminishing their support for collective security and shortenening the era of American global hegemony. Russian information and propaganda campaigns are continuous, ongoing, and relatively inexpensive. Russia can afford to keep trying these campaigns until they are either suitably dissuaded from doing so or until such campaigns are successful. Russia can, of course, escalate the level of the nonconventional attack. Russia can employ—and has—cyberattacks and other hybrid warfare to reduce the defensive capabilities of target nations. Russia has employed such tactics successfully in both the 2008 Russian-Georgian War and the 2014 Russian intervention in Crimea and Ukraine. Direct Russian cyber and information warfare paired with military actions is one potential model for future conflict. One can reasonably expect that in any future confrontation between a Western nation or nations, Russia will be very likely to use similar tactics. Therefore, Western nations must prepare a suitable response.

Defense of the Baltic Nations

The Baltic nations are under the clearest threat from Russian aggression. The Russian desire to reassert hegemonic domination over the Baltic nations, in addition to the presence of sizable Russian minorities in these nations, align Russian realist goals with domestic and ideational forces pushing Russian foreign policy to be more assertive. Moreover, the Baltic nations are particularly vulnerable to Russian bullying due to 1) the small size of their populations and armed forces, 2) their proximity to Russia and 3) their location on the periphery of the NATO alliance.

Defense of the Baltic nations must be a combination of extending the NATO strategic nuclear deterrence over the Baltic nations, a NATO commitment to conventional defense of the Baltic nations, and a robust effort to blunt Russian asymmetrical warfare aimed at the Baltic populations. Common to most assessments is the need for NATO to better prepare against Russian aggression aimed at the Baltic nations. NATO must increase its counter-information and counter-propaganda efforts in order to blunt the continuous efforts of Russian information campaigns. The battle for "hearts and minds" is now constant, ongoing, and important. NATO must seek to increase its coordination of resistance to Russian information campaigns by aligning Baltic nations, Scandinavian nations, and NATO members into a collective defense. Scholars and analysts agree that NATO must also seek to add more conventional deterrence in the Baltic nations. The stationing of rapid deployment troops must not only increase but also become more permanent. Greater intelligence capabilities must also be positioned in the Baltic nations. Russian attempts at stirring up revolt from the ethnic-Russian minorities must be resisted, and resisting such campaigns requires a robust commitment of intelligence assets. In short, the Baltic nations are vulnerable to Russian pressure; NATO needs to meet that pressure by displaying a firm commitment to defend the Baltic NATO partners.

Mastriano makes recommendations on how NATO can shore up the conventional military defense of the Baltic nations and help deter Russian aggression. First, the West must recognize that the Russian threat to the Baltic nations is both from fomenting a "hybrid ethnic uprising" as well as a conventional military attack from across the border.[15] Given the speed with which a Russian conventional attack could occur, NATO needs to develop a reliable early warning capability. Mastriano suggests that NATO's Intelligence Fusion Center (NIFC) should partner with the Baltic Intelligence Center (BIC) to provide a permanent forward intelligence that could signal the start of Russian aggression.

Second, NATO must work with its Baltic nation allies to "increase the size, survivability, mobility and lethality of the Baltic armed forces."[16] Fundamental to this goal would be an increase in each nation's defense spending coupled with the United States supplying surplus equipment to the Baltic nations.

Third, given the hybrid nature of the Russian threat, Special Forces capability is needed. An adaptive Special Forces could work with local security to counter a Russian campaign focused on starting an ethnic uprising. Special Forces would also be valuable in resisting any covert military actions linked to Russian aggression, such as transferring volunteers from Russia into the Baltic nations or Russian actions to form local Baltic militias.

Fourth, NATO must maintain a forward presence in the Baltic nations. Mastriano specifically recommends at least one brigade in each Baltic nation with cooperation in this deployment from Sweden and Finland.[17] To coordinate these forces Mastriano suggests the establishment of a permanent US headquarters in the region.

Last, to demonstrate capability and commitment, NATO should hold annual Deploy Forces to the Baltics (DEFORTIC) exercises. In essence, NATO needs to fight fire with fire and demonstrate to Putin that Russian military exercises will be met with a similar display from NATO.

Helmus et al. suggest a series of actions that the West can carry out to meet the threat of Russian information and propaganda campaigns to the Baltic nations, particularly through social media. First, Western nations must highlight and "block" Russian propaganda and information campaigns. They demonstrate that crowd-sourced sites, local media, and European assets (such as the European Union East StratCom Task Force) have the capability to identity, track, and block Russian influence and fake news on social media.[18] They suggest that Western governments both take advantage of social media to counter Russian campaigns (e.g., by buying Google ads) and also pressure social media companies (such as Facebook) to police malign and hostile content, particularly coming from fake accounts tied to Russian sources. This will also require the Western nations to develop analytic methods to track Russian media.[19] Second, Western nations should commit to a campaign to build the resilience of at-risk populations, such as the Baltic nations. This would include such measures as training journalists, raising awareness of fake news on social media among the population, and establishing crowd-sourced fact-checking websites.

Third, Helmus et al. recommend expanding and improving local and original content to compete with Russian-sourced information (this idea is similar to Van Herpen's idea of the West creating a media channel to act as a counter to pro-Russian media). The idea is for media allied and/or controlled by Western nations to continually provide local and original content that appeals to target populations and is an alternative to Russian-sourced content. Fourth, Western nations need to empower influencers on social media, particularly those with a pan-European identity. Fifth, funding for alternative media content must be provided. This includes production and distribution of content in the local language. Sixth, and related, the West must support and train Russian-language journalists and journalism. Seventh, the Western nations must commit to producing and distribution a greater amount of Russian-language programming.[20]

Eighth, the West needs to "better tell the U.S., North Atlantic Treaty Organization, and European Union story."[21] They suggest promoting the positives of Western economic, security, political, and cultural stories as a constant information campaign. Ninth, and more related to the conventional defense of the Baltic nations, effective public relations should be coordinated with the Enhanced Forward Presence (EFP) of NATO troops. Ninth and last, NATO needs to convey a clear and convincing message of the strategic importance of the NATO alliance and its presence in the Baltic nations.[22]

Gotkowska and Szymanski make some specific recommendations which all focus around a common theme: NATO should avoid a scenario in which Russia feels tempted to "test the west."[23] NATO should maintain a deterrence posture in the Baltic nations that is robust enough to reduce any Russian doubts about the NATO commitment. Along these lines they suggest that first, Poland and the Baltic nations should maintain (in the case of Poland and Estonia) or increase (Latvia and Lithuania) defense spending to 2 percent of GDP. The Baltic nations should also increase their strategic communication and coordination. Further, all NATO members in the region, including Poland, should invest in supportive measures of each other nation. Second, NATO should coordinate with the non-aligned nations of Sweden and Finland to provide for a more collective defense of the Baltic Sea region. NATO needs to convince Sweden to increase its defense spending, offering to Sweden the idea that Swedish coordination with NATO's collective defense of the Baltic Sea would create great returns in Swedish defense. NATO should also encourage Sweden and Finland to develop their own capabilities further in countering Russian propaganda and information warfare. Perhaps as another goal, Sweden and Finland could coordinate some of their efforts with the Baltic nations. Third, the NATO command structure in the region needs to be more concentrated, particularly into a single chain of command. This would increase the speed with which NATO forces could be dispatched to the Baltic nations in times of a crisis.[24]

NATO and Eastern Europe: Ukraine as the Flash Point
The primary concern in Eastern Europe for NATO is the continued regional conflict in Ukraine. As Mastriano puts it, "the Ukraine crisis

provides an opportunity to demonstrate the post–Cold War relevancy of these organizations [i.e., NATO and the Organization for Security and Cooperation in Europe-OSCE] by exhibiting solidarity, cooperation, and resolve against a re-emergent regional threat."[25] Of course, both organizations have already responded to the crisis. NATO has placed additional bases in Eastern Europe, held more military exercises in the region, provided training and funding for the Ukrainian armed forces, and deployed additional forces to the region. The OSCE has sent monitoring and observer missions to Ukraine and opened up communication between Ukraine and Russia.

The great difficulty of US-led action to defend Ukraine is that Ukraine is not a NATO member and yet simultaneously of great security concern to Russia. In short, Ukraine (and Eastern Europe in general) is in Russia's backyard, and Russia therefore takes a great interest in its affairs. Russia sees Eastern Europe as a natural part of the Russian sphere of influence, and from a realist perspective Russia also sees Eastern Europe as a buffer zone, one which Russia has watched erode since the fall of the Soviet Union. The NATO and EU incursions into the Baltic nations and other Eastern European states alarm Russia. From a social constructivist perspective, the presence in East European nations of Russian minorities and/or ethnicities with which Russians have an affinity creates a pressure on Russian foreign policy to extend its influence in the region. From a domestic politics perspective, the *siloviki* and other national interests inside Russia have a desire to maintain influence in the region. Thus, all of the drivers of foreign policy point to Russian action to protect its interests in Eastern Europe.

Therefore, the United States needs to defend against Russian military action, be it overt or covert as it was in Crimea in 2014, and also "exploitation by foreign actors [i.e., Russia] of NATO members' internal vulnerabilities and the security vacuum of European countries not belonging to NATO."[26] It is the Russian hybrid threat that should be of the most concern, for it is Russian hybrid action that effectively led to the prolonged conflict in Ukraine and Russian seizure of Crimea. If NATO does not want a repeat of such actions, or even the eventual defeat of the Ukrainian government, it must meet this hybrid threat head on. If and when Russia launches another hybrid threat, NATO must be ready with. "deterrence, defense, and de-escalation."[27] NATO's Very High Readiness Joint Task Force (VJTF) could be the answer. The idea is that the VJTF could bolster local law enforcement services, increase border security, provide humanitarian support, or whatever else is needed to accomplish two goals: 1) provide space and time for the local government to "concentrate on nonmilitary aspects of the threat it faces"[28] and 2) maintain a presence in the physical space that would prevent Russian hybrid units from controlling that same space. Any use of the Rapid Action Plan (RAP) or deployment of the VJTF is bound to incur a reaction from Russia, which will argue that any NATO presence in a nation on Russia's border is a violation of the Conventional Forces Europe Treaty. This should not however deter NATO from deploying when necessary. The duplicitous and hidden nature of Russia's hybrid warfare seeks to delay any serious response, much as what happened in Crimea. The United States and NATO must respond faster in the future.

Central Asia: The Limits on Western Responses

Russia considers Central Asia as lying within its natural sphere of influence. By most indications, this Russian assessment cannot be directly challenged by regionals actors, such as China, or by global actors, such as the United States. The influence of Western powers in Central Asia typically takes two forms: long-term diplomatic and economic ties between a particular Central Asian country and a particular European power tied to a colonial past (e.g., India and the United Kingdom) and, more recently, American military intervention into the region as part of the global war on terror (e.g., American-led intervention in Afghanistan, American ties to Pakistan). Neither of these relationships fundamentally challenges the Russian hegemonic position in the region. As such,

Western responses to Russian actions in the Caucasus and Central Asia are quite limited.

Russian intentions toward Central Asia are primarily realist: Russian foreign policy focuses on stabilizing the region and extending Russian ties, be they through diplomacy, arms sales, economic activity, or energy transfer. Moreover, even if Western powers wanted to check or reduce Russian influence in the region, there is a limit to what they could do. Central Asia is very close and important to Russia while the region is very far and lacking in great importance to the West. A recurrence of Western powers directly confronting an expanding Russian Empire, such as what took place during the Great Game between the British and Russian Empires in the second half of the nineteenth century, is highly improbable.

More likely is that the People's Republic of China will be the next balancer of Russian influence in Central Asia. China could reasonably extend the hegemony that it has in South Asia and Southeast Asia over portions of Central Asia as well. Russian courtship of India should be seen more as a Russian balancing act against a rising China than a balancing act against a distant American landlord. This is convenient for the West, much as it was during the Cold War, because it drains the attention and resources of both Russia and China, leaving the Western powers to take up matters elsewhere in the world.

This is not to say that the United States and its allies should not invest some resources in the region. Ariel Cohen emphasizes that the US has interests in preventing international terrorism and that the Caucasus region is an active source of terrorist recruitment.[29] In general, Cohen suggests that the US expand its contacts with nations in the region, primarily in intelligence, border security, law enforcement and counterterrorism. The goal would be to expand "cooperation with other foreign law enforcement and intelligence services for the collection of, prevention, and disruption of terrorist operations."[30] In short, the United States has a common interest with Russia in stabilizing the region and reducing its contribution to global terrorism. Cooperation and/ or collaboration with Russia in the region toward this end is a solid recommendation and one that has been proposed to resolve issues in the Caucasus as well.[31]

Middle East and North Africa: West Still in the Driver's Seat

Russian diplomatic overtures in the Middle East and North Africa are one of its least important vectors of foreign policy. Putin is probing for opportunities in Saudi Arabia, Iran, Israel, and elsewhere, but there is little probability that Russia will gain any sizable amount of influence in the region. As long as Russia does not firmly take a side in the simmering Sunni-versus-Shia conflict (one that is primarily driven by conflict between Saudi Arabia and Iran over hegemony in the region), and there is no indication that Russia wishes to do so, Russia will mainly be on the sidelines. This is not to say that Russia will abandon its Syrian proxy in the region, nor pass up any opportunity to expand its relations, as it did with arms sales to Turkey. Though in general, Russia has little to gain through involvement in the complicated politics and international relations of the Middle East and North Africa.

As such the Western powers still are in the driver's seat in regard to this region. Economic, diplomatic and military ties between the United States and countries such as Israel, Saudi Arabia, the UAE, and others bind these countries together much more so than any are bound to Russia. Even Russian ties to Iran might not be as important to that nation as the long-term economic and diplomatic relations Iran has with Europe.

Therefore, given the minor presence of Russian action in the Middle East and North Africa, the West should not over-react to Russian overtures. The Russian bases in Syria do extend the Russian military presence, but not in a way that compromises Western actions in the region. Moreover, Western relations with countries such as Saudi Arabia, Israel, and others should concentrate more on economic needs (such as access to oil transfers), managing the proxy Sunni-Shia conflict in Yemen so that it does not escalate into direct conflict between Saudi Arabia and Iran, reducing terrorism emanating out of and exacerbated by the Palestinian conflict with Israel, and stabilizing and filling the power vacuum in Eastern Syria and Western Iraq. This latter issue has led to some, albeit not a lot, of coordination if not cooperation between Russia and the United States in the elimination of ISIS. Generally, Western policy in the region should focus more on the West's inherent economic and security interests in the region and less on whatever maneuvers Russia is making in the region, as the Russian capability to extend itself into the Middle East and North Africa is very limited, at least for the foreseeable future.

CONCLUSION

The United States and its Western allies must respond to acts of Russian aggression through active deterrence, defense, and engagement. The core principle is to demonstrate a readiness to defend security commitments. This now must extend to the deterrence and defense against hybrid attacks from Russian information and propaganda campaigns. This requires a continuous cyber presence in the Baltic nations and Eastern Europe similar to the continuous presence of conventional forces. It also requires the West to develop the capabilities and assets to detect and counter Russian cyber intrusions and direct cyberattacks.

On a related manner, Western nations must detect and resist Russian information campaigns within their own nations. Russia seeks to destabilize the West in order to give itself more freedom to influence events in Eastern Europe and elsewhere. Further, Putin seeks to destabilize the West to decrease its collective will to both defend its allies and also to maintain sanctions against Russia. Putin needs to shake off the sanctions as part of his efforts to improve the Russian economy, with an end goal of using economic strength and energy transfers to fund the rebuilding of the Russian military. To this end he has not yet been successful. The United States and its allies do not have to directly oppose Putin's rearmament plans, but they do need to oppose Russian aggression and interference that lays the groundwork for a renewed Russian armed forces to exploit.

NOTES

1. Stent, "Putin's Power Play in Syria," 106.
2. Toal, *Near Abroad.*
3. Monaghan, *Power in Modern Russia.*
4. Charap and Colton, *Everyone Loses.*
5. Tsygankov, *Russia's Foreign Policy.*
6. Stephen K. Wegren, editor, *Putin's Russia: Past Imperfect, Future Uncertain,* 7th Edition (New York, Rowman and Littlefield, 2019).
7. Oliker et. al., *Russian Foreign Policy in Historical and Current Context,* 23.
8. Kofman, "Raiding and International Brigandry."
9. Oliker et. al., *Russian Foreign Policy in Historical and Current Context,* 25.
10. Van Herpen, *Putin's Propaganda Machine,* 275–280.
11. Marta Kepe, "NATO: Prepared for Countering Disinformation Operations in the Baltic States?" June 7, 2017. The RAND Blog, https://www.rand.org/blog/2017/06/nato-prepared-for-countering-disinformation-operations.html, accessed May 29, 2019.
12. Douglas C. Lovelace Jr., *Hybrid Warfare and the Grey Zone Threat,* Series on Terrorism: Commentary on Security Documents, vol. 141 (New York, Oxford University Press, 2016).
13. Lovelace Jr., *Hybrid Warfare and the Grey Zone Threat,* 246–249.
14. Ibid., 275.
15. Mastriano, *A U.S. War College Assessment on Russian Strategy in Eastern Europe and Recommendations on how to Leverage Landpower to Maintain the Peace,* 131.
16. Ibid.
17. Ibid., 133.
18. Helmus et. al., *Russian Social Media Influence,* 75–76.
19. Ibid., 91.
20. Ibid., 85–88.
21. Ibid., 88.
22. Ibid., 90–91.
23. Gotkowska and Szymanski, *Russia and the Security in the Baltic Sea Region,* 8.
24. Ibid., 8–10.

25. Mastriano, *A U.S. War College Assessment on Russian Strategy in Eastern Europe and Recommendations on how to Leverage Landpower to Maintain the Peace*, 19.
26. Ibid., 88.
27. Ibid., 89.
28. Ibid., 90.
29. Cohen, *Russia's Counterinsurgency in North Caucasus*, 73–77.
30. Ibid., 75.
31. Chalyi, "Approaches in Resolving the Conflict over the States In-Between."

Index

About the Author

Neal G. Jesse is a professor of political science at Bowling Green State University. He holds a PhD from UCLA and a BA from UCSB. Dr. Jesse's previous publications include *Small States in the International System: At Peace and at War, Ethnic Conflict: A Systematic Approach to Cases of Conflict, Beyond Great Powers and Hegemons: Why Secondary States Support, Follow, or Challenge*, and *Identity and Institutions: Conflict Reduction in Divided Societies.* He has published articles in several journals such as *International Political Science Review, International Studies Quarterly, Political Psychology*, and *Electoral Studies.*

Cambria Rapid Communications in Conflict and Security (RCCS) Series

General Editor: Geoffrey R. H. Burn

The aim of the RCCS series is to provide policy makers, practitioners, analysts, and academics with in-depth analysis of fast-moving topics that require urgent yet informed debate. Since its launch in October 2015, the RCCS series has the following book publications:

- *A New Strategy for Complex Warfare: Combined Effects in East Asia* by Thomas A. Drohan
- *US National Security: New Threats, Old Realities* by Paul R. Viotti
- *Security Forces in African States: Cases and Assessment* edited by Paul Shemella and Nicholas Tomb
- *Trust and Distrust in Sino-American Relations: Challenge and Opportunity* by Steve Chan
- *The Gathering Pacific Storm: Emerging US-China Strategic Competition in Defense Technological and Industrial Development* edited by Tai Ming Cheung and Thomas G. Mahnken
- *Military Strategy for the 21st Century: People, Connectivity, and Competitipauon* by Charles Cleveland, Benjamin Jensen, Susan Bryant, and Arnel David
- *Ensuring National Government Stability After US Counterinsurgency Operations: The Critical Measure of Success* by Dallas E. Shaw Jr.
- *Reassessing U.S. Nuclear Strategy* by David W. Kearn, Jr.
- *Deglobalization and International Security* by T. X. Hammes
- *American Foreign Policy and National Security* by Paul R. Viotti

- *Make America First Again: Grand Strategy Analysis and the Trump Administration* by Jacob Shively
- *Learning from Russia's Recent Wars: Why, Where, and When Russia Might Strike Next* by Neal G. Jesse
- *Restoring Thucydides: Testing Familiar Lessons and Deriving New Ones* by Andrew R. Novo and Jay M. Parker
- *Net Assessment and Military Strategy: Retrospective and Prospective Essays* edited by Thomas G. Mahnken, with an introduction by Andrew W. Marshall

For more information, visit www.cambriapress.com.

www.ingramcontent.com/pod-product-compliance
Lightning Source LLC
Chambersburg PA
CBHW031128270326
41929CB00011B/1544